DATE DUE

JE 30 07			
MR 50 '98			

DEMCO 38-296

THE
CLOISTER
WALK

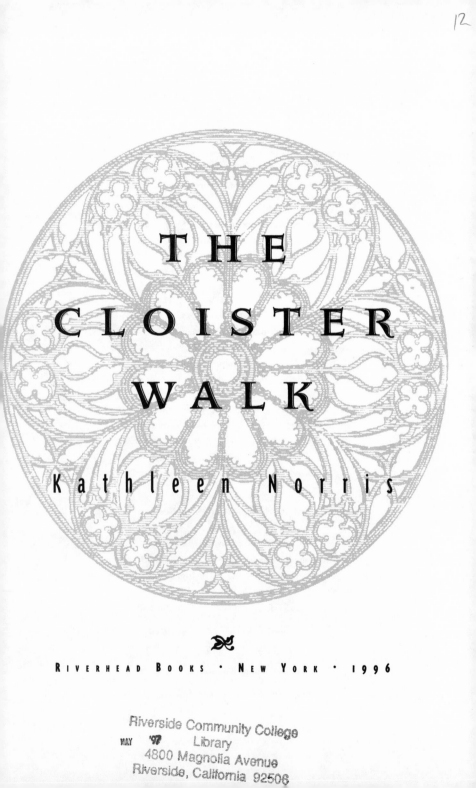

THE CLOISTER WALK

Kathleen Norris

RIVERHEAD BOOKS · NEW YORK · 1996

"My Very First Dad," © 1987 North Dakota Council on the Arts and COMPAS. Used with permission.

Excerpt from "Protestant Easter," from *Live or Die* by Anne Sexton. Copyright © 1966 by Anne Sexton. Reprinted by permission of Houghton Mifflin Co. All rights reserved.

Excerpt from "For People with Problems About How to Believe," from *An Oregon Message* by William Stafford. Copyright © 1987 by William Stafford. Reprinted by permission of HarperCollins Publishers, Inc.

Excerpts from the Grail Psalms, © 1963, 1986 by Ladies of the ~~...~~ f GIA, Inc., exclusive agent. ~~...~~ ved.

OKS

nam's Sons

Publishers since 1838

200 Madison Avenue

New York, N. Y. 10016

Copyright © 1996 by Kathleen Norris.

Published simultaneously in Canada.
Library of Congress Cataloging-in-Publication Data

Norris, Kathleen, date.
The cloister walk / Kathleen Norris.
p. cm.
ISBN 1-57322-028-0 (alk. paper)
1. Monastic and religious life. 2. Catholic Church—Liturgy.
3. Norris, Kathleen, date. 4. Spiritual life. I. Title.
BX2435.N57 1996
255—dc20 96-863 CIP

Printed in the United States of America

1 3 5 7 9 10 8 6 4 2

This book is printed on acid-free paper. ♾

Book design by Deborah Kerner

CONTENTS

For the children:

CHRISTINA, JACQUELINE,
LILLIAN, A.J., AND MIKEY

Ten years ago, when I became a Benedictine oblate, I knew two
things: I didn't feel ready to do it, but I had to act, to take the
plunge. I also had no idea where it would lead. An oblation is an
abbreviated yet powerful profession of monastic vows; you attach
yourself to a particular monastery by signing a document on the
altar during Mass, in which you promise to follow the Rule of St.
Benedict insofar as your situation in life will allow. A married
woman such as myself, for example, who makes frequent visits to
a monastery, will follow the Rule in a far different way than the
men and women who commit their lives entirely to a monastic
community. One thing I did not know was exactly how I had come
to be here. Having moved twelve years before from New York City
to my grandparents' house in western South Dakota seemed to have
something to do with it. And I'd begun to realize that the apprenticeship as a writer that I'd embarked on in my early twenties
was in essence a religious quest. (For years literature had seemed
an adequate substitute for religion in my life.) The fact that I'd been
raised a thorough Protestant, with little knowledge of religious orders, and no sense of monasticism as a living tradition, was less an
obstacle to my becoming an oblate than the many doubts about

the Christian religion that had been with me since my teens. Still, although I had little sense of where I'd been, I knew that standing before the altar in a monastery chapel was a remarkable place for me to be, and making an oblation was a remarkable, if not incomprehensible, thing for me to be doing.

The word "oblate" is from the Latin for "to offer," and Jesus himself is often referred to as an "oblation" in the literature of the early church. Many people now translate "oblate" as "associate," and while that may seem to describe the relationship modern oblates have with monastic communities, it does not adequately convey the religious dimension of being an oblate. Substituting the word "associate" for "oblation" in reference to Jesus demonstrates this all too well; no longer an offering, Jesus becomes a junior partner in a law firm. The ancient word "oblate" proved instructive for me. Having no idea what it meant, I appreciated its rich history when I first looked it up in the dictionary. But I also felt it presumptuous to claim to be an "offering" and was extremely reluctant to apply to myself a word that had so often been applied to Jesus Christ. The monk who was my oblate director, guiding my studies of the Rule (a period that was supposed to last a year but rambled on for nearly three), waited patiently for me to sort out my muddle. Finally I said to him, "I can't imagine why God would want me, of all people, as an offering. But if God is foolish enough to take me as I am, I guess I'd better do it." The monk smiled broadly and said, "You're ready."

Once I became an oblate, I found that I'd gained an enormous family. Benedictines are everywhere, and like a good family, they keep interfering in what I like to pretend is my own life. A chance encounter at an American Benedictine Academy convention led to my applying to the Institute for Ecumenical and Cultural Research at St. John's Abbey and University in Collegeville, Minnesota, and then spending not one, but two nine-month terms there. I had often heard Benedictines refer to their Liturgy of the Hours (also called the Divine Office) as "the sanctification of time," but had not much idea of what this could mean until I'd attended the liturgies at St. John's on a daily basis for many months.

Gradually my perspective on time had changed. In our culture, time can seem like an enemy: it chews us up and spits us out with appalling ease. But the monastic perspective welcomes time as a gift from God, and seeks to put it to good use rather than allowing us to be used up by it. A friend who was educated by the Benedictines has told me that she owes to them her sanity with regard to time. "You never really finish anything in life," she says, "and while that's humbling, and frustrating, it's all right. The Benedictines, more than any other people I know, insist that there is time in each day for prayer, for work, for study, and for play." Liturgical time is essentially poetic time, oriented toward process rather than pro-ductivity, willing to wait attentively in stillness rather than always pushing to "get the job done." Living at St. John's, I was surprised to discover how much the monastic world was giving me a new perspective on many aspects of my life, not only time, but mar-riage, family, living in a small town, clothing, and the vagaries of the literary world.

The Cloister Walk is a result of my immersion into a liturgical world, and in it I have tried to replicate for the reader the rhythm of saints' days, solemnities, and feasts that I experienced when I first came to St. John's in the fall of 1991. The book leaves the monastery, as I did, for family reunions, for work, for life at home in a small town in western South Dakota, and for worship at two Presbyterian churches there, Hope and Spencer Memorial. It also returns to the monastery, where for me, everything comes together. One pleasant surprise for me in writing this book is the way that my marriage came to weave in and out of it. It seems appropriate, as my life vows are not to a monastery but to matrimony, and marriage has for me been a primary instrument of conversion, "a school for love," to employ Benedict's metaphor for the monastery.

I've been a devoted reader since childhood and have been surprised to discover that what Benedict termed *lectio divina,* and many contemporary Benedictines call "spiritual reading," has given me a new appreciation for the contemplative potential of the reading process. *Lectio* is an attempt to read more with the heart than with the head. One does not try to "cover" a certain amount of material so much as surrender to whatever word or phrase catches the attention. A slow, meditative reading, primarily of the scriptures, *lectio* respects the power of words to resonate with the full range of human experience. As a monastery is a place in which the scriptures come to permeate all aspects of one's life, I have included in this book many quotations from the Bible. I feel this requires an explanatory note for the reader who, like the person I was for many years, may not have kept up an acquaintance with the Bible, and possibly thinks of it only as a weapon that Christians use against anyone who disagrees with them. Media sound bites can give the impression that this is the purpose of the Bible. But in the world the Benedictines have introduced me to, the scriptures constitute, as Paul Philibert, O.P., has described it in *Seeing and Believing,* "a demanding ecology of thought, imagination, decision, and action," words that are "awake during our rest and our silences, active in our reflection . . . effective in our actions in cooperation with others, [and that] cut through all our excuses."

Christianity, like Judaism and Islam, is a religion of the book, and for some seventeen hundred years the daily Christian liturgy has woven the Bible into the lives of monks and nuns. Monastic worship is essentially Hebraic; every day you recite the psalms, and you listen, as powerful biblical images, stories, and poems are allowed to flow freely, to wash over you. Doctrine and dogma are effectively submerged; present, but not the point. When I quote from scripture in this book, I am not trying to convince the reader that I have some hold on the truth. I am telling the story of the Liturgy of the Hours as I have experienced it, as "an open door, which no one is able to shut" (Rev. 3:8). I quote the Bible in the spirit of the great poet and theologian of the early church, Ephrem the Syrian, who said: "Scripture brought me to the gate of paradise, and the mind stood in wonder as it entered."

DAWN

*Somehow myself survived the night/And entered with
the Day . . .* —Emily Dickinson

*Abba Poeman said concerning Abba Prior that every day he
made a new beginning.*—THE SAYINGS OF THE
DESERT FATHERS

In the Orthodox tradition, the icon of Wisdom depicts
a woman seated on a throne. Her skin and her clothing
are red, to symbolize the dawn emerging against the deep, starry
blue of night.

For years, early morning was a time I dreaded. In the process
of waking up, my mind would run with panic. All the worries of
the previous day would still be with me, spinning around with old
regrets as well as fears for the future. I don't know how or when
the change came, but now when I emerge from night, it is with
more hope than fear. I try to get outside as early as possible so that
I can look for signs of first light, the faint, muddy red of dawn.

September 3

GREGORY THE GREAT

Every commandment is about love, and all of them add up to one commandment.—FROM A HOMILY OF GREGORY THE GREAT

It feels right to come back to the monastic liturgy on this day, to settle in with Gregory after the rush of moving to St. John's, the jumble of unpacking, the jumble of Gregory's life on my mind as I walk up the hill. Wealthy young Roman sells his estates, founds several monasteries, and gives to the poor. Dedicated monk turns reluctant diplomat and, in a time of plague, is elected bishop of Rome. Vigorously defends Jews' right to their synagogues, writes all we know of the life of Benedict. Fire, famine, earthquake; Rome sacked four times in twenty years. In 593, Gregory negotiates a truce.

I recall that on this day two years ago, I was in a hermitage, my marriage strained nearly to the breaking point. I felt as hard and dry as the bristly grasses of early fall, as exhausted as the drought-stricken trees around me. Then Gregory reminded me of the greatness of souls, how their true strength can emerge in the worst of times, when the known world is collapsing. "My mind divided," he said of himself, "torn to pieces by so many problems."

At vespers that night we had heard from Jeremiah: "I have loved you with an age-old love . . . Again I will build you, and you shall be built," words that renewed in me the stirrings of memory and desire. As I walked back to the hermitage in the dusk, I was suddenly glad, and not despairing, that in just a few days I'd be back with my husband, to take up life in the ruins.

I did not know that it would lead us here, to this crisp morning, my husband asleep in the apartment on the river, myself hurrying up the hill to morning prayer. That I would go to my study after prayers and begin to write poems again for the first time in three years.

ST. JOHN'S ABBEY LITURGY SCHEDULE

7 A.M.—Morning Prayer
Noon—Noon Prayer
5 P.M.—Eucharist
7 P.M.—Vespers

11:30 A.M.—Saturday Eucharist
10:30 A.M.—Sunday Eucharist

THE RULE
AND ME

Few books have so strongly influenced Western history as The Rule of St. Benedict. Written in the sixth century, a time as violent and troubled as our own, by a man determined to find a life of peace and stability for himself and others, it is a brief (ninety-six pages in a recent English translation), practical, and thoughtful work on how human beings can best live in community. Its style is so succinct that it is sometimes taught in law schools as an example of how to legislate simply and well. But the true power of the book, as with the Gospel it is based on, lies in its power to change lives.

I met the Rule by happy accident, when I found myself staying in a small Benedictine convent during a North Dakota Council on the Arts residency at a Catholic school. The women were pleasant enough, and I soon learned that the convent was indeed a heavenly place to return to after a day with lively schoolchildren. I felt it necessary to tell the sisters, however, that I wasn't much of a churchgoer, had a completely Protestant background, and knew next to nothing about them. I said they'd have to tell me if I did anything wrong. In many ways my response was typical of a modern person with little experience of church as an adult; I had the nagging fear that people as religious as these women would find me wanting, and be judgmental.

The sisters listened politely and then one of them said, with a wit I'm just learning to fathom, "Would you like to read our Rule? Then you'll know if you've done something wrong." "Sure," I said, always a sucker for a good book. She found me a copy, along with a book on Benedictine spirituality that the women were studying. As I went upstairs to begin reading, several of the sisters settled down to watch television, and I appreciated the irony. I began to think that my stay with them would work out fine.

What happened to me then has no doubt happened to many unsuspecting souls in the fifteen-hundred-plus years that Benedictines have existed. Quite simply, the Rule spoke to me. Like so many, I am put off by religious language as it's manipulated by television evangelists, used to preach to the converted, the "saved." Benedict's language and imagery come from the Bible, but he was someone who read the psalms every day—as Benedictines still do—and something of the psalms' emotional honesty, their grounding in the physical, rubbed off on him. Even when the psalms are at their most ecstatic, they convey holiness not with abstraction but with images from the world we know: rivers clap their hands, hills dance like yearling sheep. The Bible, in Benedict's hands, had a concreteness and vigor that I hadn't experienced since hearing Bible stories read to me as a child.

Benedict's Prologue has an appealing, familial tone, and indeed Benedictine communities function as families. Contrary to what one might expect, he writes: "We hope to set down nothing harsh, nothing burdensome." (This, I later learned, is a far cry from earlier monastic rules, some of which are harshly, even paranoiacally, punitive.) Benedict is refreshingly realistic in his understanding and acceptance of people as they are. "The souls of all concerned," he reminds us, "may prompt us to a little strictness in order to amend faults and safeguard love."

The Rule surprises people who expect the ether that often wafts through books on spiritual themes, the kind of holy talk that can make me feel like a lower life form. Benedict knows that practicalities—the order and times for psalms to be read, care of tools, the amount and type of food and drink and clothing—are also spiritual concerns. Many communal ventures begun with high hopes have foundered over the question of who takes out the garbage. Over and over, the Rule calls us to be more mindful of the little things, even as it reminds us of the big picture, allowing us a glimpse of who we can be when we remember to love. Benedict insists that this remembering is hard work needing daily attention and care. He writes for grown-ups, not people with their heads in the clouds. "No one shall be excused from kitchen duty," Benedict says, making exceptions only for the sick or those people engaged in the urgent business of the monastery. Today, that means that the Benedictine scholar with the Ph.D. scrubs pots and pans alongside a confrere who has an eighth-grade education, the dignified abbot or prioress dishes out food and wipes refectory tables after the meal.

I first encountered the Rule in the mid-1980s, when my husband and I were barely hanging on as freelance writers in an isolated, rural area. We were not alone in our economic uncertainty; everyone in the region was severely affected by what was termed "the farm crisis." The distress was not merely economic, but social and emotional as well, and the church I had recently, and reluctantly, joined was, like other local institutions, in considerable turmoil. Among its members were bankers as well as farmers going through bankruptcy, and tensions ran high. It surprised me to find that a sixth-century document spoke so clearly to our situation, offering a realistic look at human weakness, as well as sensible and humane advice for us, if we truly wished to live in peace with one another.

I was also surprised, as I hadn't read the Bible in years, at how much of Benedict's advice came straight from scripture. In his prologue, he takes that enticing question of Psalm 34, "Which of you desires life, and covets many days to enjoy good?" and states that God has already given us the answer in the very next verses of the psalm: "Keep your tongue from evil, your lips from speaking deceit. Depart from evil, and do good; seek peace, and pursue it" (Ps 34:12–14). It was good to be reminded, as I thought of the conflicts in my town and church and family, that peace is not an easy thing, but something that must be struggled for.

In a marriage, in a small town, in a monastery, it is all too easy to let things slide, to allow tensions to build until the only way they can be relieved is in an explosion that does more harm than good. Benedict's voice remains calm—persevere, bear one another's burdens, be patient with one another's infirmities of body or behavior. And when the "thorns of contention" arise in daily life, daily forgive, and be willing to accept forgiveness. Remember that you are not the center of the universe but, to use Benedict's words, "keep death daily before your eyes."

HILDEGARD OF BINGEN

"What I do not see I do not know," Hildegard wrote to a monk late in her life. "I see, hear, and know simultaneously, and learn what I know as if in a moment. But what I do not see I do not know, for I am not learned." At our first seminar I tell my colleagues at the Ecumenical Institute, mostly college professors on sabbatical, that this seems to me a poetic way of knowing, that poets are indeed at the mercy of what they see.

In a way, I tell them, it might also describe me, a poet who is "not learned." I have no advanced degrees and have never worked in academia. When my first book was published in 1971, I turned down a job in a college English department, because I couldn't see myself as a teacher. I didn't know it at the time, but this was a vocational decision; I became a freelance writer instead. Some eyebrows go up. I explain that my "research" at the Institute will be primarily experiential, and will be centered on attending the daily Liturgy of the Hours at the monastery. The eyebrows stay up.

I talk about the way Hildegard captures in this letter the path of knowledge that I'm most familiar with, in which thoughts and images constellate, converging, sometimes violently, in the subconscious. The sounds of words and the silence of images are more important at this stage than sense or "meaning." In composing a poem, one often seems to move directly from ignorance to revelation, instantly from a muddled sense of things to a clear picture, with only the vaguest sense of how it happened. Experience is the ground of this way of knowing. But if visionaries and poets are at the mercy of what they see, they are also called to articulate it. And this requires them to employ another form of knowledge, the linear thought that enables them to communicate their experience to others. As with most human endeavors, the key to employing these complementary elements of human intelligence is balance.

Cardinal Newman, in referring to the Benedictines as the most poetic of religious orders, has helped me to understand one aspect of their attraction for me. I've often sensed that the rhythms of monastic life, which now, as in Hildegard's time, are set to a liturgical pace, foster a way of knowing that values image over idea, the synthetic over the analytical, the instantaneous over the sequential, the intuitive and associative over the formal and prescribed. If, as Jean Leclercq has put it, monastic culture is "more literary than speculative," it also reflects what I mean by a poetic way of knowing.

A line from Hildegard's sequence for the virgin martyr Ursula: "The girl has no idea what she means," has great resonance for me. Although it is the crowd that speaks, mocking the young woman as she is put to death—as legend has it, for being a Christian and for refusing to become the concubine of Attila the Hun—I see the mockery transformed, in Hildegard's hands, into a statement of defiance. Poets understand that they do not know what they mean, and that this is a source of their strength. I wonder, if in our modern, literal-minded age, being able to declare "what I do not see I do not know" is a mark, even a cornerstone, of a poet's faith. I do not mean that we're pragmatists, like Thomas, who asked to see and touch Christ's wounds, but rather that writing teaches us to recognize when we have reached the limits of our language, and our knowing, and are dependent on our senses to "know" for us.

The discipline of poetry teaches poets, at least, that they often have to say things they can't pretend to understand. In contending with words, poets come to know their power, much the way monastics do in prayer and *lectio*. We experience words as steeped in mystery, forces beyond our intellectual grasp. In the late twentieth century, when speculative knowledge and the technologies it has spawned reign supreme, poets remain dependent on a different form of knowledge, perhaps akin to what Hildegard termed seeing, hearing, and knowing simultaneously. I wonder if what made Hildegard very much a twelfth-century person is part of what makes poets in the twentieth century seem both anachronistic and necessary.

I am not well received. Something is off, a tension I can't name. I won't know for weeks how disastrous it will be.

Before my husband embarked on his South Seas journey, he installed a large National Geographic map of the region on the stark white wall by the kitchen table. When he called last night, he'd just arrived in Rarotonga, in the Cook Islands. I found the words on the map, and fingered them as we spoke. I finger them again, at breakfast, to keep him in my presence. It's our fifteenth anniversary. He's staying at the Paradise Inn.

We didn't pick our wedding day for any particular reason. We eloped, continuing what has become a family tradition, on my mother's side; both my grandmother Totten and my mother eloped when young—probably too young—and then built of this folly marriages that endured for close to sixty years. We've had just one church wedding within the last seventy years, and it resulted in our one divorce.

One day, in a library reference room, I became curious to know if the date of our wedding had any significance in the Christian tradition. When I discovered that it was the feast of Archangels, I got the giggles and left before the librarian would have to throw me out.

I have saved up things to tell David: a monk who'd complained to me about the resistance to change he'd encountered at work, who said, "It's the well-worn idol named, 'But we've never done it that way before!'" Exasperated, he'd said, "And people wonder how dogmas get started!" David laughs; he knows this is the feast of archangels, and tells me that he's discovered that in the native religion of Tonga, whales are the messengers of the Gods, performing a function much like the eagle in Lakota religion, or angels in Christianity. In Nuku'alofa, which means, "The City Where Love Lives," he purchased an amulet of a whale's fluke, representing the divine messenger who moves between our world and that of the Creator, who lives at the bottom of the sea. The woman who sold it to him said it had been blessed by a Methodist bishop, but he could also take it to a priest of the old religion. "I did," he said. "It cost me a six-pack of beer and a carton of cigarettes," he says, happily. I am happy to think of him walking around paradise wrapped in blessings.

At morning prayer, the psalms seem suited to the archangels. Psalm 29, for Michael, the power of God: "The Lord's voice resounding on the waters, the God of Glory thunders; the Lord on the immensity of waters . . ." And for Gabriel, Psalm 25, a quiet prayer of hope and trust. For Raphael, a psalm that I love, 147: "The Lord builds up Jerusalem, and brings back Israel's exiles. And heals the broken-hearted; and binds up all their wounds."

Michael—who is as God; Gabriel—God's messenger; Raphael—God's healing. They say what angels always say, "Do not fear."

THE
DIFFERENCE

Once, as I was preparing an omelet, I turned to the friend standing in the kitchen of my apartment at the Ecumenical Institute and asked him, "How do you like your eggs?" I glanced up from chopping green onions to find him looking dazed but pleased, as if I had just suggested that we run off to Paris for the weekend. "You know," I said, puzzled by his silence, "runny or well-done?" And then it hit me: he's a monk, which means that no one ever asks him how he likes his eggs. For most of his adult life he has dined communally, eating whatever is put before him.

My monastic friends are often at pains to counteract the romantic image of the monk or nun, insisting, rightly, that they are ordinary people. Every once in a while, however, the difference asserts itself, a reminder of the fact that the monastic world is not like the world that most of us inhabit. To eat in a monastery refectory is an exercise in humility; daily, one is reminded to put communal necessity before individual preference. While consumer culture speaks only to preferences, treating even whims as needs to be granted (and the sooner the better), monastics sense that this pandering to delusions of self-importance weakens the true self, and diminishes our ability to distinguish desires from needs. It's a price they're not willing to pay.

But in a consumer culture, monastic people must be vigilant, remaining intentional about areas of life that most of us treat casually, with little awareness of what we're doing. One year at the American Benedictine Academy convention, an abbot, speaking on the subject of "The Monastic Archetype," suddenly dropped all pretense to objectivity and said he was troubled by the growing number of cereals made available for breakfast in his community. "How many kinds of cereals do we need," he asked, "in order to meet genuine health needs without falling into thoughtless consumerism?" The audience of several hundred Benedictine men and women broke into applause, obviously grateful that he'd captured, in one seemingly trivial example, an unease that many of them share about the way they live in contemporary America. One monk, a former abbot, said that he wasn't as concerned with the number of cereals available as he was with the cafeteria-style of eating adopted by his community. "When we serve ourselves," he said, "we do not exemplify monastic values." He wondered if eating family-style, sharing from a common bowl, waiting to be served and then to serve one's neighbor, was a practice monastic people could afford to lose.

A friend who is a retired corporate executive, and a Benedictine oblate, has pointed out to me that monastic, family-style management differs greatly from management as practiced by a corporation. While this difference sometimes results in Benedictines raising inefficiency to an art form, I've come to value the monastic witness to a model of institutional behavior that is not "all business," that does not bow down before the idols of efficiency and the profit motive. Now that corporations are constructing ready-made "communities," in the form of gated and guarded suburban enclaves, the difference between monastic community and corporate culture has become all the more evident.

What *The New York Times* recently termed "the fastest growing residential communities in the nation" are private developments created out of fear of crime and urban chaos. Fear is not easily contained, and it is not surprising to find that these developments also manifest a fear of individual differences that might spring up within the enclave itself, requiring a draconian set of rules that attempt to provide for every eventuality. Outdoor clotheslines, satellite dishes, and streetside parking are often prohibited, and in some communities, a pet dog who strays from its own yard is zapped by an electronic monitor. While strict regulation of such things as the colors of house paint, the height of hedges, the type of gardens or flower beds, and the number and size of hanging planters for the front porch may give the severely anal-retentive a place to call home, I find it a sad commentary on our ability to accept the responsibility of freedom. I suspect that it is also an experiment doomed to failure, as people discover that it is not easy to live according to a corporate model, and that their private governments, schools, and police forces provide more tyranny than security. The question asked by Tacitus when the well-to-do citizens of ancient Rome began fleeing the troubles of the city by retreating behind the walls of their guarded villas—"Who will guard the guards?"—is still a good one.

The Romans lost everything to barbarian invaders. Ironically, it is another legacy of the fall of Rome, the Benedictine monastery, that is still going strong fifteen hundred years later. As a young man, Benedict had abandoned the decaying city. "[Putting] aside his father's residence and fortune," his biographer Gregory the Great tells us, "and desiring to please God alone," Benedict adopted the life of a hermit in the countryside. But his renown as a spiritual man soon attracted others, and in accommodating them, establishing a monastery and writing a rule for their way of life, Benedict was able to serve the world in ways that a "private community" cannot. He took it for granted that the world would come to monks. "A monastery is never without guests," he said, implying that a true monastery is never so shut off from the world as to stop attracting guests.

The modern guest who partakes of Benedictine hospitality soon discovers that it entails a remarkable freedom to be oneself. If you start to sing Ramones songs in a loud voice at three in the morning, chances are someone will ask you to quiet down. But then, again, maybe not. The responsibility is yours; rules and regulations are kept to a minimum. In fact, the "customary" of a monastery—a book that contains, in written form, the everyday customs and traditions of the place—reveals that Benedictines themselves live free from much written legislation. The customary of one of the largest monasteries in the world is little more than a sketchy outline. One monk told me, "This is because the minute you write something down, you set it in stone. And that's dangerous, because then someone will want to enforce it." Because they operate as families, Benedictines can claim a culture that is primarily oral rather than written, more dependent on lived experience than explicit codes of conduct.

I once heard a monk who has doctorates in both canon and civil law explain that Benedict had taken one of the strengths of Roman society, a passion for civil order, and had converted it into legislation for a way of life that integrates prayer, work, and communality so flexibly that it is still relevant to twentieth-century needs. It may be more relevant now than ever. "While Benedict respected the individual," he said, "he recognized that the purpose of individual growth is to share with others." It was refreshing to hear a good legal mind with soul, another reminder of the monastic difference: "We live in vigil," the monk said, "working at love in common living. Monastic life is meant to be lived in vigil, in *koinonia,* or, a community of love. And it looks toward eternal life, where love will be completed." I don't know many tough-minded lawyers who talk like this.

Benedictines often remind me of poets, who while they sometimes speak of the art of poetry in exalted terms also know that little things count, that in fact there are no things so "little" as to be without significance in the making of a poem. Monastic life also requires paying attention to the nitty-gritty. "We know that details matter," another monk once told me, "and we'll tinker with our liturgy of the hours, trying a minute of silence after each psalm, after discovering that ninety seconds is too long. But we are still an experiment, after all these years, and we resist codifying." The great experiment of Christian monasticism has taken so many forms that it is hard to characterize: now, as in the fourth century, monastic people live as hermits, in loosely organized clusters of hermits, as members of cloistered communities, and in communities in constant contact with the world. They are urban, rural, and they live in wilderness; they work as pastors (and as counselors, teachers, nurses, doctors, and massage therapists) and they pray as contemplatives. At times in the Middle Ages, "monastic cities" existed, inhabited by monks and their students, soldiers, and families of merchants, servants, farmers, and artisans, a situation that several modern monasteries have emulated loosely, taking in artists who practice their craft in exchange for room and board, or allowing widows, married couples, and families to participate more fully in monastic life without making lifelong vows. Time will tell what works, and what doesn't; after a millennium and a half, Benedictines can afford to take the long view.

I was intrigued to discover that there are fussy monastic rules that predate that of Benedict, notably *The Rule of the Master,* in which fear and suspicion predominate, revealing an overwhelmingly negative view of both the world outside the monastery, and the motives of individuals within it. Predictably, the author of this rule attempts, in the words of one commentary, "to regulate everything in advance, to foresee every possible case." Benedict appears relaxed and humane by comparison, more laissez-faire, much more trusting of individual discretion: "Whoever needs less should thank God and not be distressed," he writes in the section about distribution of goods in the monastery, but he adds that "whoever needs more should feel humble because of his weakness, not self-important because of the kindness shown him. In this way, all the members will be at peace." From the earliest days in the Egyptian desert, monastic life has attracted all classes of people. And this means, as Benedict was quick to realize, that equal treatment does not translate into equality; what is an unpleasantly hard bed to someone raised in wealth might be a luxury to a shepherd used to sleeping on the ground. As recently as the 1930s, monastic novices raised on American farms, who had slept all their lives on straw-filled ticking, got their first experience of mattresses and sheets in the monastery. (This cultural phenomenon, by which monastic deprivation becomes a form of luxury, is much in evidence today in the thriving Benedictine monastaries of the Third World, making Benedict's wisdom on the subject of need more relevant than ever.)

The ongoing Benedictine experiment demonstrates a remarkable ability to take individual differences into account while establishing the primacy of communal life. I find this most evident when a Benedictine community is deciding whether or not to accept a candidate. Questions that would be primary in the business world—what are this person's credentials and skills, what will they add to the organization's efficiency and productivity?—are secondary, if they're raised at all. Even the question of "acceptability," which is so often a mask for prejudice, is muted. People are simply asked to consider whether or not this person has a monastic vocation for that particular community. The fact that you might not like the person, certainly not enough to want to live with them for the rest of your life, is not supposed to be a factor. The monastic value of not judging others, of giving them the benefit of the doubt, can become extremely painful at a time like this, because once a person becomes a part of the community, they are family.

Most monasteries now employ psychological screening methods for candidates, and the discipline of the novitiate tends to weed out the severely maladjusted. But I've often been touched by the way in which monastic communities, like strong families, can accommodate their more troubled members. Every monastery I know contains at least one borderline person, who may be socially retarded (or just extremely repressed), who has minimal brain damage, who suffers from a mental illness such as manic-depression, or who is ravaged by Alzheimer's, or even, in the words of one monastic friend, who may simply be "surpassingly strange." And it is good to see the many ways that communities find to make room. While monastic people are not conventionally nice to each other—as family, they can be brutally honest, taking liberties that outsiders find shocking—I've often witnessed support for their more disturbed members in the form of prayers, and daily acts of patient, loving-kindness that would put many families to shame. Benedictines do make use of psychiatrists and drugs such as Prozac, but I sometimes wonder if the sustained love of a community doesn't help just as much.

Contemporary American Benedictines, like the culture they live in tension with, are struggling with questions of diversity. Communities founded by Swiss or German monastics a century or more ago are contending with the loss of old customs, as their newest members—of Mexican, Laotian, Vietnamese ethnicity—bring new customs with them. Several Benedictines who teach novitiate classes in both men's and women's communities, have said to me that one of the biggest problems monasteries currently face is people who come to them having no sense of what it means to live communally. Schooled in individualism, often having families so disjointed that even meals in common were a rarity, they find it extremely difficult to adjust to monastic life. "They want to be alone all the time," one formation director said to me of his current novices. "I have to force them to do things as a group."

Monasticism is a way of life, and monasteries are full of real people. In considering the great tensions that have always existed in the monastic imperative—between structure and freedom, diversity and unity, openness to the world and retreat from it—monks are better off when they retain the ability to laugh at themselves. One monk, when asked about diversity in his small community, said that there were people who can meditate all day and others who can't sit still for five minutes; monks who are scholars and those who are semiliterate; chatterboxes and those who emulate Calvin Coolidge with regard to speech. "But," he said, "our biggest problem is that each man here had a mother who fried potatoes in a different way." Differences between individuals will either be absorbed when the community gathers to act as one, or these communal activities become battlegrounds. As one monk, a liturgist, once said to me, "Go to the dining room and to prayers, and you'll find out how a monastery is doing."

When I think of all that monasteries have survived in the 1500-plus years of their existence—pirate raids, bandits, wars and revolutions, political and social upheavals of all kinds, dictators, tyrants, confiscation, foreclosure, martyrdom at the hands of kings, as well as co-opting by the wealthy and powerful—I find it amazing that they're still here. "We're as persistent as weeds," one Benedictine friend says. "We just keep springing up." I suspect that it is the difference, the adherence to monastic bedrock, what one sister calls the "non-negotiables" in the face of changing circumstances, that makes monasticism so indestructible. Monastic communities traffic in intangibles—worship, solitude, humility, peace—that are not easily manipulated by corporate concerns, not easily identified, packaged, and sold. It will be interesting to see how monastic communities fare in a world which gives more and more power to large, multinational corporations.

I expect they'll survive, with their difference, the absurdity of faith that attracts people to a communal way of life and gives them the strength to persevere in it. "The basis of community is not that we have all our personal needs met here, or that we find all our best friends in the monastery," I once heard a monk say. In fact, he added, his pastoral experience with married couples had taught him that such unreasonably high expectations of any institution, be it a marriage or a monastery, was often what led to disillusionment, and dissolution of the bond. "What we have to struggle for, and to preserve, is a shared vision of the *why,*" he said, "why we live together. It's a common meaning, reinforced in the scriptures, a shared vision of the coming reign of God."

September 30

JEROME

We hear from Jerome today, at morning prayer, a section of the Prologue to his commentary on Isaiah. He was a contentious man: "Ignorance of Scripture is ignorance of Christ," he booms, and his words shatter our sleepy silence. Jerome was the hard-edged, brilliant fellow who first translated the Hebrew scriptures into Latin. And, judging from his letters and his life, he may have been one of the most irascible people who ever lived.

Jerome is a saint feminists love to hate, and to quote: "Now that a virgin has conceived in the womb and borne to us a child . . . now the chain of the curse is broken. Death came through Eve, but life has come through Mary. And thus the gift of virginity has been bestowed most richly upon women, seeing that it has had its beginning from a woman."

This is typical of the way in which the Christian biblical interpreters of the late fourth century—Jerome and then Augustine, not long after—made a connection between Eve and Mary. We've lost the wonder that these words must have had for those who first heard them; now we sigh, discouraged, hearing only the seeds of our well-worn, ludicrous sexual double standard which dictates that women must be either virgins or whores, either blessed or cursed, while men are simply sexual athletes, slaves of lust. (And, don't forget, Christian boys and girls, everyone is a temple of the Holy Spirit.)

As with most of these writings from a time so distant from our own, it is difficult to read without reading into it our modern frustrations, difficult to discern the complexities that resist our simplistic interpretations. To me, this passage reflects a fear of women that is thoroughly comprehensible: if Eve is the mother of the living, she is also mother of the dead. One of the most astonishing and precious things about motherhood is the brave way in which women consent to give birth to creatures who will one day die. That they do this is an awesome thing, as is their virginity, their existence in and of themselves, apart from that potential for bearing life and death. That we all begin inside a woman and must emerge from her body is something that the male theologians of the world's religions have yet to forgive us for.

The truth about Jerome is that he was an equal-opportunity curmudgeon. He despised both men and women, but women fascinated him more. Maybe because he genuinely believed that in them, as in Mary, lay the beginnings of salvation. Jerome's friendships with women—Paula, her daughter Eustochium, Marcella—certainly saved him from much hardship. These learned, powerful women had taken their considerable wealth out of the Roman Empire's reach in order to found monasteries and scholarly enterprises such as Jerome's. Without their friendship and financial support, his translation of the Bible would not have been possible.

It is clear from Jerome's correspondence that his friendships with these women were abiding and deep. I like to think that they inspired him to give the women of the New Testament a theological import that is radical, even now. Whenever I hear of conservative seminarians (Roman Catholic or Protestant) who bristle at the mention of Mary Magdalene as a model for the apostles, I think of Jerome's typically tart comment on the subject: "The unbelieving reader may perhaps laugh at me for dwelling so long on the praises of mere women; yet if he will but remember how holy women followed our Lord and Saviour and ministered to Him out of their substance, and how the three Marys stood before the cross and especially how Mary Magdalene—called the tower from the earnestness and glow of her faith—was privileged to see the rising Christ first of all before the very apostles, he will convict himself of pride sooner than me of folly. For we judge people's virtue not by their sex but by their character . . ."

Jerome's own character was notoriously difficult. As Peter Brown has dryly noted, he was a man "of pronounced ascetical views," not at all shy about advising his lady friends on the virtues of going without baths, of aspiring to "holy knees hardened like a camel's from the frequency of prayers," and of sleeping on cold floors, full of groans and tears. Who wouldn't cry?

The hymn we sing in Jerome's honor is a pleasant, generic hymn in praise of the saints, entitled "Who Are These Like Stars Appearing," and it amuses me greatly to envision Jerome, of all people, shining like a star, and hating every minute of it. As we're leaving the church, I mention this to one of the monks. "Ah, poor Jerome," he said, "forced to smile and sing for all of eternity. Maybe that's his punishment." One of the theology students has overheard us. "The feast of St. Jerome," he says, "Wickedness is in the air."

October 1

THÉRÈSE

OF THE CHILD JESUS

It's always a relief to come to St. Thérèse after Jerome: from the bitter to the sweet, from the brutally ridiculous to the offhandedly sublime. For a few years, in the 1870s and early 1880s, Thérèse and Emily Dickinson were contemporaries. Thérèse was thirteen when Dickinson died, and already determined to join the Carmelite convent at Lisieux.

As Emily Dickinson was known to be attracted to the company of children—they were the eager recipients of cookies and gingerbread that she baked and lowered in baskets from the window of her room—I love to think that she might have enjoyed a conversation with the four-year-old Thérèse, whose response to being offered a handful of ribbons from which to choose was to say, simply, "I choose all."

Both Thérèse and Emily Dickinson did choose all, I think, and in doing so gave up almost everything. First Corinthians attracted them both; I suspect it is where each woman found her calling. Emily Dickinson, attracted to Paul's confession of "weakness and much fear and trembling," his knowing "nothing but Christ crucified," speaks in her poems of daily crucifixion, of "newer—nearer

Crucifixion." Near the end of her life, she wrote in a letter: "When Jesus tells us about his Father, we distrust him. When he shows us his Home, we turn away, but when he confides to us that he is 'acquainted with Grief,' we listen, for that also is an Acquaintance of our own."

Commenting on First Corinthians in her autobiography, Thérèse laments that for a long time she could not find herself in any of the members which Paul describes in the epistle—not a martyr (that's a matter of opinion), not an apostle, but an insignificant young nun who was known in her convent mainly for her tendency to fall asleep during the Liturgy of the Hours. Remembering, suddenly, to be the bold child who chooses all, she states, "I have found my calling: my call is love," and writes: "In the heart of the Church, my mother, I will be love, and thus I will be all things . . ."

This is the reading in the breviary for this day, and the text I had expected to hear at morning prayer. Instead, I am startled awake by Thérèse in another mode: "For a long time," she says, "I have wondered why the good Lord has preferences . . . I was surprised to see the Lord give extraordinary favors to saints who had offended him." (She may be referring here to St. Jerome.) Why these saints, she wonders, blessed all their lives by God's interfering presence, when there are so many people Thérèse considers to be unimaginably poor, "dying without even hearing the name of God . . ."

She finds her answer in the "book of nature" that Jesus has given her. Contemplating the diversity of flowers, she writes, "I have come to realize, that the radiance of the rose and the whiteness of the lily do not take away the fragrance of the little violet or the delightful simplicity of the daisy." She decides that "perfection consists in being what God wants us to be."

It was a decision that was to cost her dearly. Emerging out of the narrow confines of nineteenth-century Jansenism, a thickly pious little girl, adored and spoiled by her parents and older sisters, she rushed headlong into the wide spaces of sanctity, only to be confined again by tuberculosis, a disease in which the lungs become brittle over time, and are finally coughed out. With a temerity equal to that of Paul (and Emily Dickinson), she addressed Jesus frequently towards the end of her life, saying "My little story, which was like a fairy tale, has turned into prayer."

Thérèse was then twenty-four, and close to death. At Easter of 1896, the year before she died, she herself had become impoverished by the loss of a sense of God's presence that had been with her all her life. She saw this as grace, that God should permit her to be overwhelmed by impenetrable darkness. Again, she addresses God: "Lord, your child has understood your divine light: she asks pardon for her brothers, and consents to eat for as long as you wish it the bread of sorrow, and she will not rise from this table, which is filled with bitterness, where poor sinners eat, until the day you have appointed. Further, can she not say in their name . . . 'Have pity on us, Lord, for we are poor sinners.' " Thérèse concludes, boldly, "I told [the Lord] that I am happy not to enjoy heaven here on earth in order that he may open heaven for ever to poor unbelievers."

Here a saint emerges, an astonishing brat who dares to speak thus to God, in a voice that Emily Dickinson might well recognize as kindred to her own. (I can hear them talking, perhaps in the Elysian Fields: "My business is to love . . . My business is to sing," Emily says, and Thérèse replies, "My call is love . . . love embraces every time and every place." From the confines of a room in Amherst, a drafty cell at the Carmel in Lisieux, each woman might be said to have traveled extensively.) I believe that Thérèse became a uniquely valuable twentieth-century saint, a woman who can accept even the torment of doubt, as she lay dying, as a precious gift, who turns despair into a fervent prayer for others. I think of her as a saint for unbelievers in an age of unbelief, a voice of compassion in an age of beliefs turned rigid, defensive, violent.

Late in the morning, I emerge from my study in the basement of the library to find buses of the Guardian School Bus company disgorging flocks of brightly dressed children, who with their wary-looking teachers and weary parents, are waiting—jumping, dancing, screaming, running, slapping hands and knees—on the steps of the abbey church. Soon they'll take a tour of the woods and no doubt collect some red and golden leaves. I notice in the courtyard by the guest wing of the monastery that tough little roses are still in bloom, despite the hard frost.

October 2

GUARDIAN ANGELS

It has to do with us, this feast. What we long for, and see, and do not see. "And so the angels are here," says St. Bernard, whispering like a child.

Two crows interpose themselves between me and the golden trees—ash, oak—between the blood-red maple and a full moon grown pale in a cloudless blue. Their cries, on the chill wind, come as mystery, much like the question Bernard tosses up to God: "What are we, that you make yourselves known to us?"

JEREMIAH
AS WRITER:
THE NECESSARY
OTHER

The Benedictine monks of St. John's Abbey practice what is known as *lectio continua,* reading through whole books of the Bible, a section at a time, at morning and evening prayer. They read through the entire New Testament in this way every year, and during the time I've spent with them—eighteen months over the last three years—we also listened to Genesis, Ruth, Tobit, Esther, Job, the Song of Songs, Hosea, Jonah, and large portions of the books of Exodus, Samuel, Kings, and Isaiah. The most remarkable experience of all was plunging into the prophet Jeremiah at morning prayer in late September one year, and staying with him through mid-November. We began with chapter 1, and read straight through, ending at chapter 22:17. Listening to Jeremiah is one hell of a way to get your blood going in the morning; it puts caffeine to shame.

The monastic discipline of listening aims to still body and soul so that the words of a reading may sink in. Such silence tends to open a person, and opening oneself to a prophet as anguished as

Jeremiah is painful. On some mornings, I found it impossible. Like one of my monk friends, who had the duty of reading the prophet aloud through some particularly grim passages, I felt like shouting, "Have a Nice Day!" to the assembly. Easier to mock a prophet than to listen to him.

On other days, I became angry, or was reduced to tears, perhaps a promising sign that something of Jeremiah's grief had broken through my defenses. The command in chapter 4:3, "Break up your fallow ground," stayed with me long enough to elicit a response in my journal. The ancient monastics recognized that a life of prayer must "work the earth of the heart," and with their acceptance of the painful, and even violent nature of this process in mind, I wrote, "And as I take my spade in hand, as far as I can see, great clods of earth are waiting, heavy and dark, a hopeless task. First weeds will come, then whatever it is I've planted. I feel the struggle in my knees and back."

One beneficial effect of *lectio continua* is that it enables a person to hear the human voices of biblical authors. It becomes obvious, for instance, that Paul's letters are actual letters, meant to be read aloud, and in their entirety, to church congregations. The monks, in keeping that tradition alive, are also helping Paul's words to live in the present. Paul's theological wheel-turning can lose me—Oscar Wilde once described Paul's prose style as one of the principal arguments against Christianity—but hearing Paul read aloud in the monk's choir allowed me to take an unaccustomed pleasure in the complex play Paul makes of even his deepest theology. To hear the joke working its way through 1 Corinthians 1:21 is to get the point: "For since in the wisdom of God the world did not come to know God through wisdom, it was the will of God through the foolishness of the proclamation to save those who have faith." Hearing the passage read slowly one night at vespers,

I suddenly grasped the exasperation there, and God's good humor, and it made me laugh.

Listening to the Bible read aloud is not only an invaluable immersion in religion as an oral tradition, it allows even the scripture scholars of a monastic community to hear with fresh ears. A human voice is speaking, that of an apostle, or a prophet, and the concerns critical to biblical interpretation—authorship of texts, interpolation of material, redaction of manuscript sources—recede into the background. One doesn't forget what one knows, and the process of listening may well inform one's scholarship. But in communal *lectio,* the fact that the Book of Jeremiah has several authors matters far less than that a human voice is speaking, and speaking to you. Even whether or not you believe that this voice speaks the word of God is less important than the sense of being sought out, personally engaged, making it possible, even necessary, to respond personally, to take the scriptures to heart.

Taking Jeremiah to heart, day in day out, I got much more than I bargained for. I found it brave of these Benedictines, in late-twentieth-century America, in a culture of denial, to try to listen to a prophet at all. The response of the monks was illuminating, and sometimes comical. "Know what you have done," Jeremiah shouted at us one morning (2:23), but before we could get over the ferocity of that command—it's so much easier to live *not* knowing what we've done—the prophet had gone on to a vivid depiction of Israel as a frenzied camel in heat, loudly sniffing the wind, making directionless tracks in the sand. This was imagery we could smell; the poetry of scripture at its earthy best.

Monks are not used to being compared to camels in heat, but they took it pretty well. I noticed eyebrows going up around the choir, and then a kind of quiet assent: *well, there are days.* Monks know very well how easy it is to lose track of one's purpose in life, how hard to maintain the discipline that keeps (in St. Benedict's words) "our minds in harmony with our voices" in prayer, the ease with which aimless desire can disturb our hearts. "Stop wearing out your shoes" (2:25), Jeremiah said, and we sat up straight. This was something a crusty desert father might have said to a recalcitrant young monk who thought that some other monastery might suit him better, or whose restlessness was preventing prayer: get hold of yourself, settle down. *Stop wearing out your shoes.* Good advice for us in America, in a society grown alarmingly mobile, where retreats and spirituality workshops have become such a hot consumer item one wonders if seeking the holy has become an end in itself.

One day, not long after we'd begun to read Jeremiah, and it was dawning on us that we had a long, rough road ahead, a monk said to me: "We haven't read a prophet for a while, and we need to hear it. It's good for us." Another said he was glad to be reading Jeremiah in the morning, and not at evening prayer, when there are more likely to be guests. "The monks can take it," he said, "but most people have no idea what's in the Bible, and they come unglued."

Coming unglued came to seem the point of listening to Jeremiah. The prophet, after all, is witness to a time in which his world, the society surrounding the temple in Jerusalem, meets a violent end, and Israel is taken captive to Babylon. Hearing Jeremiah's words every morning, I soon felt challenged to reflect on the upheavals in our own society, and in my life. A prophet's task is to reveal the fault lines hidden beneath the comfortable surface of the worlds we invent for ourselves, the national myths as well as the little lies and delusions of control and security that get us through the day. And Jeremiah does this better than anyone.

The voice of Jeremiah is compelling, often on an overwhelmingly personal level. One morning, I was so worn out by the emotional roller coaster of chapter 20 that after prayers I walked to my apartment and went back to bed. This passionate soliloquy, which begins with a bitter outburst on the nature of the prophet's calling ("You enticed me, O Lord, and I was enticed"), moves quickly into denial ("I say to myself, I will not mention him, I will speak in his name no more. But then it becomes like fire burning in my heart, imprisoned in my bones"). Jeremiah's anger at the way his enemies deride him rears up, and also fear and sorrow ("All my close friends are watching for me to stumble"). His statement of confidence in God ("The Lord is with me like a dread warrior") seems forced under the circumstances, and a brief doxology ("Sing to the Lord, praise the Lord, for he has delivered the life of the needy from the hands of evildoers") feels more ironic than not, being followed by a bitter cry: "Cursed be the day that I was born." The chapter concludes with an anguished question: "Why did I come forth from the womb, to see sorrow and pain, to end my days in shame?"

Listening to that dazzling convergence of the prophet's call with his pain and his hope, I realized suddenly that the prophet Jeremiah had become part of a remarkable convergence in my own life, a synchronicity of blessings and curses that had shattered certain boundaries that had long held me secure. For much of that fall, I experienced the most intense and prolonged writing period of my life. Poems were coming almost every morning and, unlike my earlier work, they came out whole, and nearly finished. As I hadn't written any poetry for several years, I was extremely grateful.

But at the same time that I was experiencing this rush of poetic energy, I was also experiencing bitter failure in my attempts to fit in with the rest of the "resident scholars" at the Institute. That was our official title, although I'm not a scholar in the conventional sense, and often find myself ill at ease in the academic environment. Denise Levertov once said that "the substance, the means of art, is incarnation, not reference but phenomena," and like many poets, I'd much rather read a poem out loud than discuss it. Having to talk about what I do, what poets do, tends to make me stupid.

Two years before at the Institute, my attempts to explain myself and what I was doing there had been received by the group with a bemused toleration. One exchange I will never forget took place at a seminar that I'd been dreading because I had no idea how to conduct a seminar. I spoke on the topic of "Incarnational Language" in such a manner that one man fell asleep; maybe he, at least, had found me suitably academic. I hadn't given much thought to a precise definition of "incarnational language"; examples and stories attract me so much more, but they didn't seem to be what people wanted to hear. "You said the liturgy is like a living poem. What makes it like a poem?" one woman asked, and I replied, "Did I say that?" Apparently, I'd blurted it out during my so-called lecture, and had to try to remember what in the world I'd meant, while suppressing the sudden emergence of Emily Dickinson into my consciousness, whispering, "All men say, 'What' to me."

During the discussion period, one colleague, clearly frustrated with my response to a comment he'd made, said, "Kathleen, you could have come back at me much harder on that." He then proceeded to list several points I might have made, and I nodded my assent to most of them. Finally, I said, "You know, Bill, I might have come up with all that, if I had more time, maybe two or three weeks. A month. I'm no good on my feet, I'm a slow thinker." At least we all left that seminar wide awake. Uneasy, but awake.

During my second residency at the Institute, however, simple unease became a mean spirit. I suspect that I made a gravely wrong move early in the term, something I've not been able to identify, which led to distrust, misapprehensions, a tangle of unfortunate presumptions and graceless gestures that soon became impossible to unravel. None of us seemed capable of acting our best. A clique formed, which of course divided us into those within and those without. Discussions bristled with unspoken tensions, and no one had the good sense to bring them to light so that we might identify and defuse them. It was pure folly, a sorry accumulation of human failures, my own as much as anyone else's.

Scholars speak with authority, and they must, as they are trying to convince the reader that they have a worthwhile point of view. On the other hand, poets speak with no authority but that which the reader is willing to grant them. Our task is not to convince but to suggest, evoke, explore. And to be a poet, which at its root means "maker," to be a maker of phenomena, speaking without reference to authority but simply because the words are given you, is not necessarily welcome in the academic world. That fall, the Institute became my crucible. I found myself deeply, helplessly engaged in the writing of a body of poems, even as I was experiencing, full-blast, the scorn of academics for a poet in their midst. It was the monks and their liturgy that kept me sane.

Ironically, it was a desire for liturgy that had led me to risk entering an academic environment in the first place. And now I found that liturgy was saving me. Writers become extremely vulnerable when a prolonged writing spell takes hold; sustaining such intensity has driven more than one poet to nervous breakdown, and even suicide. But the powerful rhythms of Benedictine life gave me balance, a routine. And the liturgy became a place where the prophet Jeremiah could help me understand my own life, my vocation as a poet. I am not making a facile comparison between myself and a prophet. I relate the tale only because I believe it illuminates the workings of *lectio*. The monastic liturgy plunges you into scripture in such a way that, over time, the texts invite you to commune with them, and can come to serve as a mirror.

All of us, I suspect, have times when we're made to suffer simply for being who and what we are, and we become adept at inventing means of escape. My means of escape that fall happened to be few—my husband was traveling halfway around the world, I was physically unwell. But Jeremiah reminded me that the pain that comes from one's identity, that grows out of the response to a call, can't be escaped or pushed aside. It must be gone through. He led me into the heart of pain, forcing me to recognize that to answer a call as a prophet, or a poet for that matter, is to reject the authority of credentials, of human valuation of any kind, accepting only the authority of the call itself. It was as a writer that Jeremiah spoke to me, and it was as a writer I listened. I couldn't have asked for a better companion.

It was the prophet who helped me understand that there wasn't much I could do about my situation, except to wait it out. I watched ice form on the river outside my window one Sunday afternoon and felt a loneliness more intense than any I could remember since childhood. The day had grown incredibly still—I spent much of that fall in solitude—and the silence was so deep it seemed poised at the edge of eternity. When it became too much to bear, words came to me: "the necessary other, a reminder and reproach; the ground of winter, watchful and chill, no longer looking for what is not there."

I found this image of winter's encroachment curiously hopeful. Nearly empty, I could not hope to fill myself—certainly not with human companionship, although when it did come that fall even small acts of kindness and hospitality were resplendent—and I began to sense that this was exactly as it should be. God wanted me empty, alone, silent, and watchful. I was suffering from both severe laryngitis and a lame leg, and had to laugh at myself, wondering if I really were so dense that God had to resort to these extremes in order to get me to shut up and be still.

I spent fruitful hours meditating on what it might mean to be a "necessary other." The phrase seemed to define Jeremiah, and the prophetic role. I also wondered if it might not help to serve to define the otherness of the poet, an otherness that typically emerges in childhood. Jeremiah 13:16—"When you look for light, he turns it into gloom,/and makes it deep darkness"—brought back to me a childhood image of God, which had led to nothing but trouble in my cheery, 1950s Protestant Sunday school. We'd been asked to paint a picture of heaven, and my effort, an image of God's throne surrounded by clouds, was a dismal failure. The newsprint cracked under all the layers of paint I had applied, in an attempt to get the image dark enough. It wasn't until I stumbled across Gregory of Nyssa in my mid-thirties that I discovered that my childhood image had a place within the Christian tradition.

Many people experience such otherness in childhood, but those who find their otherness integral to a calling—to religious life, to ministry, to the arts—learn to adjust to it as a permanent condition. William James, in *The Varieties of Religious Experience,* quotes novelist Alphonse Daudet on the death of his brother: "My father cried out so dramatically: 'He is dead, he is dead!' While my first self wept, my second self thought, 'How truly given was that cry, how fine it would be at the theatre.' I was then fourteen years old . . . Oh, this terrible second me . . . how it sees into things, and how it mocks!"

When artists discover as children that they have inappropriate responses to events around them, they also find, as they learn to trust those responses, that these oddities are what constitute their value to others. They can make people laugh, or move them to tears. Under such circumstances, the second, mocking self can make the journey to adulthood extremely difficult and lonely, and artists are notorious for *not* making it, for becoming monsters of ego instead of human beings.

It doesn't help that others often encourage artists to think of themselves as somehow more special, sensitive, "creative" than other mortals. This is false doctrine. There is but one creator, and "creating" is the very thing that artists cannot do. The gifts of the human imagination that artists employ operate equally in science and scholarship, teaching and philosophy, business and mathematics, ranching, preaching, engineering, mothering and fathering. Still, it can't be denied that artists interact strongly with their world, and that there is a measure of suffering involved as they come to a mature understanding of their communal role.

The romanticizing of the artist, of course, has a flip side, a culture that often demeans, ridicules, or dismisses them, and artists soon learn that a strong ego is necessary if they are to practice their art. They learn that they must invent themselves, and in boldly appropriating for their art the raw material of their own lives, they are well served by a level of self-assurance and self-confidence that others find daunting, and often misread as self-satisfaction, or the annoying self-aggrandizement of the artist manqué. I suspect that this was part of my trouble at the Institute that fall. When I spoke as an artist, I was being heard as an artiste, a throwback to what Louise Bogan once termed "the disease of Shelleyism."

The popular, nineteenth-century image of the poet-as-Romantic; the lone rebel, free of restraint, seized by holy imagination, has proved dangerous for poets in this century. It has overshadowed the poet's ancient communal role as historian, prophet, storyteller, and has mystified and idealized the writing process. But although poetry is taught notoriously badly in our schools and is no longer at the center of popular culture as it was even as recently as Tennyson's time, the culture still has need of the poet-as-other. In fact, expectations of artists can run very high. The biologist Lewis Thomas has said that "poets, on whose shoulders the future rests," are needed to help us make our way through "a wilderness of mystery . . . in the centuries to come." The theologian John Cobb, in commenting on the history of art from the Byzantine age to the present, says that "the power that can transform, redeem, unify and order has moved in a continuous process from a transcendent world into the inner being of artists themselves."

This is dangerous for artists to contemplate, that the culture that trivializes and spurns them would also, paradoxically, look to them for hope of transformation. Walter Brueggeman, in a book on the prophets entitled *Hopeful Imagination,* suggests that "a sense of call in our time is profoundly countercultural," and notes that "the ideology of our time is that we can live 'an uncalled life,' one not referred to any purpose beyond one's self." I suspect that this idol of the autonomous, uncalled life has a shadow side that demands that we resist the notion that another might be different, might indeed experience a call. Our idol of the autonomous individual is a sham; the truth is we expect everyone to be the same, and dismiss as elitist those who are working through a call to any genuine vocation. It may be that our culture so fears the necessary other that it has grown unable to identify and name real differences without becoming defensive about them.

I think this explains our mania for credentials, which allow us a measure of objectivity in assessing differences. Credentials measure what is quantifiable; they represent results. A call, on the other hand, is pure process; it cannot be measured, quantified, or controlled by institutions. People who are called tend to violate the rules in annoying ways. Young professors clinging to the tenure track do not like to hear that Denise Levertov has taught at Stanford, despite having little formal education. It offended several of my Institute colleagues that a university had invited me for a week-long residency as a "poet and theologian." My last formal course on the Bible was in eighth grade. How could I be a theologian? What good are the rules, the boundaries of our precious categories—"theologian," "scholar"—if poets can violate them at will? Ironically, while the Institute's director, Patrick Henry, has a deep commitment to breaking down the barriers between artists and academics, during that semester he found himself contending with personality clashes that made such bridge-building extremely difficult.

The poet, as a "necessary other," is free to speak, and indeed must speak, in ways that scholars cannot. But that freedom comes at a considerable price. During that fall at the Ecumenical Institute, I began to suspect that just as monastic discipline looks to many people like restriction but ends in freedom, so what looks like the untrammeled freedom of the artist is, in fact, an exacting form of discipline. To employ yet another analogy, I'll use Robert Frost's famous comment that writing free verse is like playing tennis without a net. What he meant by that is that it's damned difficult. Imagine playing tennis *well* without a net. And doing it not only with your writing, but your very life.

The danger of going out of bounds is real. Poetry is a vocation without many guidelines for formation, and poets are often people who lack the religious underpinnings that might help them to take in stride both the intense seclusion of the writing process and the safe return to "the world." Without such underpinnings, they've often turned to drugs or alcohol to help them manage the highs and lows; many poets' lives, since the late nineteenth century, have been demonstrations of William Blake's axiom: "The road of excess leads to the palace of wisdom," aptly titled one of the Proverbs of Hell.

When I was beginning to write poetry in college, in the 1960s, it seemed as if, for contemporary poets, madness and suicide were the primary occupational hazards. Religion itself was dangerous for some, a goad to the manic-depressive roller coaster. (John Berryman and Anne Sexton are tragic examples.) It seemed that the best one could do was to take what one of my teachers called "the artist's road to redemption," and find salvation through writing. This worked for me for years.

That it worked so well for so long is a credit to the nature of the poetic call. Art is a lonely calling, and yet paradoxically communal. If artists invent themselves, it is in the service of others. The work of my life is given to others; in fact, the reader completes it. I say the words I need to say, knowing that most people will ignore me, some will say, "You have no right," and a few will tell me that I've expressed the things they've long desired to articulate but lacked the words to do so.

By what authority does the poet, or prophet, speak? How dare the poet say "I" and not mean the self? How dare the prophet say "Thus says the Lord"? It is the authority of experience, but by this I do not mean experience used as an idol, as if an individual's experience of the world were its true measure. I mean experience tested in isolation, as by the desert fathers and mothers, and also tried in the crucible of community. I mean a "call" taken to heart, and over years of apprenticeship to an artistic discipline, developed into something that speaks to others.

The Oxford Companion to the Bible suggests that the emotional power of Jeremiah 20, and several other chapters in the book that evoke the tensions of a prophet's calling, comes from the fact that "behind the apparently untroubled certainty of 'Thus says the

Lord,' there may lie a host of unresolved questions and deep inner turmoil." It's no wonder. Jeremiah grieves—"Is there no balm in Gilead? Is there no physician there? Why then has the health of my poor people not been restored? O that my head were a spring of water, and my eyes a fountain of tears, so that I might weep day and night for the slain of my poor people!" (8:22; 9:1)—but if he grieves, he must also speak words of unspeakable violence—"[your friends] shall fall to the sword of their enemies while you look on" (20:4)—to the very people he loves; he must plead to God on their behalf: "We look for peace, but find no good; for a time of healing, but there is terror instead" (14:19).

In our own time we look for peace and healing, but our newspapers are filled with tales of violence and rage. And Jeremiah holds this world up to us, as a mirror. Hearing his words every morning, as personal as my response to Jeremiah sometimes was, I also recognized, in the months that we took his body blows at morning prayer, the public dimension of his prophecy and of our response. Jeremiah's lament over a land so ravaged that even the birds and animals have fled has a powerful resonance in an age in which species are rapidly disappearing, and the threat of nuclear warfare remains. His bleak image of death "cutting down the children in the street, young people in the squares, the corpses of the slain like dung on a field, like sheaves behind the harvester, with no one to harvest them" (9:20–21) could have come from a *Newsweek* story on Bosnia, or Rwanda, or inner-city America. Much as the people of Judah who worshiped at the temple, Americans tend to think of themselves as good, religious people, and their nation as morally superior. Yet child prostitution thrives, hunger and homelessness plague us, in many of our cities death by gunshot is the number-one cause of death for young men, and violent crime is such that people of all ages do not feel safe in their homes, or on neighborhood streets.

The contemporaneity of Jeremiah made me reflect on our need for prophets; I'd sit in the monks' choir and let the naive thoughts come: *it really is this bad, and if people heard it they would want to change; they'd have to change.* Of course it was Jeremiah himself who'd bring me back to earth, to the bitterness of his call, when God tells him: "You shall speak to them and they will not listen; you shall call and they shall not answer" (7:27). Yet a prophet speaks out of hope and, like all the prophets, Jeremiah's ultimate hope is for justice, a people made holy by "doing what is right and just in the land" (33:15). As the carriers of hope through disastrous times, prophets are a necessary other. And we reject them because they make us look at the way things really are; they don't allow us to deny our pain.

In the Book of Jeremiah we encounter a very human prophet, and a God who is alarmingly alive. Jeremiah makes it clear that no one chooses to fall into the hands of such a God. You are chosen, you resist, you resort to rage and bitterness and, finally, you succumb to the God who has given you your identity in the first place. All that fall, when Jeremiah's grief and my own impossible situation cast me into deep loneliness, I was grateful to be sustained by the liturgy that had brought me to Jeremiah and insisted that I listen to him.

And on the feast of St. John Lateran, in early November, a feast commemorating the dedication of a Roman basilica erected by the Emperor Constantine, and traditionally referred to as "the mother church of Christendom," the words of Psalm 46—"God is within, it cannot be shaken"—suddenly revealed God to me as a place, both without and within. In my notebook I wrote: "In naming my-

self as a 'necessary other,' I finally accept the cross of myself, a burden I've carried ever since childhood, and felt so acutely in my
teens. The cross of difference, of being outside, always other. But
now, I am free to take it on. It seems appropriate, on this feast."

At morning prayer, we heard these words from Ephesians 2:
"So you are no longer strangers and aliens, but you are citizens with
the saints and also members of the household of God, built upon
the foundation of the apostles and prophets, with Christ Jesus as
the cornerstone." The altar gleamed, bone-white, before the dark
wood of the monks' choir, and I could dare to conceive of the
Church as refuge, a place to find the divided self made whole, the
voice of the mocker overcome by the voice of the advocate. It is
still a sinful Church—how could it be otherwise?—but the words
of its prophets and apostles had led me to this sanctuary, and I
could dare to imagine it as home, a place where there is no "other."

November 1 and 2

ALL SAINTS, ALL SOULS

The monks are decorating the church and baptistry with vigil lights and greenery. The two who've been assigned to place relics in the baptistry are engaged in a bidding war: "Trade you one Lucy for two Saint Ritas, one Bonaventure for three Peter Damians." I pretend to be shocked. "You *Catholics,*" I say, as I pass by, and they glare at me, pretending to be offended.

Photismos is a word I've learned today, from Father Godfrey, an ancient word for baptism. I like the way it shares a root with photosynthesis, the way the saints might be said to have heeded the command in 1 John 3, to "come to light."

At morning prayer, in the Book of Revelation, a new song is spoken of. St. Bernard laments, "The saints want us to be with them, and we are indifferent. . . . Let us long for those who are longing for us," he pleads, and I think of human weakness turned into strength, human folly become the wisdom of God.

On All Souls, the mood is somber. We say the Office for the Dead, we ask for mercy. We pray for "the faithful departed," but out of habit I add "and the unfaithful," or, as one of the eucharistic prayers puts it, "those whose faith is known to you alone," those whose stories are a messy, long departure. Louise Bogan, who said to a friend, "The gift of faith has been denied me," Anne Sexton, who told a priest, "I love faith, but have none," John Berryman, who wrote, "I would like if possible to be buried in consecrated ground."

They told it well, but darkly. Now the feasts wheel round, in the dark of the year. All Saints, All Souls, all song and story.

November 16

GERTRUDE THE GREAT

It is good to be asked to dine with other people; I've had too little of that lately. But the Benedictine women at St. John's, who have come from monasteries as far away as Australia and South Africa to work or to study, have decided to celebrate the Feast of St. Gertrude in a big way, and I'm one of several Benedictine oblates whom they've invited for a festal meal followed by vespers in the grad school dorm. I've been looking forward to it for days.

At morning prayer we hear from Gertrude's Fourth Spiritual Exercise, a prayer I find as touching as it is various: "Deliver me from timidity of spirit and from storminess. . . . From all heedlessness in my behavior, deliver me O Lord." I do not know Gertrude's writing well, but I know the story. In the year 1260, at the age of four, she entered the great monastery of Helfta in Saxony, and received an education there—she wrote in both Latin and her native German. But she was for years, as she later put it, a nun in name only: frivolous, vain, inattentive to the Divine Office.

When she was twenty-six, she endured a month of restlessness, with a deeply troubled mind. Then one night, as she was walking in the monastery at dusk, in the deep silence after compline, an older nun approached. Gertrude bowed to her, as prescribed in the

49

Rule of Benedict: "Whenever sisters meet, the junior asks her senior for a blessing." But when Gertrude looked up, she saw the face of the youthful Christ, a boy of about sixteen. "Courteously and in a gentle voice," she later wrote, "he said to me: 'Soon will come your salvation; why are you so sad?' "

The older nun passed by, and Gertrude was changed forever. I have a busy morning, and race to noon prayer. On such a day, the brief reading and silent response is welcome, a door that opens onto the still point, where my heart is. Today we hear from the Song of Songs: "Arise, my love . . . let me see your face and hear your voice . . . For your voice is sweet, and your face is lovely."

The word "lovely" resonates through the choir, poignant among the celibates. If Christ speaks to them, I suppose it is now, but this is beyond my grasp. I miss my husband—his voice, his face—though it's been two months since I have seen him, and his face has grown indistinct in my mind. Nevertheless, I hold him there, for a moment, and the distance between us is as nothing.

My afternoon is full of errands, annoying but necessary. It ends more pleasantly, at a lecture in which a monk, a historian, remarks that "church history for a long time was largely a cosmetic process, which," he says, slowly, savoring the words, "if you were remarkably stupid, could be edifying." In describing the environment surrounding the creation of the magnificently illuminated Lindisfarne Gospel in the seventh century, he says, "Everyone lived in the sticks, nothing was going on. They had enormous amounts of time and could enjoy figuring things out." It sounds good.

I hurry home and change into a simple dress of bright green flannel. I add a scarlet and gold scarf made of sari cloth. God, the laughter. I hear it as soon as I enter the dorm. Women are cooking, chopping vegetables, washing paring knives and serving spoons, transforming the homely little communal kitchen into a place of feast. My offerings, homemade bread and a magnum of champagne, are accepted with joyful exclamation. One of the grad students pokes his head in the door and says, "My, Sister Julie, you're looking sultry tonight." Julie, a highly spirited and pretty young woman, replies with mock confusion: "Sultry? Why? Is my face broken out?" as she good-naturedly shoos the young man out.

At dinner, discussion turns toward something I've noticed that Benedictines seldom talk about, that is, the angelic nature of their calling. Their Liturgy of the Hours is, at root, a symbolic act, an emulation of and a joining with the choirs in heaven who sing the praise of God unceasingly. To most people even to think of such things seems foolish, and Benedictines are well aware that their motives are easily misinterpreted, labeled as romanticist or escapist. "Anyone who knows us knows we're down to earth," one sister says. "We have to be, to live in community as we do."

But one of the Australian sisters insists that Benedictines "be willing to admit to the angelic charism. The best thing we can do," she says, "is to praise." I tell the story of a monk I know who dreamed one night that armed men in uniform had entered the abbey church, and when he tried to stop them from approaching the altar, they shot him. As he lay by the altar, he saw Christ standing before him. "Am I dead?" the monk asked, and Christ nodded and answered, gravely, "Yes." "Well, what do I do now?" the monk inquired, and Christ shrugged and said, "I guess you should go back to choir."

The laughter comes as blessing; women, youthful and aged, with nubile limbs and thick, unsteady ankles, graceful, busy hands and gnarled fingers slowed by arthritis, making a joyful noise. Our talk is light-hearted, easy as we clear the table.

So that we might sing vespers together, one sister has brought booklets that her home community devised for "Evening Praise,

Common of Monastic Women." Its cover is filled with their names: Scholastica, Walburga, Hildegard, Mechtild, Gertrude, Lioba, Julian, Hilda. The antiphon is from the Song of Songs: "Set me as a seal on your heart, for love is stronger than death."

Our reading is from Gertrude, a recasting of the ceremony of monastic profession: "I profess, and to my last breath I shall profess it, that both in body and soul, in everything, whether in prosperity or adversity, you provide for me in the way that is most suitable . . . with the one and uncreated wisdom, my sweetest God, reaching from end to end mightily and ordering all things sweetly."

I am pleasantly distracted by the echo from "O Wisdom," one of the antiphons I am just learning to sing, that we will be singing in choir a month from now. *All things, sweetly.* I find my place in the booklet as our leader intones, "Jesus called them away to be alone with him." To be alone with Jesus is something I can hardly fathom, but the words we sing in response are words that have in some sense been realized in these holy women, past and present. I am aware of a difference between us, although we share in some sense a monastic call; maybe it is our very differences that have drawn us together to celebrate Gertrude tonight. "They arose and went to the mountain," we sing, identifying ourselves with the disciples at the Transfiguration: "They went to be alone with him, and when they raised their eyes, they saw no one but Jesus."

EXILE, HOMELAND, AND NEGATIVE CAPABILITY

Exile, like memory, may be a place of hope and delusion. But there are rules of light there and principles of darkness. . . . The expatriate is in search of a country, the exile in search of a self.
—Eavan Boland, OBJECT LESSONS

Negative capability . . . [is being] capable of being in uncertainties, mysteries, doubts without any irritable reaching after fact and reason.—John Keats

A strange thing happens when I enter an elementary school classroom as a visiting artist, to read some poetry and eventually get the kids to write. It has much less to do with me as an individual than with the power of poetry, and may also be a side effect of the simple fact that I come to the children knowing very little about them. With me, they are suddenly handed a fresh slate. But no matter if the school is rich or poor, in the country, a suburb, or city, I've found that the kids that the teacher might have described as "good students" will inevitably write acceptable but unexceptional poems and stories. The breathtaking poems come from left field, as it were, from bad students, the ones the

53

teachers will say don't usually participate well in classroom activities.

One day, when I was engaged with fifth-graders in a working-class neighborhood in North Dakota, I glanced down at a boy's paper and saw the words "My Very First Dad," and that alerted me that something very personal, very deep was going on. I no longer remember what my assignment had been, but I know it was nothing as invasive as "write a poem about someone in your family." Most likely it was an open-ended challenge to work with similes. Given the freedom to write about anything at all, this boy had chosen to write about his "very first dad," and while I left him alone to work it out, I did have several conversations with him. He was pleased, and surprised, when I pointed out to him that his similes were so good they had quickly led him into the deeper realm of metaphor. He'd written of his father: "I remember him/like God in my heart, I remember him in my heart/like the clouds overhead,/and strawberry ice cream and bananas/when I was a little kid. But the most I remember/is his love,/as big as Texas/when I was born."

The boy said, rather proudly, that he had been born in Texas, but otherwise told me nothing of his story. It was his stunned teacher who filled me in. She said things that did not surprise me, given my previous experience as an artist-in-residence—"He's not a good student, he tries, but he's never done anything like this before"—but then she told me that the boy had never known his father; he'd skipped town on the day he was born.

Oddly enough, hearing this was gratifying. Just a poet's presence in that classroom, on behalf of similes and metaphors (officially, to justify my presence in terms recognized by the educational establishment, that's what I was "teaching"), had allowed this boy to tell the adults in his life—his teacher, his mom, his stepfather—

something they need to know, that a "very first dad" looms large in his psyche. Like God in his heart, to quote the poem, a revelation from the depths of this boy's soul.

There are no prescriptions, no set of rules that will produce a poem like this; no workshop could teach a method that would replicate exactly what went on between me and the students in that room. But I have some idea as to how and why it happened. A teacher once told me that having an artist come to her classroom was like letting a cat in—and I'll risk a bad pun by saying that I think it's more like dropping a catalyst into a chemical solution in order to stimulate a reaction.

What *is* happening in that classroom, when the poet acts as a catalyst? Well, first of all, before I ask students to write, we always have a long discussion about rules. I tell them that for this adventure of writing poetry, we can suspend many of the normal rules for English class. No, you don't have to write within the margins; no, you don't have to look a word up in the dictionary to make sure you're spelling it right—we'll do that later. For now just write the word the way you think it's spelled so you don't interrupt the flow of writing; you can print or use cursive (that's a *big* issue in third grade); you can doodle on your paper; you can scratch things out (here I show them my own rough drafts, so they can see that I mean it); you can write anonymously or even make up a name for yourself as a poet.

If you're really stuck, I tell them, you can collaborate and work on a poem with someone else who's also stuck. This means you can *talk* in the classroom, so long as you don't disturb your neighbor. As we're working, I often have to reassure a student that it's all right not to finish a poem if you really can't. You can let it sit for a while and maybe come back to it, or maybe not. And if you really get carried away by an assignment, it's all right not to go on to my next one—just keep going with what you're doing, *take your time.* (Often, by this time the students are looking at me gratefully but a bit warily, wondering if they've fallen into the hands of a lunatic.)

We talk about the ways this kind of writing differs from learning spelling or math, where there are right and wrong answers. I tell the kids that in what we'll be doing, there *is* no one right answer, not even a right way or wrong way to do it. And if, in a particular writing assignment, I do suggest some rules to follow, I always say, if you can think of a way to break these rules and still come out with a really good poem—go right ahead. I see this as a way to get beyond paying lip service to children's creativity and encouraging them to practice it. By now the good students may be feeling lost. They're often kids who have beaten the system, who have become experts at following the rules in order to get a good grade. And now, maybe for the first time, they're experiencing helplessness at school, because the boundaries have shifted; without rules to follow, they're not sure how to proceed. They may sulk, or even cry, although they usually come around and have a good time.

But it's the other students, the bad students, the little criminals, who often have a form of intelligence that is not much rewarded in school, who are listening most attentively. It's these kids, for whom helplessness and frustration are the norm at school, and often in life—maybe their mom's boyfriend got drunk and abusive the night before—who take to poetry like ducklings to water. And sometimes, as with that fifth-grade boy, they find that adopting a poetic voice can be a revelation. It's as if they're free to speak with their true voice for the very first time. It is always a gift—to the teacher, the class, and to me—to have a child lead us into the heart of poetry. That boy spoke to our own loneliness and exile and reminded us that our everyday world is more mysterious than we know: who would have guessed that an ordinary boy, in an ordinary classroom in North Dakota, was walking around with a love, and a loss, as big as Texas in his heart?

Often, when I'm working in an elementary classroom, my mind pitches back to my own school days. I enjoyed school wholeheartedly until third grade. My mother was an elementary-school teacher, and that may have helped me develop early on a sense of what was expected of me, and the confidence that I could learn new things. Then, as we moved from adding and subtracting to multiplying and dividing, I had my first taste of failure. I'd grown used to counting on my fingers and panicked when the numbers became so big so fast, literally untouchable. I became enormously frustrated trying to grasp concepts that remained tantalizingly out of reach. I still excelled at English and found spelling easy. But I began to fall behind in math.

One day, in fourth grade, I had an epiphany about the nature of numbers, and a peculiar taste of otherness—the unmistakable sense that I'd seen something that my teacher, and the other students, could not see. My teacher that year prided herself on being tough. She had warned us on the very first day of school that she expected us to work, and to work hard. That was fine with me; I wanted to learn. As I was one of the better students in English, however, my teacher seemed unable to forgive me for being so backward in mathematics. I believe she thought that if she pressured me enough, even ridiculed me from time to time, I would simply apply myself and learn. Thus, one day, in exasperation at some muddle I'd made with a math problem on the blackboard, an experience that always terrified me, she grabbed my chalk, solved the problem, and said, in a sarcastic voice, "You see, it's simple, as simple as two plus two is always four."

And, without thinking, I said, "That can't be." Suddenly, I was sure that two plus two could not possibly *always* be four. And, of course, it isn't. In Boolean algebra, two plus two can be zero, in base three, two plus two is eleven. I had stumbled onto set theory, a truth about numbers that I had no language for. As this was the early 1950s, my teacher had no language for it either, and she and the class had a good laugh over my ridiculous remark. I staggered away from my epiphany and went back to my seat, feeling certain of the truth of what I'd seen but also terribly confused. Briefly, numbers had seemed much more exciting than I had been led to believe. But if two plus two was always four, then numbers were too literal, too boring, to be worth much attention. I wrote math off right then and there, and, of course, ended up with a classic case of math anxiety.

In a way, though, this experience had a positive side, as the beginning of my formation as a poet. Whenever definitions were given as absolutes, as *always,* I would have that familiar tingle— *that can't be*—and soon learned that I could focus on the fuzzy boundaries, where definitions give way to metaphor. Even though "negative capability," like set theory, was a term I wasn't to hear for years, I had stumbled onto it as a way of being, a way of thinking, a way of intelligence that largely defined me. It was there in that ambiguous world that I resolved to dwell.

I have since met visual artists who as children were so intent on playing with the shapes of numbers and letters that they fell behind in both English and math, to the despair of their teachers, who recognized that these were intelligent children. Yet visual intelligence, even more than poetic intelligence, can be a handicap in this culture. Years ago, when I was a kindergarten aide at a Quaker school, one little girl demonstrated a capacity for attention unusual at the age of five; every afternoon, she would paint huge blocks of color onto newsprint, working for nearly an hour. Then she would ask me to hang the painting to dry so that she could work on it again the next day. The teacher and I were fascinated but soon found that we had to protect her from the other children, who, once they noticed that her paintings didn't "look like anything," made fun of them. The girl, remarkably, was undeterred, already adept at exile.

And once, when I was visiting a second-grade classroom and the children were showing me drawings they'd done in celebration of fall, a restless, untidy little boy reluctantly retrieved his from the bottom of a pile of papers. The drawing depicted a man throwing a football, with the ball shown in every stage of the arc. It was the way an engineer might depict a football pass, but the boy (and I suspect, his teacher) was convinced that he had done the drawing "wrong." I wondered if his exile had begun, and where it would lead him.

Working with children on the writing of poetry has led me to ponder the ways that most of us become exiled from the certainties of childhood; how it is that the things we most treasure when we're young are exactly those things we come to spurn as teenagers and young adults. Very small children are often conscious of God, for example, in ways that adults seldom are. They sing to God, they talk to God, they recognize divine presence in the world around them: they can see the Virgin Mary dancing among the clouds, they know that God made a deep ravine by their house "because he was angry when people would not love him," they believe that an overnight snowfall is "just like Jesus glowing on the mountaintop." Yet these budding theologians often despise church by the time they're in eighth grade.

In a similar way, the children who un-selfconsciously make up songs and poems when they're young—I once observed a three-

year-old singing a passionate ode to the colorful vegetables in a su-
permarket—quickly come to regard poetry as meaningless and irrelevant. I began to despise mathematics when I sensed that I was
getting only part of the story, a dull, literal-minded version of what
in fact was a great mystery, and I wonder if children don't begin
to reject both poetry and religion for similar reasons, because the
way both are taught takes the life out of them. If we teach children
when they're young to reject their epiphanies, then it's no wonder
that we end up with so many adults who are mathematically, po-
etically, and theologically illiterate.

Some teachers still require children to copy bad nineteenth-
century verse as a handwriting exercise. And in most classrooms
I've been in, the teacher assumes that she is "teaching" the students
the ordinary tools of language that are in fact the basis of human
intelligence. Once, in a fourth-grade classroom, after I'd talked
about metaphor, made up some silly examples on the board, and
also read and discussed several deeply metaphorical poems, I asked
the students to come up with metaphors of their own. The teacher
warned me, "This isn't a subject they've studied," but I replied,
"They'll know how to do it, they just don't know the word for it
yet." She and I had our own epiphanies that day, and that class
turned out to be one of the best I ever worked with.

As children grow older and are asked to analyze poetry, they
are taught that separating out the elements in the poem—images,
similes, metaphors—is the only way to "appreciate" it. As if the
poem is somehow less than the whole of its parts, a frog students
must dissect in order to make it live; as if the purpose of poetry is
to provide boring exercises for English class. The metaphorical intelligence that has pulled disparate elements together to make the
poem is of no consequence. Clearly it has not been taught, in most

classrooms I've visited, as one of the more intriguing elements of the human imagination.

And do we do any better when it comes to the teaching of religion? The liturgical scholar Gail Ramshaw makes a valuable distinction between theology and liturgy: theology is prose, she says, but liturgy is poetry. "If faith is about facts," she writes, "then we line up the children and make them memorize questions and answers . . . But if we are dealing with poetry instead of prose . . . then we do not teach answers to questions. We memorize not answers but the chants of the ordinary; we explain liturgical action . . . we immerse people in worship so that they, too, become part of the metaphoric exchange."

Metaphor has been so degraded in our culture that it may be difficult for people to conceive of worship as a "metaphoric exchange." But as a poet I am willing to explore the implications. How would it change our understanding of worship if, from the time they were small, children were taught to value and explore the possibilities of Keats's "negative capability" in themselves? They might better understand faith as a process, and church tradition as not only relevant but strikingly alive.

The ancient understanding of Christian worship is that, in the words of the liturgical scholar Aidan Kavanagh, it "gives rise to theological reflection, and not the other way around." We can see the obvious truth of this by shifting our attention to poetry, and entertaining the notion that one might grow into faith much as one writes a poem. It takes time, patience, discipline, a listening heart. There is precious little certainty, and often great struggling, but also joy in our discoveries. This joy we experience, however, is not visible or quantifiable; we have only the words and form of the poem, the results of our exploration. Later, the thinkers and definers come along and treat these results as the whole—*Let's see; here she's used a metaphor, and look, she's made up a rhyme scheme. Let's stick with it. Let's teach it. Let's make it a rule.* What began as an experiment, a form of play, an attempt to engage in dialogue with mystery, is now a dogma, set in stone. It is something that can be taught in school.

Let's return to our classroom setting, only this time we'll be exploring faith as well as poetry. A poem, as Mallarmé once said, is not made of ideas but of words, and faith also expresses itself through that which is lived, breathed, uttered, left silent. If faith, like poetry, is a process, not a product, then this class will be messier than we can imagine. To make the poem of our faith, we must learn not to settle for a false certitude but to embrace ambiguity and mystery. Our goal will be to recover our original freedom, our childlike (but never childish) wisdom. It will be difficult to lose our adult self-consciousness (here the discipline of writing can help us), difficult not to confuse our worship with self-expression. (All too often the call for "creativity" in worship simply leads to bad art.)

We will need a powerful catalyst. In any institution, while there's always the sacred "way we've always done it," and certainly a place for the traditions that such an attitude reflects, there is also a spirit at work that has more to do with being than with doing.

Poets are immersed in process, and I mean process not as an amorphous blur but as a *discipline*. The hard work of writing has taught me that in matters of the heart, such as writing, or faith, there is no right or wrong way to do it, but only the way of your life. Just paying attention will teach you what bears fruit and what doesn't. But it will be necessary to revise—to doodle, scratch out, erase, even make a mess of things—in order to make it come out right.

When it comes to faith, while there are guidelines—for Christians, the Bible and the scaffolding of the church's theology and tradition—there is no one right way to do it. Flannery O'Connor once wisely remarked that "most of us come to the church by a means the church does not allow," and Martin Buber implies that discovering that means might constitute our life's work. He states that: "All [of us] have access to God, but each has a different access. [Our] great chance lies precisely in [our] unlikeness. God's all-inclusiveness manifests itself in the infinite multiplicity of the ways that lead to him, each of which is open to one [person]." He illustrates this with a story about Rabbi Zusya, who said, a short while before his death, "In the world to come I shall not be asked: 'Why were you not Moses?' I shall be asked: 'Why were you not Zusya?'" The rabbi is not speaking of a vague "personal spirituality" that allows him to be Zusya alone; he knows himself to be a part of the people of Israel.

For myself, I have found that being a member of a church congregation, and also following, as I am able, the discipline of Benedict's Rule, has helped me to take my path toward God without falling into the trap of thinking of myself as "a church of one." I have also found that the Benedictines are a good illustration of Buber's point. Although their members follow a common way of life, monasteries do not produce cookie-cutter monks and nuns. Just the opposite. Monasteries have a unity that is remarkably unrestrained by uniformity; they are comprised of distinct individuals, often memorable characters, whose eccentricities live for generations in the community's oral history.

The first time I went to a monastery, I dreamed about the place for a week, and the most vivid dream was of the place as a chemistry lab. Might religion be seen as an experiment in human chemistry? And the breath of the divine as the catalyst that sparks reactions and makes our humble institutions work as well as they do, often despite ourselves? Imagination and reason, those vital elements of human intelligence, are adept at dismantling our delusions. Both bring us up against our true abilities and our limitations. But we've gotten ourselves into a curious mess in the modern world. We've grown afraid of the imagination (except as a misguided notion of a "creativity" granted to a few) and yet are less and less capable of valuing rationality as another resource of our humanity, of our *religious* humanity. We end up with a curious spectrum of popular religions, a rigid fundamentalism at one end, and New Age otherworldliness, manifested in "angel channeling workshops," on the other. And even religious institutions—I'll speak here of the Christian churches, because they are what I know—often manifest themselves as anything but Christ's humble body on earth. What gets lost in all of this is any viable sense of the sacred that gives both imagination and reason room to play.

Can poets be of any use here? I believe so, though I'm not sure of the reasons why. I may be doodling. But the sense of the sacred is very much alive in contemporary poetry; maybe because poetry, like prayer, is a dialogue with the sacred. And poets speak from the margins, those places in the ecosystem where, as any ecologist can tell you, the most life forms are to be found. The poet Maxine Kumin has described herself as "an unreconstructed atheist who believes in the mystery of the creative process," while my husband, who is both a lyric poet and a computer programmer, declares himself to be "a scientific rationalist who believes in ghosts." If, as Gail Ramshaw has said, "Christianity requires metaphoric thinking," if, as a Benedictine liturgist once said to me, the loss of the ability to think metaphorically is one of the greatest problems in liturgy today, maybe the voices of poets are the ones we need to hear.

I hear many stories these days from people who are exiled from their religious traditions. They, also, speak from the margins. Many, like me, are members of the baby-boom generation who dropped religious observance after high school or college, and are now experiencing an enormous hunger for spiritual grounding. One woman wrote to me to say that she felt a great longing for ritual and community; she said she wanted to mark the year with more than watching the trees change. She'd joined some political organizations and a women's service club but found that it wasn't enough. She was afraid to even think of joining a church—the Bible makes her angry, more often than not—but she thought she might have to.

There is no set of rules for her to follow, but only the messy process of life to be lived. Since what she's seeking is salvation, and not therapy, not political or social relevance, I suspect that she might eventually find what she is looking for in the practice of prayer and in communal worship. And if things work as they should, whatever healing needs to happen, whatever larger social dimension she needs to address, will grow organically out of those experiences, that community. But how does she get from here to there?

She may be closer than she knows. The Anglican bishop John V. Taylor has said, "Imagination and faith are the same thing, 'giving substance to our hopes and reality to the unseen.' The whole Bible endorses this, and if believers talked about faith in these terms they would be more readily understood." In the Book of Deuteronomy, the commandment of God is revealed not as an inaccessible mystery but as "something very near to you, already in your mouths and in your hearts; you have only to carry it out" (Deut. 30:14). And in the Gospel of Luke, Jesus says, "The coming of the kingdom of God cannot be observed, and no one will announce, 'Look, here it is!' or, 'There it is.' For, behold, the kingdom of God is within you" (Luke 17:20–21).

The boy who wrote about his absent father had a story to tell. His heart was in exile, and the catalyst of poetry helped it come home. And what of the catalyst of faith? Drawing both from our reason and our capacity for negative capability, faith might help us see that our most valuable experiences are always those which leave us, as the sculptor and critic Edward Robinson has said, with "an unaccountable remainder . . . 2 plus 2 equals 5 experiences" that remind us that our relationships with each other and the world are more mysterious than we care to admit. In the universe God made, the real world we call home, love is bigger than Texas, and even death itself, and 2 plus 2 might be 0, 11, or even 4.

NEW YORK CITY:
THE TRAPPIST
CONNECTION

Advent began magnificently at St. John's. The long summer of Ordinary Time had dragged on and on, and several monks commented that they were ready for a change of season. For people who live by the liturgical year, the transition into Advent can be as physically invigorating as the shift from summer into fall, and on that first Sunday of Advent, in late November, the air was charged with expectation.

St. John's has a custom that I believe to be rare among monasteries; they always invite a person from outside the monastic community to do the first reading at their Sunday Mass. This person also carries the great book of scriptures into the sanctuary, and leads the liturgical procession. At St. John's, this includes all the monks who are in residence, well over a hundred, who walk in, two by two. The liturgy director had tapped me for the first reading that Sunday, and warned that the procession would be even longer than usual, as the abbots of over twenty European monasteries were visiting and would follow the St. John's community down the aisle.

I succumbed to the temptations of a minor demon, who suggested that with all of the basic black in evidence, a touch of color would be appropriate. I wore a scarlet dress. And just before the service began, as I walked with the liturgy director from the sacristy to the head of the long line of monks, one of them, a good friend, winked at me and whispered, "A scarlet woman—we'll give those abbots something to talk about when they get home."

Walking at the slow pace set by the liturgy director, I soon felt the astonishment that often comes to me during worship, whether I'm with the congregation of a little country church, or Benedictines in a magnificent monastery chapel. It is the wonder that I should be there at all. My faith was non-existent, or at least deeply submerged, for so long a time, but liturgy pulled me back. As so often happens, on this day worship reinforced my conviction that *only* Christ could have brought all of us together, in this place, doing such absurd but necessary things.

My text that morning was from Isaiah and, as always, when I am granted the great privilege of reading him aloud in worship, I am grateful. Grateful that such poetry exists, that it tastes so good in the mouth, grateful that my messy, stormy life has led to this calm sea. Being a lector is a unique experience; it feels nothing like reading poems, my own or anyone else's, to an audience. And it's certainly not a performance; no emoting, or the monks would have my hide. The Liturgy of the Word is prayer. You pray the scriptures with, and for, the people assembled, and the words go out to them, touching them in ways only God can imagine. The words are all that matter, and you send them out as prayer, hoping to become invisible behind them.

The words on that first Sunday of Advent were from Isaiah 63: "Why do you let us wander, O God, from your ways, and harden our hearts so that we fear you not?" The passage is an honest rendering of the human condition, a desperate prayer for God's presence, a recognition that we fall apart, and our world falls apart, when God is absent from our hearts. Why *are* our hearts so hard? Can God rend them, like the heavens, and change us for the good?

The next day, when I had to fly to New York City, Isaiah proved a good traveling companion. He permeates the readings of early Advent, and as I walked in Manhattan, those words seemed to come to life before me: "The lofty city God . . . casts to the dust. The foot tramples it, the feet of the poor, the steps of the needy." From a bus I glimpsed an old woman seated on layers of clothing on a patch of damp ground in front of the Plaza Hotel, an incarnation of Isaiah's judgment against another city: "Instead of perfume there shall be a stench . . . instead of beauty, shame. Your young men shall fall by the sword and your warriors in battle. And her gates shall lament and mourn; ravaged, she shall sit upon the ground." Being in the city is good for my monastic soul. If anything, the desert monks' command to "pray without ceasing" seems easier there; the need is so obvious, so constant.

I had a number of obligations in the city, several of them public, and the next morning, when I realized that my last haircut, a freebie from one of the graduate students at St. John's, was growing out badly, I decided to go in search of an inexpensive beauty salon. I left my friends' apartment on West Eighty-first Street, and walking south, passed several places strong on elegant, spare decor, the false simplicity that merely means "expensive." Finally, I found a place that was busy—moms with kids coming and going, along with elderly women who looked as if they'd lived in the neighborhood for many years. This was promising, as was the sign in the window, "Haircuts, $8.00 and up."

Within minutes, the receptionist had handed me over to a middle-aged man—hyper, gay, extremely extroverted—who lost no time in sweeping me into a chair and fluffing my hair with his fingers. Immediately he scowled and grumbled, "Whoever did your last haircut?" I shrugged and said, "Ah, the price was right. It was given to me for nothing by a delightful young nun. I suspect she's a much better nun than she is a hair stylist."

"A nun?" he said, and paused. Then he smiled, as if he suddenly thought much better of me and my unkempt hair. "Some of my best customers are nuns, and former nuns. I just love them. They're good people." Then he asked, "Do you know the Trappists?" Bemused, I said, cautiously, "Yes, I know some Trappists." "Well, have you ever been to Spencer, Mass? The monastery there?" "No," I said. "I've heard of the place, but I've never been there."

The man then began to praise the monks of Spencer, his tongue seeming to move as fast as his scissors. He'd been isolated, ostracized in his small hometown in the South, and made to feel unwelcome in the church he was raised in. So, years ago, he'd come to New York City. He'd written off religion, he told me. Then he met a Catholic priest who'd engaged him in a small group studying the Bible, and one year they went to Spencer for Holy Week. "Boy, did I love that," he said, "just sitting in that church, the way they let you come to church with them. They don't preach at you, they let you experience it for yourself." He stilled the scissors for a moment and said, "You know, I've never felt so close to God before or since. It blew me the fuck away."

I caught his eye in the mirror and nodded, "Yes," I said, "I know what you mean."

LOS ANGELES: THE O ANTIPHONS

The O Antiphons are verses that are sung or chanted preceding the Magnificat ("My soul magnifies the Lord, my spirit rejoices in God my Savior . . .") at vespers during the last week of Advent, from December 17 through 23. Each one addresses Christ by a different title: "O Wisdom," "O Adonai," "O Root of Jesse," "O Key of David," "O Radiant Dawn," "O King of Nations," "O Emmanuel." The chant tones are uncommonly beautiful, and combine with an uncommon wealth of imagery to fulfill one role of chant, that is, to engage us more fully, more bodily, with our faith each time we hear or sing them.

I seldom get to sing the O antiphons with a monastic community, but during one residency at St. John's, it looked as if I might make it nearly through all seven before I left for the family Christmas in Honolulu. I grew up only dimly aware of the Advent season. We usually had an Advent calendar, but even in the 1950s, before Christmas had become the consumer feeding frenzy that it is now, the push to celebrate Christmas overshadowed the subtleties of Advent. It is through my affiliation with the Benedictines that

I've learned how much the Advent season holds, how it breaks into our lives with images of light and dark, first and last things, watchfulness and longing, origin and destiny.

It was my destiny, that Advent, to submit to my publisher's request that I stop in Los Angeles for a few days before going on to Hawaii. I set about looking for a place in Los Angeles where I could hear the O Antiphons. The publicist couldn't help me; his job was arranging interviews and putting me in a tony hotel in Beverly Hills, thinking, as he cheerfully put it, that it would make a nice contrast with the monastery, and give me something to write about.

I knew that the people most likely to be singing the antiphons would be Roman Catholic or Episcopalian religious communities that pray vespers every night. Through a friend I obtained the name of a professor of nursing at a Catholic college in Los Angeles, who said that she could take me to such a community.

When I checked into the hotel, the clerk told me, as if it were significant, that my room had a view of the Hollywood Hills. I had no idea what this entailed, but it sounded good and I was glad to see the sinuous horizon, the graceful folds of land. The hills became my companion, especially at twilight, and in the blue light before dawn, when their human habitations seemed far less significant than the subtleties of changing light. I sang the O Antiphons, all seven of them, to the Hollywood Hills.

The woman hired by my publisher to escort me to my interviews picked me up in an old Buick convertible. I couldn't imagine a better vehicle in which to see the city. The woman explained that her public relations work was part-time, that she was a writer, too. "What do you write?" I asked. "Television game shows," she replied. She was trying to sell her latest to one of the big networks. Her roommate, she told me, wrote unauthorized celebrity biographies. Bristling with gossip about the recent arrest of Heidi Fleiss for running a prostitution ring, she said she'd heard that Fleiss had paid several million in cash for a mansion. I said, "I didn't know there were that many fucks in the world worth paying for." This seemed to shock the woman; apparently she'd been told I was a religious writer.

But I didn't much care. The sun, the ride in the open air, the California breeze after a cloistered Minnesota fall had put me in a reckless mood for my live interview on Pacifica radio. "Do you consider yourself a Christian?" my host asked. I sighed and said, "My problem with that is that so many people who publicly identify themselves as Christians are such jerks about it." The woman laughed, as did the people in the sound booth behind her. "Especially now," I continued, "when all that Christmas cheer is being rammed down our throats. It's enough to make a saint scream." I said I often wondered if being a Christian was something we could, or should, claim for ourselves; that if being a Christian meant incarnating the love of Christ in my own life, then maybe it would be best to let others tell me how well, or how badly, I'm doing. I spoke briefly about what Advent meant to me, and then confessed that I had schemed for months to find the O Antiphons in the city. I doubt that it was the looniest interview the woman had all day, but it had its moments.

My guide and I left the radio station and went in search of Mt. St. Mary, the college where I was to meet my professor. I'd been given explicit directions, but as we climbed high above Brentwood, the woman kept asking, "Are you sure we keep going? I don't think there's anything more up here." Finally, as promised, we saw the nuns' retirement center ahead, and kept climbing until we had come to a tiny jewel of a campus. The L.A. woman was stunned; "Why, it's a whole little world up here," she exclaimed,

"I had no idea." "Catholics are good at this," I said, and we parted company.

The view was stunning—the entire L.A. basin, the channel islands and Catalina. I found the nursing school and not one but two friendly women who were planning to take me to the O Antiphons. Vespers was at 5 P.M., and it was not quite 4, so one of the women asked if I'd like to first take a brief hike further up the mountain, past the convent and onto the fire road. It seemed a fine idea to me, and we took off.

Soon we could see, far below us, a small section of what she told me was the Santa Monica freeway. Then we left the traces of civilization behind. The air was lively with the lingering scent of juniper mixed with that of other vegetation I did not recognize. We never made it to the summit, because at one turn we encountered two coyotes, a male and a female. We stared at them, and they at us, and then they slipped away, down the hill. We decided to turn back and leave them to their pursuits.

I was overcome with the wonder of having come all the way from western South Dakota, via Minnesota, only to find myself alone with coyotes in Los Angeles. Breathing in the delicious air, taking in the snow-capped peaks of mountains to the east and the breadth of the Pacific to the west, I understood for the first time the beauty of the place; why it was people had thought it was a paradise.

In the chapel, an elderly sister, who brought us booklets so we could follow the vespers service, whispered, loudly, "Who are you?" But when we began to answer, she waved our words away, "Don't bother, I'm hard of hearing," she said, adding as she shuffled down the aisle, "It doesn't matter, we're all God's children." The antiphon that night, December 21, was "O Oriens": "O Radiant Dawn, brightness of light eternal, and sun of all justice; O come and illumine those who live in deep darkness, in the shadow of death." It passed too quickly.

After the service, several sisters gathered around us and would not hear of our leaving until they'd fed us. I'd hoped to find a dazzling ethnic restaurant in Los Angeles, but the meat loaf, mashed potatoes, and steamed zucchini we were served went down just fine. The hospitality of the nuns was dazzlement enough. Younger sisters briefed us on the community's history; they have the top of the mountain because in the mid-1920s a nun had been determined to buy it. People thought she was crazy to buy a lot of scrub brush on top of an isolated mountain way out in ranch country. The elderly of the community, dignified women in wheelchairs, the former president of the college among them, were introduced to us as other sisters, and several students assisted them with their meals, and with mobility.

The western wall of the dining room was mostly glass, to take advantage of the view. As the darkness intensified, I sensed that we were floating between the stars above and the lights below. One of the sisters, an octogenarian with an impossibly youthful demeanor, leaned on her cane and said to me, "Imagine our being here, with all this, just like the rich people."

"Sister, I said, "you *are* the rich people."

BORDERLINE

"Dear Kathy,
I feel hurt because you wrote a book and I didn't. Happy for
you and I try read your book and I was bored with it. Mom
and dad and everybody talking about it. I feel left out but it
will pass. Hope you understand how I feel about your book.
I telling you how I feel and I starting to cry while I write this
letter."

This comment on my book *Dakota*, which became a surprise best-seller in 1993, is by far the best response I received. It bored my sister Becky. Not for the first time in our relationship, she became a kind of *amma* for me, a desert mother challenging my complacency, allowing me to see the world (and myself) in a new light. By calling me back to the important things in life, my sister seemed as wise and stern as Amma Syncletica, a desert monastic of fourth-century Egypt, who said that "it is impossible for us to be surrounded by worldly honor and at the same time to bear heavenly fruit." Syncletica sums up, I believe, the difficulty writers have in America in surviving success: to keep bearing fruit one must keep returning, humbly, to the blank page, to the uncertainty of the writing process, and not pay much heed to the "noted author" the world wants you to be. Becky's letter was a godsend—reading it over, I found myself released from much of the tension induced by sudden notoriety, the rigors of a book tour stretched out over nearly two years; too much travel, too much literary hoohah.

Becky's life has been a kind of desert. When she was born, the doctors at Bethesda Naval Hospital gave my mother too strong a dose of anesthesia. Having already given birth to two children, she knew something was wrong when she couldn't push enough to release the baby from the birth canal. Precious oxygen was lost. My mother recalls one doctor saying to another, "You got yourself into this mess; let's see you get yourself out." While the doctors squabbled, my sister's brain was irreversibly damaged.

Becky is diagnosed as "borderline." She is intelligent enough to comprehend what happened to her when she was born. She is not intelligent enough to learn mathematical computation. A tutor my parents hired when Becky was in third grade told us that Becky could grasp a concept long enough to work out several problems in the course of an hour-long session, but that by the next week she'd have forgotten what she'd learned and have to start all over. Her teachers had been passing her along; there were no "special ed" programs then, and no one knew what to do with her, or where she belonged. Becky's life has been lonely in ways that most of us could not comprehend.

Yet our family ties are strong, and for years we've acted as Becky's advocates within the educational and medical establishment, sometimes taking consolation in the fact that Becky is a good enough judge of human nature to wrap psychiatrists round her little finger. Several times, when she's been given a tranquilizer or some other drug she didn't like, she's learned enough about the contraindications to fabricate symptoms so that the doctor would be forced to change her prescription. When she realized that alcoholic families were fashionable—or at least "in" with therapists—she convinced one psychologist that her mother was an alcoholic. (My mother is the sort of person who, on a big night out, might order a bit of crème de menthe.) In order to survive in her desert, my sister has often resorted to being a con artist: you get what you want by telling people what they want to hear.

She learned all this, of course, in the bosom of our family. Our parents decided when Becky was very young that she didn't belong in an institution but with us. I believe that being raised with myself and a brother, both older, and one younger sister was good for Becky. I know being raised with Becky was good for me. Very early on, I had to learn to respect her intelligence, although it was very different from mine. I also came to respect her tenacity. When she was two years old, and learning to walk was still beyond her capabilities, she became adept at scooting around the house, always with a security blanket in hand. I also had to learn to discern the difference between what Becky was truly incapable of knowing and what she was simply trying to get by with. When she destroyed my first lipstick by writing with it on a brick wall, I took off after her. She yelled, "You can't hit me, I'm retarded." She learned that she was wrong.

When I was in high school, I began to discover how much my sister and I had in common. We were both in difficult situations—I was a shy, ungainly newcomer at a prep school where many of the students had been together since kindergarten, and Becky had a particularly unsympathetic teacher. On coming home from school, she'd immediately go to her room, and play mindless rock music—"Monster Mash" is one that I recall—while she danced around the room (and sometimes on her bed). She talked to herself, incessantly and loudly. The family accepted all this as something Becky needed to do.

One day, as Becky carried on her usual "conversations," with her teacher, with other girls in her class, with a boy who'd made fun of her, I was doing homework in the next room and realized that I, too, needed release from daily tensions, a way to daydream through the failed encounters and make them come out right. Usually I lost myself in reading or practicing the flute, but sometimes I listened to music—Joan Baez, the Beach Boys, Bob Dylan, Frank Sinatra, Verdi overtures—and imagined great careers for myself, great travels, great loves. I didn't have the nerve to stomp around my room and yell as my sister was doing, but our needs were the same.

We were both struggling with our otherness, although I did not know it then. Rejection comes to everyone, of course, but for those who are markedly different from their peers, it is a daily reminder of that difference. To most people, my sister and I didn't seem to have much in common, but I knew from that day on that we were remarkably alike. If nothing else, this insight helped me to survive the intensely competitive atmosphere of my prep school. I knew that getting a D on a math test was not the worst thing in the world. And when I got an A-plus in English, when my writing won praise from my teachers, I could put it in perspective. I knew there were other kinds of intelligence that were just as valuable, and needs that could not be satisfied in school.

Our parents are nearing eighty years of age and, while they often seem to have more energy as the years go by, the fact of their mortality looms large for their children. Becky, God bless her, is incapable of hiding her fears. We went for a walk one Christmas Eve not long ago, and she said, out of the blue: "I don't want Mom and Dad to die. I worry about what will happen to me." "It scares me, too," I replied. "But *everyone* is scared to think about their parents dying." I'm not sure I convinced Becky on that score—she tends to think that she's alone in her suffering, and all too often in her life that has been the case. But I believe I did manage to reassure her that her brother and sisters would not abandon her.

As we walked through a light Manoa Valley rain—bright sunlight, prickles of moisture on bare skin—I remembered the two little girls who used to hide in their rooms every afternoon after school. How good it is to have those difficult years behind us. Becky will tell you that she's "slow." I guess I've always been fast by comparison. What does it matter, on the borderline? We're middle-aged women now, and our parents are old. As for the future, human maturity being what it is, the slow process of the heart's awakening, I sometimes wonder if Becky is better equipped for it than I.

THE CHRISTMAS
MUSIC

For nearly twenty years, my immediate family has lived as a three-generation commune in Honolulu. The arrangement is not uncommon there, because of the many Japanese- and Chinese-Americans, for whom such family structures are traditional. Many of my high school friends had grandparents living at home. For my family, the venture began as a way for everyone to have a place to live in the face of Hawaii's exorbitant housing prices, and at first it spanned four generations—my father's mother lived there for a time. But over the years, the family has found many reasons to value this way of life. "There's always somebody home at my house," one niece told her kindergarten teacher, who had asked how she might reach family members during the day. (With two ministers, a financial planner, a jazz musician, and a law office manager, there's only one person who works on a nine-to-five schedule.) And one year, I was touched to hear my four-year-old nephew call out, "Anybody! Anybody!" when he was in some kind of jam and needed help. I was one of four family members who responded (three adults and a teenager), and I thought to myself, there are worse ways to learn about trust in this world.

My parents, while they were worried at first about becoming

free baby-sitters, tell me that they can't imagine any other way to have grandchildren except on the intimate, daily basis they currently enjoy. The commune has seen two deaths—my grandmother Norris and aunt Kathleen—and four births, of my three nieces and one nephew. We recently sent our first fledgling out into the world; the oldest niece has graduated from high school and is adjusting to life in a college dorm. The family also has survived for years the Christmas visits of myself and my husband. We're forgiven for lingering well into January, putting off our return to winter, as I bake bread and my husband cooks a splendid Christmas dinner, including chocolate mousse from scratch. (One niece, on having her first taste at the age of three, asked why she couldn't have it *every* day.)

For many years, Christmas with my family meant going to hear my dad's Dixieland band play in the hotels in Waikiki, on Sunday afternoons and in the early evenings, five to nine P.M. the rest of the week. The band, and the music itself, had become a kind of ministry for my dad. He's a preacher's kid, after all. They always attracted a group of dancers, mostly middle-aged couples, and I loved to watch the complicated steps—the Balboa, the Charleston—done with such evident ease. On Christmas Eve, they'd get couples stopping in for a few dances before going to Mass, but for other people, my dad's version of "O Holy Night"—with the band's singer, Sydette, in a sexy silver lamé cocktail dress, and him on cello—was about all the religion they were going to get. And people took it seriously; the dance floor would clear, the cabaret would quiet down. It was so serious, in fact, that the song occasioned the only act of violence the band witnessed in over ten years at the club. One year a tipsy couple remained on the dance floor, moving suggestively, clinging to each other more than dancing, and a bodybuilder—one of those intensely muscular men who was unbelievably light on his feet when doing the fox trot with his wife—lost his temper. "This is religious music, dammit," he said, picking up the couple and depositing them, more or less gently, on a sofa. Sydette and my dad kept on going.

One year, on December 30, the Feast of the Holy Family, the piano player, already weakened by cancer, played one last boogie-woogie. His Our Lady of Perpetual Help medal swayed to the beat, a gold pendant shaped like a scallop shell, an ancient symbol of pilgrimage. My mother reminisced that day about her very first dance, the Fireman's Ball in Lemmon, South Dakota, in an auditorium long gone. The vanished music, the happy dancers, herself the happiest in her first grown-up dress. The bass player, Jerry, a comedian to break your heart, got serious for a moment and did a searing rendition of "St. James' Infirmary." Cold, stark death, death and devotion. My dad's gritty cornet solo brought it home.

Both the piano player and Jerry died before the year was out, Jerry from complications of diabetes, at only thirty-seven years of age. The room—the Esprit Lounge, of all things—remains fixed in my memory, a cabaret with a view of the ocean. And music that lingers in the afterglow of sunset, as the first star of evening appears over the Pacific. Living in a monastic environment all that fall had made me see many things in a new light. Dixieland jazz, for example, now seemed the most Benedictine, the most communal of ventures. Each individual in the band is recognized as such, in fact is required to play a solo, but not to improvise to the extent that the others are left out. The band begins and ends each song together.

Not long ago, on the afternoon of New Year's Eve, when the band played for a senior citizens' dance on the waterfront, at Aloha Tower, it turned into a reunion for former fans who don't get out much any more. An elderly black man that my mother and I remembered as a regular at the old Garden Bar at the Hilton, where the band played on Sundays for more than twenty years, embraced a former dancing partner. Then he set down his cane and danced with her. "Dad better watch it, Mom," I said. "When that sort of thing happened around Jesus, all hell broke loose." But I don't know that she heard me; she was eyeing the crowd for a dancing partner of her own. A few years before, when she turned seventy, she got new ballroom dancing shoes, to replace the pair she'd worn out.

My favorite photograph of my parents, taken not long after they eloped, shows two pretty young people dressed in style, who most likely had no idea of the moral courage their marriage would require of them. They were still vain children—Mom's showing off her great legs, Dad his rascal grin—but they soon found that matrimony would plunge them headlong into the strenuous process of redemption, in which even the worst things may eventually work to the good. It took my father a long time to settle into marriage, and my mother learned the hard way, as she once told me, that the only way to hold on to those you love is to let them go. As of this writing, they've been at it for going on fifty-eight years.

I inherited my father's promiscuous nature. He falls in love easily, he's the sort of man who easily turns strangers into friends. And he doesn't like to lose people. His fidelity to friendship is such that in his late seventies, he still corresponds with high school and college friends, including his first girlfriend. I also inherited my mother's stability, her commitment to the sacred vows of matrimony. All of it has helped. That year, my sister-in-law said about of them, "They have large human hearts, getting larger. As they age, they're becoming more intensely themselves, and it's so good. Good for them, good for us, good for the children to see."

January 2

BASIL THE GREAT
AND GREGORY OF NAZIANZUS

Gregory and his friend Basil met as students in Athens in the mid-fourth century, and later lived together as monks in Cappadocia. Basil wrote a Rule for monasteries that is still followed in the Orthodox world today. Grounding monastics firmly in private and communal prayer, as well as manual work, he also gave a high priority to their care of the needy; he legislated flexibly enough to provide for a mix of contemplation and action in monastic life. Basil himself founded a number of hospitals, orphanages, and residences for the poor, and was termed "the Great" by the populace of Caesarea, when, shortly before becoming the bishop of the city, he gave away much of his inheritance in famine relief, and served food to the destitute.

In one of Gregory's orations, "De pauperum amore" (On the love of the poor), he supports his friend Basil's soup kitchens by asking the rich to express their gratitude to God in gracious giving, without prejudging the needy. It is not unlike some of the last sermons of the martyred archbishop of El Salvador, Oscar Romero. At any rate, Gregory's view of the common good is still relevant, and increasingly endangered in a world that idolizes private wealth.

"Let us put into practice," Gregory says, "the supreme and primary law of God. He sends down rain on just and sinful alike and to earth's creatures he has given the broad earth, the springs, the rivers, and the forests. . . . He has given abundantly to all the basic needs of life, not as a private possession, not restricted by law, not divided by boundaries, but as common to all, amply and in rich measure."

PASSAGE

I spent some time, over Christmas, sorting through a box of mementoes, some of my own from college, and many more that my mother has saved for me since I was a child, among them several bills from Providence Hospital, in Washington, D.C., dating from the late 1940s. This is where, at the age of six months, I came close to dying. I had shrunk to twelve pounds.

I owe my life to the doctors and nurses there, and to Sir Alexander Fleming, the man who discovered penicillin. After using the drug successfully on soldiers during World War II, doctors thought it might work as well on infants. They felt that I would die without massive doses of it, and my grandfather Totten, who was a doctor, signed papers approving the experimental treatment that saved my life. Before we moved from Washington, when I was nearly seven years old, my mother took me to see the surgeon who had operated on me. Pulling a heavy book off a shelf, he showed me the pages where Baby X's treatment was recorded. He told me that I'd become so accustomed to the shots that the nurses would come in, turn me over and give me the dose, and I wouldn't even wake up.

He also said something I'd long heard from my parents and grandparents, that the reason I lived was because I had the will to live—"You were a fighter," the doctor said. Not until I was in my thirties did I realize that this was not the whole truth. Babies are drawn to pretty things, and if dying is as full of light as those who've come closest to it say, I may have wanted to die, to follow the blue light, which is my image for it, and maybe a memory, although I was only six months old.

Before I had language, I'd had the most intense engagement of my life, a frustration I contend with by writing. Had I been rejected from heaven? Surely I was poor enough to make it, then, all the way through the needle's eye. It was a Catholic hospital, and my mother tells me that the nurses—mostly nuns in those days, Sisters of Charity—loved to hold me. Surely they were praying; one of them may have baptized me in secret. My mother came every day as well, to hold me and to sing. It was my mother, and the nuns, the surgeon, and the nurse who fed me a bottle all through the operation—these people working helplessly, with all their hope and skill—who called me back. It was their world I learned to want, like a Dorothy who, having seen Oz, can call Kansas home.

For me, for years afterward, there were nightmares, and screaming fits induced by motor noises and lights that triggered memories of my hospital stay. Once, when my favorite baby-sitter, a maternal teenager named Lillian, came to the house dressed all in white I had such a tantrum that she went home and changed. My mother says that my eyes seemed sad to her when I was a baby, sadder and older than those of other children. And when I first encountered the words "eschatology" and "teleology," reading Kierkegaard at the age of sixteen, I looked them up in the dictionary and knew they were mine in a way most words were not.

Today, we are baptizing our little nephew. He's seven months old, chubby, thoroughly healthy. Ever since we came here for Christmas, I've listened for him in the morning. Like the birds, he begins to sing at first light, and together, they make the most joyous music—the baby, the birds—cooing and calling, as if life depended on it. We've planned the ceremony for late in the afternoon of Epiphany, at home, after our two ministers—my brother (Disciples of Christ) and his wife (Episcopalian) have returned from their church duties.

The baby's tired and cranky, he has no way of knowing that we are passing through hell. We renounce the forces of evil, and he cries out. As the godmother, I am holding him, and he's fussy, squirming; I have to hold on tight:

Our words wash over you, and you brush them away. The candle catches your eye, your mother's hair and fingers transparent in its light. You want the candle, you want the food your mother has become for you, you want to go down into this night at her breast. Poor little baby, water on your hair, chrism on your forehead, dried milk on your chin. Poor, dear little baby; hold on.

THE PARADOX
OF THE PSALMS

Pain—is missed—in Praise
—Emily Dickinson

Church meant two things to me when I was little: dressing up and singing. I sang in choirs from the time I was four years old and for a long time believed that singing was the purpose of religion, an illusion that was rudely swept away by the rigors of catechesis. Church was also a formal affair, a matter of wearing "Sunday best" and sitting up straight. Like the girl in Anne Sexton's "Protestant Easter, *8 years old*" I knew that "when he was a little boy / Jesus was good all the time," and I made a confused attempt to connect his story with what I saw around me on Sunday morning: "They pounded nails into his hands. / After that, well, after that / everyone wore hats . . . / The important thing for me / is that I'm wearing white gloves."

I have lately realized that what went wrong for me in my Christian upbringing is centered in the belief that one had to be dressed up, both outwardly and inwardly, to meet God, the insidious notion that I need be a firm and even cheerful believer before I dare show my face in "His" church. Such a God was of little use to me in adolescence, and like many women of my generation I simply stopped going to church when I could no longer be "good," which for girls especially meant not breaking rules, not giving voice to anger or resentment, and not complaining.

Not surprisingly, given their disruptive tone, their bold and incessant questioning of God ("How long, O Lord, will you hide yourself forever?" [Ps. 89:46]), the psalms were largely excluded from Sunday worship when I was a girl, except for a handful of the more joyful ones selected as suitable for responsorial reading. The wild and often contradictory poetry of the psalms is still mostly censored out of Christian worship in America, though Catholics, Episcopalians, Lutherans, and other mainstream Protestants hear snippets every Sunday. In worship services that lack a liturgical structure one hears less of the exacting music of poetry than lax, discursive prose that provides the illusion of control over what happens in church, and in the human heart. And the Pentecostal churches that allow for more emotional response in their worship try to exercise control by sentimentalizing emotions. Their "psalms" are likely to be pop tunes about Jesus.

Not having been to church for some twenty years following high school, I rediscovered the psalms by accident, through my unexpected attraction to Benedictine liturgy, of which the psalms are the mainstay. A Benedictine community recites or sings psalms at morning, noon, and evening prayer, going through the entire Psalter every three or four weeks. As I began to immerse myself in monastic liturgy, I found that I was also immersed in poetry and was grateful to find that the poetic nature of the psalms, their constant movement between the mundane and the exalted, means, as British Benedictine Sebastian Moore has said, that "God behaves in the psalms in ways he is not allowed to behave in systematic theology," and also that the images of the psalms, "rough-hewn from earthy experience, [are] absolutely different from formal prayer."

I also discovered, in two nine-month sojourns with the St.

John's community, that as Benedictine prayer rolls on, as daily as marriage and washing dishes, it tends to sweep away the concerns of systematic theology and church doctrine. All of that is there, as a kind of scaffolding, but the psalms demand engagement, they ask you to read them with your whole self, praying, as St. Benedict says, "in such a way that our minds are in harmony with our voices." Experiencing the psalms in this away allowed me gradually to let go of that childhood God who had set an impossible standard for both formal prayer and faith, convincing me that religion wasn't worth exploring because I couldn't "do it right."

I learned that when you go to church several times a day, every day, there is no way you can "do it right." You are not always going to sit up straight, let alone think holy thoughts. You're not going to wear your best clothes but whatever isn't in the dirty clothes basket. You come to the Bible's great "book of praises" through all the moods and conditions of life, and while you may feel like hell, you sing anyway. To your surprise, you find that the psalms do not deny your true feelings but allow you to reflect on them, right in front of God and everyone. I soon realized, during my first residency at St. John's, that this is not easy to do on a daily basis. Before, I'd always been a guest in a monastery for a week or less, and the experience was often a high. But now I was in it for a nine-month haul, and it was a struggle for me to go to choir when I didn't feel like it, especially if I was depressed (which, of course, is when I most needed to be there). I took great solace in knowing that everyone there had been through this struggle, and that some of them were struggling now with the absurdity, the monotony of repeating the psalms day after day.

I found that, even if it took a while—some prayer services I practically slept through, others I seemed to be observing from the planet Mars—the poetry of the psalms would break through and touch me. I became aware of three paradoxes in the psalms: that in them pain is indeed "missed—in Praise," but in a way that takes pain fully into account; that though of all the books of the Bible the psalms speak most directly to the individual, they cannot be removed from a communal context; and that the psalms are holistic in insisting that the mundane and the holy are inextricably linked. The Benedictine method of reading psalms, with long silences between them rather than commentary or explanation, takes full advantage of these paradoxes, offering almost alarming room for interpretation and response. It allows the psalms their full poetic power, their use of imagery and hyperbole ("Awake, my soul, / awake lyre and harp, / I will awake the dawn" [Ps. 57:8]), repetition and contradiction, as tools of word-play as well as the play of human emotions. For all of their discipline, the Benedictines allowed me to relax and sing again in church; they allowed me, as one older sister, a widow with ten children, described it, to "let the words of the psalms wash over me, and experience the joy of just being with words." As a poet I like to be with words. It was a revelation to me that this could be prayer; that this could be enough.

But to the modern reader the psalms can seem impenetrable: how in the world can we read, let alone pray, these angry and often violent poems from an ancient warrior culture? At a glance they seem overwhelmingly patriarchal, ill-tempered, moralistic, vengeful, and often seem to reflect precisely what is wrong with our world. And that's the point, or part of it. As one reads the psalms every day, it becomes clear that the world they depict is not really so different from our own; the fourth-century monk Athanasius wrote that the psalms "become like a mirror to the person singing them," and this is as true now as when he wrote it. The psalms remind us that the way we judge each other, with harsh words and acts of vengeance, constitutes injustice, and they remind us that it is the powerless in society who are overwhelmed when injustice becomes institutionalized. Psalm 35, like many psalms, laments God's absence in our unjust world, even to the point of crying, "How long, O Lord, will you look on?" (v. 17). I take an odd comfort in recognizing that the ending of Psalm 12 is as relevant now as when it was written thousands of years ago: "Protect us forever from this generation / [for] . . . the worthless are praised to the skies" (vv. 7–8).

But this is not comfortable reading, and it goes against the American grain. A writer, whose name I have forgotten, once said that the true religions of America are optimism and denial. The psalms demand that we recognize that praise does not spring from a delusion that things are better than they are, but rather from the human capacity for joy. Only when we see this can we understand that both lamentation ("Out of the depths I cry to you, O Lord" [Ps. 130:1]) and exultation ("Cry with joy to the Lord, all the earth" [Ps. 100:1]) can be forms of praise. In our skeptical age, which favors appraisal over praise, the psalms are evidence that praise need not be a fruit of optimism. But Benedictine communities draw their members from the world around them and naturally reflect its values to some extent. Women in American society are conditioned to deny their pain, and to smooth over or ignore the effects of violence, even when it is directed against them. As one sister said to me, "Women seem to have trouble drawing the line between what is passive acceptance of suffering and what can transform it." This is the danger that lies hidden in Emily Dickinson's insight that "Pain—is missed—in Praise": that we will try to jump too quickly from one to the other, omitting the necessary but treacherous journey in between, sentimentalizing both pain and praise in the process.

The sister, speaking of the women she counsels—displaced homemakers, abused wives, women returning to college after years away—says, "It doesn't help that the church has such a lousy track record here. We've said all these crappy things to people, especially to women: 'Offer it up,' or 'Suffering will make you strong.' Jesus doesn't say these things. He says, 'This will cost you.' "

Anger is one honest reaction to the cost of pain, and the psalms are full of anger. Psalm 39 begins with a confident assertion of self-control: "I will be watchful of my ways / for fear I should sin with my tongue" (v. 1). The tone soon changes in a way familiar to anyone who is prone to making such resolutions only to watch them fall apart: "The prosperity [of the wicked] stirred my grief. / My heart was burning within me. / At the thought of it, the fire blazed up / and my tongue burst into speech . . ." (vv. 2–3). Typically, although judgment is implied in calling another person wicked, the psalmist's anger is directed primarily at God, with the bitter question, "And now, Lord, what is there to wait for?" (v. 7).

Many Benedictine women find that the psalms provide an outlet for such anger; the psalms don't theologize or explain anger away. One reason for this is that the psalms are poetry, and poetry's function is not to explain but to offer images and stories that resonate with our lives. Walter Brueggemann, a Lutheran theologian, writes in *Israel's Praise* that in the psalms pain acts both as "the locus of possibility" and "the matrix of praise." This is a dangerous insight, as risky as Dickinson's. There's a fine line between idealizing or idolizing pain, and confronting it with hope. But I believe that both writers are speaking the truth about the psalms. The value of this great songbook of the Bible lies not in the fact that singing praise can alleviate pain but that the painful images we find there are essential for praise, that without them, praise is meaningless. It becomes the "dreadful cheer" that Minnesota author Carol Bly has complained of in generic American Christianity, which blinds itself to pain and thereby makes a falsehood of its praise.

People who rub up against the psalms every day come to see that while children may praise spontaneously, it can take a lifetime for adults to recover this ability. One sister told me that when she first entered the convent as an idealistic young woman, she had tried to pretend that "praise was enough." It didn't last long. The earthy honesty of the psalms had helped her, she says, to "get real, get past the holy talk and the romantic image of the nun." In expressing all the complexities and contradictions of human experience, the psalms act as good psychologists. They defeat our tendency to try to be holy without being human first. Psalm 6 mirrors the way in which our grief and anger are inextricably mixed; the lament that "I am exhausted with my groaning; / every night I drench my pillow with tears" (v. 6) soon leads to rage: "I have grown old surrounded by my foes. / Leave me, you who do evil (vv. 7–8). Psalm 38 stands on the precipice of depression, as wave after wave of bitter self-accusation crashes against the small voice of hope. The psalm is clinically accurate in its portrayal of extreme melancholia: "the very light has gone from my eyes" (v. 10), "my pain is always before me" (v. 17), and its praise is found only in the possibility of hope: "It is for you, O Lord, that I wait" (v. 15). Psalm 88 is one of the few that ends without even this much praise. It takes us to the heart of pain and leaves us there, saying, "My one companion is darkness" (v. 18). We can only hope that this darkness is a friend, one who provides a place in which our deepest wounds can heal.

The psalms make us uncomfortable because they don't allow us to deny either the depth of our pain or the possibility of its transformation into praise. As a Benedictine sister in her fifties, having recently come through both the loss of a job and the disintegration of a long-term friendship, put it to me, "I feel as if God is rebuilding me, 'binding up my wounds' (Ps. 147:3). "But," she adds, "I'm tired, and little pieces of the psalms are all I can handle. Once you've fallen apart, you take what nourishment you can. The psalms feel to me like a gentle spring rain: you hardly know that it's sinking in, but something good happens."

The psalms reveal our most difficult conflicts, and our deep desire, in Jungian terms, to run from the shadow. In them, the shadow speaks to us directly, in words that are painful to hear. In recent years, some Benedictine houses, particularly women's communities, have begun censoring the harshest of the psalms, often called the "cursing psalms," from their public worship. But one sister, a liturgist, said after visiting such a community, "I began to get antsy, feeling, *something is not right.* The human experience is of violence, and the psalms reflect our experience of the world."

The psalms are full of shadows—enemies, stark images of betrayal: "Even my friend, in whom I trusted, / who ate my bread, has turned against me" (Ps. 41:9). Psalm 10 contains an image of a lion who "lurks in hiding" (10:9) that calls to my mind the sort of manipulative people whose true colors come out only behind the doors of their "lairs." Psalm 5 pictures flatterers, "their throat a wide-open grave, all honey their speech" (v. 9). As C. S. Lewis has noted in *Reflections on the Psalms,* when the psalms speak to us of lying and deceit, "no historical readjustment is required. We are in the world we know."

But all-American optimism, largely a middle-class and Protestant phenomenon, doesn't want to know this world. We want to conquer evil by being nice, and nice people don't want to soil their white gloves with the gritty anger at the heart of a cursing psalm such as 109, in which the psalmist is driven to cry out against his tormentor: "He loved cursing; let curses fall upon him. / He scorned blessing; let blessing pass him by." The imagery roils like a whirlpool, drawing us in and down: "He put on cursing like his coat; / let it soak into his body like water; / let it sink like oil into his bones . . ." (vv. 17–18).

Evidently in the Hebrew it is clear that this breathtaking catalogue of curses, as one commentary reads, "should be understood as the curses of the psalmist's enemy against him." The intent is to show the bully what it's like to have "no one show any mercy" (v. 12), how it feels to be hated. But the poem also shows us how it feels *to* hate: its curses are not just a venting of anger but a devastatingly accurate portrait of the psychology of hatred. Though the psalmist starts out speaking of love, of praying for his enemies, he fails, as we tend to do when beset by evil, to keep the love foremost.

The psalmist finally reaches out of this paranoiac maelstrom, saying, "Let the Lord thus repay my accusers" (v. 20) and recalling his own true condition: "I am poor and needy / and my heart is pierced within me" (v. 22). This most painful of psalms ends with a whisper of praise, the plea of an exhausted man for help from a God "who stands at the poor man's side / to save him from those who condemn him" (v. 31).

It is good to fall back into silence after reading this psalm out loud, to recall that it is a true prayer, in that it leaves ultimate judgment to God. But it also forces us to recognize that calling for God's judgment can feel dangerously good. It became clear to me in Benedictine liturgy that, as one sister explained, the "enemies" vilified in the cursing psalms are best seen as "my own demons, not 'enemies out there.' " But, she added, noting that the psalms always resist an attempt to use them in a facile manner, "you can't simply spiritualize all the enemies away."

Adults can be hypersensitive about admitting to offensive emotions, and children sometimes are more able to allow for the hyperbole of the psalms. I once assigned Psalm 109 in a class I was teaching, and one woman ended up reading it to her nine-year-old granddaughter, after she'd encountered her in tears. It was a hot afternoon, and the girl had ridden her bike over a mile along a dusty trail to the neighborhood swimming pool, hoping to cool off. But she arrived just as the staff was closing it, and one officious youth was short with her. Her grandmother explained that she had to study a poem about being angry, and it might help to read it aloud. But soon after she'd entered the catalogue of curses—"Let their children be wanderers and beggars / driven from the ruins of their home. / Let creditors seize all their goods . . ." (vv. 10–11)—the child cried out, "Oh, stop! Stop! He's just a college kid!"

The daily praying of the psalms helps monastic people to live with them in a balanced and realistic way, appreciating their hyperbole without taking it as prescriptive. Benedictines become so close to the psalms that they become, as more than one sister told me, "like a heartbeat." The psalms do become a part of a Benedictine's physical as well as spiritual life, acting on the heart to slow it down, something I came to know as I often came to noon prayer with my mind still racing with the work I'd interrupted. Beginning to recite a psalm such as 62, which begins: "In God alone is my soul at rest," I'd feel as if I were skidding to a halt. Like many of the psalms, it laments human falsity, those who "with their mouth . . . utter blessing / but in their heart they curse" (v. 4). But the next line: "In God alone *be* at rest, my soul," offers not only a pleasurable poetic repetition but a shift from pain into hope, a widening of horizons that is not only sound but comforting.

But daily exposure to the psalms also makes it possible to become numb to them, to read even the most stunning poetry ("By

God's word the heavens were made, / by the breath of God's mouth all the stars" [Ps. 33:6]) in such a way that you scarcely notice what you've said. But what often happens is that holiness reasserts itself so that even familiar psalms suddenly infuse the events of one's life with new meaning. One sister told me that as she prayed the psalms aloud at the bedside of her dying mother, who was in a coma, she discovered "how perfectly the psalms reflected my own inner chaos: my fear of losing her, or of not losing her and seeing her suffer more, of saying goodbye, of being motherless." She found that the closing lines of Psalm 16—"You will show me the path of life, / the fullness of joy in your presence"—consoled her "as I saw my mother slipping away. I was able to turn her life over to God."

Internalizing the psalms in this way allows contemporary Benedictines to find personal relevance in this ancient poetry. Paradoxically it also frees them from the tyranny of individual experience. To say or sing the psalms aloud within a community is to recover religion as an oral tradition, restoring to our mouths words that have been snatched from our tongues and relegated to the page, words that have been privatized and effectively silenced. It counters our tendency to see individual experience as sufficient for formulating a vision of the world.

The liturgy that Benedictines have been experimenting with for fifteen-hundred-plus years taught me the value of tradition; I came to see that the psalms are holy in part because they are so well-used. If so many generations had found solace here, might I also? The holiness of the psalms came to seem like that of a stone that has been held in the palm by countless ancestors, illustrating the difference between what the poet Galway Kinnell has termed the "merely personal," or individual, and the "truly personal," which is individual experience reflected back into community and tradition. That great scholar of mysticism, Evelyn Underhill, makes the same distinction when speaking of prayer, admitting that "devotion by itself has little value . . . and may even be a form of self-indulgence," unless it is accompanied by a transformation of the personal. "The spiritual life of individuals," she writes, "has to be extended both vertically to God and horizontally to other souls; and the more it grows in both directions, the less merely individual and therefore the more truly personal it will be."

Recent scholarship regards the psalms as liturgical poems that were used in ancient Israel's communal worship. Even individual laments such as Psalm 51, it is believed, were incorporated into a public worship setting. But praying the psalms is often disconcerting for contemporary people who encounter Benedictine life: raised in a culture that idolizes individual experience, they find it difficult to recite a lament when they're in a good mood, or to sing a hymn of praise when they're in pain.

The communal recitation of the psalms works against this form of narcissism, the tendency in America to insist that everything be self-discovery. One soon finds that a strength of the monastic choir is that it always contains someone ready to lament over a lifetime of days of "emptiness and pain" (Ps. 70:10) or to shout with a joy loud enough to make "the rivers clap their hands" (Ps. 98:8). Though, as one sister says, "we're so different I sometimes think we live in different universes, the liturgy brings us back to what's in the heart. And the psalms are always instructing the heart." This is not a facile remark. The vow of "conversion of life," which is unique to Benedictines, means that you commit yourself to being changed by the words of the psalms, allowing them to work on you, and sometimes to work you over.

A cursing psalm such as 52: "You love lies more than truth . . . you love the destructive word" (v. 3) might occasion self-recrimination, demanding that we pray it for someone who is angry with us, and also reflect on just how justified that person might be in leveling such an accusation against us. Psalm 22, which moves dramatically from pain ("My God, My God, why have you forsaken me?"[v. 1]) to prophetic praise ("All the earth shall remember and return to the Lord . . ." [v. 27]), might pose a challenge to the rational mind. What if there is no one to hear such a prayer? What if one is simply too exhausted by despair to pray it? Herein lies the gift of communal worship. "In the really hard times," says one sister, "when it's all I can do to keep breathing, it's still important for me to go to choir. I feel as if the others are keeping my faith for me, pulling me along."

It helps that the psalms themselves keep moving. In a monastic choir they inevitably pull a person out of private prayer, into community and then into the world, into what might be termed praying the news. Psalm 74's lament on the violation of sacred space: "Every cave in the land is a place where violence has made its home" (v. 20) has become for me a prayer for the victims and perpetrators of domestic violence. Watching television footage of the Los Angeles riots of early 1992 gave me a new context for the words of Psalm 55 that I encountered the next morning in the monastic choir: "I see nothing but violence and strife in the city" (v. 9). Hearing Psalm 79 ("They have poured out water like blood in Jerusalem / there is no one left to bury the dead" [v. 3]) as I read of civil war in the Balkans forces me to reflect on the evil that tribalism and violence, often justified by religion, continue to inflict on our world.

But the relentless realism of the psalms is not depressing in the way that television news can be, although many of the same events are reported: massacres, injustices to those who have no one to defend them, people tried in public by malicious tongues. As a book of praises, meant to be sung, the Psalter contains a hope that "human interest" stories tacked on to the end of a news broadcast cannot provide. The psalms mirror our world but do not allow us to become voyeurs. In a nation unwilling to look at its own violence, they force us to recognize our part in it. They make us re-examine our values.

When we want to "feel good about ourselves" (which I have heard seriously proposed as the purpose of worship), when we've gone to the trouble to "get a life," current slang suggesting that life itself is a commodity, how can we say, with the psalmist, "I am poor and needy" (Ps. 40:17) or "my life is but a breath" (Ps. 39:5)? It seems so damned negative, even if it's true. How can we read Psalm 137, one of the most troubling of the psalms and also one of the most beautiful? The ultimate song of exile, it begins: "By the waters of Babylon / there we sat and wept, / remembering Zion."

In a line that expresses the bitterness of colonized people everywhere, the psalmist continues:

> For it was there that they asked us,
> our captors, for songs,
> our oppressors, for joy.
> "Sing to us," they said,
> "one of Zion's songs."
>
> O how could we sing
> the song of the Lord
> on alien soil? (Ps. 137:3–4)

These lines have a special poignancy for women: All too often, for reasons of gender, as well as poverty and race, we find that our journey from girlhood to womanhood is an exile to "alien soil." And how do feminist women, who often feel as if we're asked to sing in the midst of an oppressive patriarchy, asked to dress pretty and act nice, read such a psalm? We may feel, as radical feminists do, that the very language we speak is an oppressor's tongue. How, then, do we sing?

If the psalm doesn't offer an answer, it allows us to dwell on the question. And as one encounters this psalm over and over again in Benedictine liturgy, it asks us to acknowledge that being uprooted and forced into servitude is not an experience alien to our "civilized" world. The speaker could be one of today's refugees or exiles, an illegal alien working in an American sweat shop for far less than the minimum wage, a slave laborer in China. When one reads the psalm with this in mind, the closing verse, containing an image of unspeakable violence against Israel's Babylonian captors, comes as no surprise: "O Babylon, destroyer, / he is happy who repays you the ills you brought on us. / He shall seize and shall dash / your children on the rock!" (vv. 8–9).

These lines are the fruit of human cruelty; they let us know the depth of the damage we do when we enslave other people, when we blithely consume the cheap products of cheap labor. But what does it mean to find such an image in a book of prayer, a hymn-book of "praises"? The psalms are unrelenting in their realism about the human psyche. They ask us to consider our true situation, and to pray over it. They ask us to be honest about ourselves and admit that we, too, harbor the capacity for vengeance. This psalm functions as a cautionary tale: such a desire, left unchecked, whether buried under "niceness" or violently acted out, can lead to a bitterness so consuming that even the innocent are not spared.

What the psalms offer us is the possibility of transformation, of converting a potentially deadly force such as vengeance into something better. What becomes clear when one begins to engage the psalms in a profound way—and the Benedictines insist that praying them communally, every day, is a good place to start—is that it can come to seem as if the psalms are reading and writing *us.* This concept comes from an ancient understanding, derived from the Hebrew word for praise, *tehilla,* that, in the words of the Benedictine Damasus Winzen, "comes from *hallal* which does not only mean 'to praise' but primarily means 'to radiate' or 'to reflect.' " He states that "the medieval Jewish poet Jehuda Halevi expressed beautifully the spirit of the Psalter when he said: 'Look on the glories of God, and awaken the glory in thee.' "

I never felt particularly glorious at morning, noon, or evening prayer in my time with the Benedictines, but I did begin to sense that a rhythm of listening and response was being established between me and the world of the psalms. I felt as if I were becoming part of a living, lived-in poem, a relationship with God that revealed the holy not only in ordinary words but in the mundane events of life, both good and bad. As I was plunged into mysteries beyond my understanding—the God the psalmist has exhorted to speech ("O God, do not keep silence" [Ps. 83:1]) suddenly speaking in the voice of the *mysterium tremendum* ("from the womb before the dawn I begot you" [Ps. 110:3])—I recognized the truth of what one sister told me. She compared Benedictine liturgy to "falling in love, because you don't enter into it knowing the depths. It's a relationship you live with *until* you begin to understand it."

In the dynamic of this liturgy one rides the psalms like a river current, noticing in passing how alien these ancient and sophisticated texts are, and how utterly accessible. When I encounter Psalm 61, which asks God to "set me on a rock too high for me to reach" (v. 2), I think of the dying ten-year-old girl in Robert Coles's *The Spiritual Life of Children,* who said as she slipped into a final coma, "I'd like to go to that high rock." When I read Psalm 131 with its image of the soul as "a weaned child on its mother's breast" (v. 2), I remember the Benedictine sister retired from a university professorship on account of a delibitating illness who said, "For so many years, I was taught that I had to 'master' subjects. But who can 'master' beauty, or peace, or joy? This psalm speaks of the grace of childhood, not of being childish. One of my greatest freedoms is to see that all the pretenses and defenses I put up in the first part of my life, I can spend the rest of my life taking down. This psalm tells me that I'm a dependent person, and that it's not demeaning."

There is much beauty in the psalms to stir up childlike wonder: the God who made whales to play with, who calls the stars by name, who asks us to drink from the stream of delight. Though as adults we want answers, we will sometimes settle for poetry and begin to see how it is possible to say, "My soul sings psalms to God unceasingly (Ps. 30:12), even if that means, in the words of one Benedictine nun, "I pray best in the dentist's chair."

The height and depth of praise urged on us in the psalms ("Let everything that lives and that breathes / give praise to the Lord" [Ps. 150:6]) can heighten our sense of marvel and awaken our capacity to appreciate the glories of this world. One Benedictine woman has told me of herself and another sister getting permission from their superior, in the days before Vatican II, to don army-surplus parkas and ski-patrol pants and go cross-country skiing in the early spring. Coming to a wooded hill, the women sank in waist-deep snow and discovered at their feet a patch of hypatia blossoms. "There'd been an early snow that fall," she said, "and those plants were still emerald green, with flower buds completely encased in ice. To me this was 'honey from the rock' [Ps. 81:16]. It was finding life where you least expect it."

Sometimes these people who live immersed, as all Benedictines do, in the poetry of the Psalter, are granted an experience that feels like a poem, in which familiar words that have become like old friends suddenly reveal their power to bridge the animal and human worlds, to unite the living and the dead. Psalm 42, like many psalms, moves the way our emotions do, in fits and starts: "Why are you cast down, my soul, / why groan within me? / Hope in the Lord, I will praise God still" (v. 5). But its true theme is a desire for the holy that, whatever form it takes, seems to be a part of the human condition, a desire easily forgotten in the pull and tug of daily life, where groans of despair can predominate. One sister wrote to me: "Some winters ago, when ice covered all the lands surrounding our priory, deer came close in search of food. We had difficulty keeping them from eating our trees and even the shrubs in our cemetery." Having been at the convent for many years, she had known most of the women buried there. One morning she woke to find that "each deer had selected a particular tombstone to lie behind, oblivious to us watching from the priory windows. The longing for God expressed at the beginning of Psalm 42, 'Like the deer that yearns / for running streams, / so my soul is yearning / for you, My God,' has stayed with me ever since."

BAPTISM
OF THE LORD:
A TALE OF
INTIMACY

True intimacy is frightening, and I was well into my marriage before I realized that I either had to seek it or live a lie. Intimacy is what *makes* a marriage, not a ceremony, not a piece of paper from the state. I have shared great intimacy with several people; my friend dying of cancer for whom I would hold (and later clean) the bowls in which she frequently had to vomit; the monk, homosexual and resolutely celibate, with whom I've shared the deepest confidences. But it is only with my husband that I feel the mystery St. Paul speaks of in Ephesians, our lives so intertwined that they feel like "one flesh."

I had forgotten how much marriage imagery there is in this feast that ends the Christmas season. "On the third day there was a wedding at Cana in Galilee," I read last night in my breviary. Cana again in the morning hymn, and "Here is my beloved" at morning prayer, and again at Mass. But why, at the end of Mass, a song about a wedding garment? Is baptism a kind of marriage?

Why, to celebrate the baptism of Jesus in the Jordan, hymn verses that echo the Song of Songs, the lover knocking on a door that is locked against him, and the night?

It brings a flood of memories that exhaust me. For years I hated weddings. I used to think it was simply a cultural prejudice against a ceremony that seemed only to celebrate sentiment and money, the barbaric custom of "giving away" a woman, as if she were not a person but property. But it ran much deeper, a fear of giving myself to anyone. And then, one night, when my husband had hidden himself away, and was found by a gentle policeman (who later told me, "M'am, your husband was so *depressed,* I never saw a man so depressed as that"), I read myself to sleep with the Song of Songs and found us there, the beloved knocking, calling, "Open to me, my sister, my love," and my own delayed response, the selfish thought, in the face of love—"I had put off my garment, how could I put it on again? I had bathed my feet; how could I soil them?" The comic scurrying, my bad timing: "I opened to my beloved, but my beloved had turned and was gone."

That night I discovered, in the "Song," a religious dimension to something I'd never fully understood. "When I found him whom my soul loves, I held him and would not let him go, until I brought him to my mother's house, into the chamber of her that conceived me." I had, in fact, brought my husband from New York City to my grandmother's house in South Dakota, the house where my mother was born, and now I wondered if this had been an attempt to build a marriage, to free us from the distractions of the city so that we could get to know each other. Maybe love needs space around it, and time. Is love fostered by time as much as it needs and fosters intimacy?

Yes, I am married, but do I know how to love? Has my heart

been shut for so long? I look up that passage in Paul. "The two will become one flesh," he says, but only after sputtering on for a good long while, trying to make explicit the comparison between marriage and Christ's love for the church. Finally, he gives up; I hear exasperation as well as wonder in his voice when he says, "This is a great mystery." I read the end of Ephesians 5 as an example of what happens when you discover a metaphor so elusive you know it must be true. As you elaborate, and try to explain, you begin to stumble over words and their meanings. The literal takes hold, the unity and the beauty flee. Finally you have to say, I don't know what it means; here it is.

A mystery indeed, elusive as prayer. For years I had chosen relationships that seemed safe, because I was choosing; in fact, I had chosen them because they didn't require commitment. It's hard to change old ways, to let myself be chosen, blessed by love, as if anointed. I don't know what it means, but after my husband had been missing for three days and I found him in the emergency room, I did not know him. Depression had turned him inside out; he looked as ravaged as the corpus on the crucifix on the wall behind him. ("I'm afraid all the time," is what he told me, a few days later, when he could speak.)

Of course, it was a Catholic hospital, Benedictine; one of our best friends, a young monk, had just become a chaplain there. Here it is, a mystery: I carry with me still the photograph of the three of us taken the summer before. My husband, our friend (who had just been ordained), and me. David had left, but I went to find him and brought him back. The three of us smiling, in the abbey courtyard. And that night, in the wine cellar, when the celebrating was done, I helped Fr. Robert wash glasses. He's an older monk whom I had yanked out of semi-retirement to help me become an oblate, and wine tasting and washing up in his cellar were part of the deal.

I'd been an oblate for a little more than a year and felt as lost as ever. Prayers were a torment, but what I knew I needed to do. My life was a hurricane, and our marriage, confused as it was, the calm at the center. "You are entering the deep, uncharted waters" is what he said to me.

January 10

GREGORY OF NYSSA

Gregory is the fellow who gives us an unforgettable account of the way in which everyday fourth-century life was permeated with theology, particularly debate concerning the nature of Christ. Everyone had an opinion, it seems. As Gregory says about Constantinople: "Garment sellers, money changers, food vendors— they are all at it. If you ask for change, they philosophize about the Begotten and the Unbegotten. If you inquire about the price of bread, the answer is that the Father is greater and the Son inferior. If you say to the attendant, 'Is my bath ready?' he tells you that the Son was made out of nothing."

What people were discussing was the controversy that had arisen concerning the divinity of Christ and his relation to God the Father, which the first official council of the Christian church, held at Nicaea, had attempted to settle just ten years before Gregory's birth. Soon, however, even bishops who had signed the Nicene Creed found that they didn't always agree on what it meant, and competing philosophies—chiefly Arianism, which held that Christ was a created being, less divine than the Father—had much popular appeal.

Born into a remarkable family—his sister Macrina and his

brother Basil the Great both founded monasteries—Gregory was the dreamer of the bunch. He appeals to me mainly because he seems equally a poet and a theologian. Discovering his *Life of Moses*, finding that Christian theology could contain such poetry, such wild and inspiring typology, was something I desperately needed at the time. I read the book slowly, not wanting to finish it.

What Gregory said of Moses, that he "entered the darkness, and then saw God in it," that in God's sanctuary "he was taught by word what he had formerly learned by darkness," seemed to me to tell an essential truth about poetry, as well as religion. It confirmed a sense that I'd held as a child of the holy as dwelling in deep darkness, despite being told by my Sunday-school teachers that "God is light." They were nice enough grown-ups and brave souls; they did their best to teach me origami. But I always sensed that they weren't giving me the full story.

As befits a poet, Gregory is a theologian of desire; he looks at Moses and sees a "bold request which goes up the mountains of desire," asking only to see the beauty of God "not in mirrors and reflections, but face to face." Gregory's own search for God seems to have been fueled more by desire than a certitude of faith. (As the church historian William Placher has said of Gregory, "For a long time he drifted through life without either a career or much religion, but he eventually found a deep faith.") I frequently take consolation in Gregory's sense that with God there is always more unfolding, that what we can glimpse of the divine is always exactly enough, and never enough.

February 2

CANDLEMAS /

PRESENTATION OF THE LORD

And Simeon blessed them and said to Mary his mother, "Behold
this child is destined for the fall and rise of many in Israel, and to
be a sign that will be contradicted (and you yourself a sword will
pierce) so that the thoughts of many hearts will be revealed."
(LUKE 2:34–35)

The darkness is still with us, O Lord. You are still hidden and the
world which you have made does not want to know you or receive
you . . . You are still the hidden child in a world grown old . . . You
are still obscured by the veils of this world's history, you are still
destined not to be acknowledged in the scandal of your death on the
cross . . . But I, O hidden Lord of all things, boldly affirm my faith
in you. In confessing you, I take my stand with you . . . If I make
this avowal of faith, it must pierce the depths of my heart like a
sword, I must bend my knee before you, saying, I must alter my life.
I have still to become a Christian.
—Karl Rahner, PRAYERS FOR MEDITATION

Today, the monks are doing something that seems futile, and a bit
foolish. They are blessing candles, all the candles they'll use during worship for the coming year. It's good to think of the light hidden inside those new candles; walking to prayer each morning in
the bitter cold, I know that the light comes earlier now. I can feel
the change, the hours of daylight increasing. The ground has been

covered by snow since Thanksgiving; in this climate, I'll seize hold of any bit of hope, even if it's monks saying prayers over candles.

The reading from Karl Rahner, at morning prayer, came as a shock. To hear so esteemed a theologian cry out, "I have still to become a Christian" was humbling. The words have stayed with me all day. I wonder if one of the reasons I love the Benedictines so much is that they seldom make big noises about being Christians. Though they live with the Bible more intimately than most people, they don't thump on it, or with it, the way gorillas thump on their chests to remind anyone within earshot of who they are. Benedictines remind me more of the disciples of Jesus, who are revealed in the gospel accounts as people who were not afraid to admit their doubts, their needs, their lack of faith. "Lord, increase our faith," they say, "Teach us to pray." They kept getting the theology wrong, and Jesus, more or less patiently, kept trying to set them straight. Except for Peter, the disciples were not even certain who Jesus was: "Have I been with you all this time, and still you do not know me?" Jesus asks in the Gospel of John, not long before he's arrested and sentenced to death.

Maybe because it's the heart of winter, and the air is so cold that it hurts to breathe, the image of the sword from Luke's gospel comes to mind as I walk back home after vespers. We've heard it twice today, at morning prayer and at Mass. I wonder if Mary is the mother of *lectio,* because as she pondered her life and the life of her son, she kept Simeon's hard prophecy in her heart. So much that came easily in the fall has become a struggle this winter. I still walk to morning prayer—it seems necessary to do—but it requires more effort now. Still I know that it is nothing that I do that matters, but what I am, what I will become. Maybe Mary's story, and this feast, tell us that if the scriptures *don't* sometimes pierce us like a sword, we're not paying close enough attention.

CELIBATE
PASSION

The Cherub was stationed at the gate of the earthly paradise with
his flaming sword to teach us that no one will enter the heavenly
paradise who is not pierced with the sword of love.
—St. Francis de Sales, TREATISE ON THE LOVE OF GOD

Celibacy is a field day for ideologues. Conservative
Catholics, particularly those who were raised in the
pre-Vatican II church, tend to speak of celibacy as if it were an idealized, angelic state, while feminist theologians such as Uta Ranke-
Heinemann say, angrily, that "celibate hatred of sex is hatred of
women." That celibacy constitutes the hatred of sex seems to be a
given in the popular mythology of contemporary America, and we
need only look at newspaper accounts of sex abuse by priests to see
evidence of celibacy that isn't working. One could well assume that
this is celibacy, impure and simple. And this is unfortunate, because
celibacy practiced rightly is not at all a hatred of sex; in fact it has
the potential to address the sexual idolatry of our culture in a most
helpful way.

One benefit of the nearly ten years that I've been a Benedictine oblate has been the development of deep friendships with celibate men and women. This has led me to ponder celibacy that
works, practiced by people who are fully aware of themselves as sex-

ual beings but who express their sexuality in a celibate way. That is, they manage to sublimate their sexual energies toward another purpose than sexual intercourse and procreation. Are they perverse, their lives necessarily stunted? Cultural prejudice would say yes, but I have my doubts. I've seen too many wise old monks and nuns whose lengthy formation in celibate practice has allowed them to incarnate hospitality in the deepest sense. In them, the constraints of celibacy have somehow been transformed into an openness that attracts people of all ages, all social classes. They exude a sense of freedom. They also genderbend, at least in my dreams. Sister Jeremy will appear as a warrior on horseback, Father Robert as a wise old woman tending a fire.

The younger celibates of my acquaintance are more edgy. Still contending mightily with what one friend calls "the raging orchestra of my hormones," they are more obviously struggling to contain their desires for intimacy, for physical touch, within the bounds of celibacy. Often they find their loneliness intensified by the incomprehension of others. In a culture that denies the value of their striving, they are made to feel like fools, or worse.

Americans are remarkably tone-deaf when it comes to the expression of sexuality. The sexual formation that many of us receive is like the refrain of an old Fugs' song: "Why do ya like boobs a lot—ya gotta like boobs a lot." The jiggle of tits and ass, penis and pectorals, assault us everywhere—billboards, magazines, television, movies. Orgasm becomes just another goal; we undress for success. It's no wonder that in all this powerful noise, the quiet tones of celibacy are lost; that we have such trouble comprehending what it could mean to dedicate one's sexual drives in such a way that genital activity and procreation are precluded. But celibate people have taught me that celibacy, practiced rightly, does indeed have something valuable to say to the rest of us. Specifically, they have helped me better appreciate both the nature of friendship, and what it means to be married.

They have also helped me recognize that celibacy, like monogamy, is not a matter of the will disdaining and conquering the desires of the flesh but a discipline requiring what many people think of as undesirable, if not impossible—a conscious form of sublimation. Like many people who came into adulthood during the sexually permissive 1960s, I've tended to equate sublimation with repression. But my celibate friends have made me see the light; accepting sublimation as a normal part of adulthood makes me more realistic about human sexual capacities and expression. It helps me to respect the bonds and boundaries of marriage.

Any marriage has times of separation, ill-health, or just plain crankiness, in which sexual intercourse is ill-advised. And it is precisely the skills of celibate friendship—fostering intimacy through letters, conversation, performing mundane tasks together (thus rendering them pleasurable), savoring the holy simplicity of a shared meal, or a walk together at dusk—that can help a marriage survive the rough spots. When you can't make love physically, you figure out other ways to do it.

Monastic people are celibate for a very practical reason: the kind of community life to which they aspire can't be sustained if people are pairing off. Even in churches in which the clergy are often married—Episcopal and Russian Orthodox, for example—their monks and nuns are celibate. And while monastic novices may be carried along for a time on the swells of communal spirit, when that blissful period inevitably comes to an end, the loneliness is profound. One gregarious monk in his early thirties told me that just as he thought he'd settled into the monastery, he woke up in a panic one morning, wondering if he'd wake up lonely every morning for the rest of his life.

Another monk I know regards celibacy as an expression of the essential human loneliness, a perspective that helps him as a hospital chaplain, when he is called upon to minister to the dying. I knew him when he was still resisting his celibate call—it usually came out as anger directed toward his abbot and community, more rarely as misogyny—and I was fascinated to observe the process by which he came to accept the sacrifices that a celibate, monastic life requires. He's easier to be with now; he's a better friend.

This is not irony so much as grace, that in learning to be faithful to his vow of celibacy, the monk developed his talent for relationship. It's a common occurence. I've seen the demands of Benedictine hospitality—that they receive all visitors as Christ—convert shy young men who fear women into monks who can enjoy their company. I've witnessed this process of transformation at work in older monks as well. One friend, who had entered the monastery very young, was, when I first met him, still suffering acutely from an inadequate and harmful sexual formation. Taught that as a monk he should avoid women, he faced a crisis when he encountered women as students and colleagues on a college faculty. Fear of his own sexual desires translated all too easily into misogyny. As a good Benedictine, however, he recognized, prayed over, and explored the possibilities for conversion in this situation. Simply put, he's over it now. I'm one of many women who count him as a dear friend, including several who became serious scholars because he urged them on.

One reason I enjoy celibates is that they tend to value friendship very highly. And my friendships with celibate men, both gay and straight, give me some hope that men and women don't live in alternate universes. In 1990s America, this sometimes feels like a countercultural perspective. Male celibacy, in particular, can become radically countercultural if it is perceived as a rejection of the consumerist model of sexuality, a model that reduces women to the sum of her parts. I have never had a monk friend make an insinuating remark along the lines of, "You have beautiful eyes" (or legs, breasts, knees, elbows, nostrils), the usual catalogue of remarks that women grow accustomed to deflecting. A monk is supposed to give up the idea of possessing anything and, in this culture, that includes women.

Ideally, in giving up the sexual pursuit of women (whether as demons or as idealized vessels of purity), the male celibate learns to relate to them as human beings. That many fail to do so, that the power structures of the Catholic church all but dictate failure in this regard, comes as no surprise. What is a surprise is what happens when it works. Once, after I'd spent a week in a monastery, I boarded a crowded Greyhound bus and took the first available seat. My seatmate, a man, soon engaged me in conversation, and it took me a while to realize that he wasn't simply being friendly, he was coming on to me. I remember feeling foolish for being so slow to catch on. I remember thinking, "No wonder this guy is acting so strange; he didn't take a vow of celibacy."

When it works, when men have truly given up the idea of possessing women, healing can occur. I once met a woman in a monastery guest house who had come there because she was pulling herself together after being raped, and said she needed to feel safe around men again. I've seen young monks astonish an obese and homely college student by listening to her with as much interest and respect as to her conventionally pretty roommate. On my fortieth birthday, as I happily blew out four candles on a cupcake ("one for each decade," a monk in his twenties cheerfully proclaimed), I realized that I could enjoy growing old with these guys. They were helping me to blow away my fears of middle age.

As celibacy takes hold in a person, over the years, as monastic values supersede the values of the culture outside the monastery, celibates become people who can radically affect those of us out "in the world," if only because they've learned how to listen without possessiveness, without imposing themselves. With someone who is practicing celibacy well, we may sense that we're being listened to in a refreshingly deep way. And this is the purpose of celibacy, not to attain some impossibly cerebral goal mistakenly conceived as "holiness" but to make oneself available to others, body *and* soul. Celibacy, simply put, is a form of ministry—not an achievement one can put on a résumé but a subtle form of service to others. In theological terms, one dedicates one's sexuality to God through Jesus Christ, a concept and a terminology I find extremely hard to grasp. All I can do is to catch a glimpse of people who are doing it, incarnating celibacy in a mysterious, pleasing, and gracious way.

The attractiveness of the celibate is that he or she can make us feel appreciated, enlarged, no matter who we are. I have two nun friends who invariably have that effect on me, whatever the circumstances of our lives on the infrequent occasions when we meet. The thoughtful way in which they converse, listening and responding with complete attention, seems always a marvel. And when I first met a man I'll call Tom, he had much the same effect on me. I wrote in my notebook, "such tenderness in a man . . . and a surprising, gentle, kindly grasp of who I am." (Poets aren't used to being listened to, let alone understood, by theologians.) As our friendship deepened, I found that even brief, casual conversations with him would often inspire me to dive into old, half-finished poems in an attempt to bring them to fruition.

I realized, of course, that I had found a remarkable friend, a

Muse. I was also aware that Tom and I were fast approaching the rocky shoals of infatuation, a man and a woman, both decidedly heterosexual, responding to each other in unmistakably sexual ways. We laughed; we had playful conversations as well as serious ones; we took delight in each other. At times we were alarmingly responsive to one another, and it was all too easy to fantasize about expressing that responsiveness in physical ways.

The danger was real, but not insurmountable; I sensed that if our infatuation were to develop into love, that is, to ground itself in grace rather than utility, our respect for each other's commitments—his to celibacy, mine to monogamy—would make the boundaries of behavior very clear. We had few regrets, and yet for both of us there was an underlying sadness, the pain of something incomplete. Suddenly, the difference between celibate friendship and celibate passion had become all too clear to me; at times the pain was excruciating.

Tom and I each faced a crisis the year we met—his mother died, I suffered a disastrous betrayal—and it was the intensity of these unexpected, unwelcome experiences that helped me to understand that in the realm of the sacred, what seems incomplete or unattainable may be abundance, after all. Human relationships are by their nature incomplete—after twenty-one years, my husband remains a mystery to me, and I to him, and that is as it should be. Only hope allows us to know and enjoy the depth of our intimacy.

Appreciating Tom's presence in my life as a miraculous, unmerited gift helped me to place our relationship in its proper, religious context, and also to understand why it was that when I'd seek him out to pray with me, I'd always leave feeling so much better than when I came. This was celibacy at its best, a man's sexual energies so devoted to the care of others that a few words could lift me out of despair, give me the strength to reclaim my life. Abundance indeed. Celibate love was at the heart of it, although I can't fully comprehend the mystery of why this should be so. Celibate passion—elusive, tensile, holy.

Februa r y 10

SCHOLASTICA

One winter night, Benedict's sister, Scholastica, was awakened by a song bird. How can this be, she thought, and she looked out the window of her cell. Three naked men were dancing in the monastery garden by the light of the moon. One whistled like a bird and made her laugh. The men were fair to look at, Scholastica thought, but she knew she needed more rest before the first prayers of the day.

Kneeling by her bed, she closed her eyes and sleepily said a prayer for the men—if they were men—that they might find shelter, clothing, and rest for their dancing feet, and if (as she suspected) they were demons, that they might return to from whence they came.

When she awoke, her cell was filled with the scent of roses. Where the men had been dancing a rose bush had sprung up and was blooming in the snow. It bloomed all that winter, and it blooms to this day.

GOOD OLD SIN

J. was horrifying me with tales of the sedate gambling places at Lake Tahoe, the ones that are prim and country-clubbed, and which cater to decent people, with dealerettes in prim black dresses, and soft Muzak, and nary a drunk on the premises, and the nice old ladies coming up to gamble in buses from the cities of the Plain. I am utterly disheartened. What has happened to good old sin? Here I am behind these walls, doing my bit and counting on the world to do its bit, with barrelhouse piano and the walleyed guys in eyeshades, with long cigars, raking in the pieces of eight, and the incandescent floozies lolling over the roulette wheels. Tell me . . . am I wasting my time?—Thomas Merton, in a 1962 letter*

The heart itself is but a small vessel, yet dragons are there, and there are also lions; there are poisonous beasts and all the treasures of evil. But there too is God, the angels, the life and the kingdom, the light and the apostles, the heavenly cities and the treasuries of grace—all things are there.—Pseudo-Macarius

It wasn't until I had encountered the writings of fourth-century monks such as Pseudo-Macarius and Evagrius of Pontus that I found a workable, useful, and healthy definition of sin, a realistic sense of the capacity for both evil and virtue that resides in the human heart. My husband and I, raised in the pietistic churches of the 1950s, received an education in sin that was not only inadequate but harmful. From the Protestants I got a list of

125

rules that were not to be broken and naively thought that as long as I wasn't breaking those rules, sin was not much of a problem for me. As a young adult, I believed that I had no conscience, a state I was fortunate to survive. From the Catholics my husband got less a sense of sin than a terrific ability to feel guilty for everything under the sun, a situation that left him less likely to recognize and contend with those things for which he might actually wish to repent.

Having grown used to the polite verbiage of modern-day counseling—we speak of "having guilt feelings" rather than actually acknowledging our guilt—I found myself delighted by the pithy language and imagery of the early monks. Here, for example, is the seventh-century monk of Sinai, John Climacus, on the subject of pride, from a book that is still read in Orthodox monasteries during Lent:

> *Pride is a denial of God, an invention of the devil, contempt for men. It is the mother of condemnation, the offspring of praise, a sign of barrenness. It is a flight from God's help, the harbinger of madness, the author of downfall. It is the cause of diabolical possession, the source of anger, the gateway of hypocrisy. It is the fortress of demons, the custodian of sins, the source of hardheartedness. It is the denial of compassion, a bitter pharisee, a cruel judge. It is the foe of God. It is the root of blasphemy.*

Welcome to the truth: that's the feeling I have when I read such a text. And the monk Evagrius, the first to write down and attempt to codify the beliefs and practices of the desert monks with regard to sin (which they called "demons" or "bad thoughts"), not only provides me with a means of understanding my own "bad thoughts" but also with the tools to confront them. His view of anger is typically sensible. Anger, he wrote, is given to us by God to help us confront true evil. We err when we use it casually, against other people, to gratify our own desires for power or control.

Considering "Good old sin," in the sense that the ancient monks understood it, exposes the vast difference between their worldview and our own. These days, when someone commits an atrocity, we tend to sigh and say, "That's human nature." But our attitude would seem wrong-headed to the desert monks, who understood human beings to be part of the creation that God called good, special in that they are made in the image of God. Sin, then, is an aberration, not natural to us at all. This is why Gregory of Nyssa speaks so often of "[returning] to the grace of that image which was established in you from the beginning." Gregory, in fact, saw it as our lifelong task to find out what part of the divine image God has chosen to reveal in us. Like the other early monks, he suggests that we can best do this by realistically determining how God has made us—what our primary faults and temptations are, as well as our gifts—not that we might better "know ourselves," or in modern parlance, "feel good about ourselves," but in order that we might become instruments of divine grace for other people, and eventually return to God.

The tragedy of sin is that it diverts divine gifts. The person who has a genuine capacity for loving becomes promiscuous, maybe sexually, or maybe by becoming frivolous and fickle, afraid to make a commitment to anyone or anything. The person with a gift for passionate intensity squanders it in angry tirades and, given power, becomes a demagogue. There is much insight in the early monastic writings that resonates well with modern psychology. Evagrius, for example, understood that the health of the soul is revealed in conscious thoughts during the day and dreams at night. The goal of the monks was to know themselves as they truly were, warts and all, and to be able to call it "good," not in order to excuse bad behavior but to accept the self without delusions. The point was to know the material you were working with, in order to give a firmer foundation to your hope for change.

Are monks wasting their time in seeking to convert themselves, and the world, from evil? Many have said so. For myself, I appreciate their realism about human beings confronted by evil, and the good sense that does not allow them to be easily fooled when evil attempts to disguise itself by adopting innocuous dress. Both the monks of the ancient tradition and contemporary monastics, it seems to me, have a refreshing sense of what really matters in human behavior. They know that the roots of sin are not to be found in the acts of gambling, drinking, dancing, smoking, playing dominoes (an activity that got my grandfather Norris fired by a Methodist church in 1919), or even in adultery or fornication. Looking deeper, they recognize, as one monk said to me, a man who'd sown plenty of wild oats before entering a monastery, that "even though I gave up fornicating years ago, pride and anger are still with me." Pride and anger were recognized by the desert monks as the most dangerous of their bad thoughts, and the most difficult to overcome. Abba Ammonas said, "I have spent fourteen years [in the desert] asking God night and day to grant me the victory over anger." In the words of Benedicta Ward, "For all sins, there is forgiveness. What really lies outside the ascetic life is despair, the proud attitude which denies the possibility of forgiveness." All committed life is ascetic, in some sense; the word originally meant an exercise, practice, or training adopted for a certain way of life. Athletes, monks, artists, musicians, married people, and celibates all learn to recognize the practices that will hinder or foster the growth of their commitment.

As for designating despair as an aspect of the sin, or "bad thought," of pride, I find it enormously helpful. Among other things, it defeats my perfectionism, my tendency to give up when I can't do things "just right." But if I accept the burden of my despair, in the monastic sense, then I also receive the tools to defeat it. I have a hope that no modern therapeutic approach can give me. "The desert fathers were convinced that the words of scripture possessed the power to deliver them from evil," writes Douglas Burton-Christie, another scholar of the early monks. "They believed that the Word of God has the power to effect what it says." Or, as Amma Syncletica wrote early in the fifth century, in a catalogue of Bible quotations to be used in times of temptation, "Are you being tried by fever? Are you being taught by cold? Indeed, scripture says, 'We went through fire and water, yet you have brought us forth to a spacious place" (Ps. 66:12). She adds, "For he said, 'The Lord hears me when I call' (Ps. 4:3). It is with these exercises that we train the soul."

ACEDIA

From Late Latin, from Greek akedia, *indifference.*
a (absence) + kedos (care)—AMERICAN HERITAGE DICTIONARY

*The malice of sloth lies not merely in the neglect of duty (though
that can be a symptom of it) but in the refusal of joy. It is allied
to despair.*—Evelyn Waugh, *Acedia,* in THE SEVEN DEADLY
SINS

*Amma Syncletica said: There is a grief that is useful, and there is
a grief that is destructive. The first sort consists in weeping over one's
own faults and weeping over the weakness of one's neighbors, in
order not to lose one's purpose, and attach oneself to the perfect good.
But there is also a grief that comes from the enemy, full of mockery,
which some call accidie. This spirit must be cast out, mainly by
prayer and psalmody.*—THE SAYINGS OF THE DESERT
FATHERS

Severe lethargy has set in, what the desert monks might
have called "acedia" or "listlessness," and in the Middle
Ages was considered sloth, but these days is most often termed "depression." I had thought that I was merely tired and in need of rest
at year's end, but it drags on, becoming the death-in-life that I
know all too well, when my capacity for joy shrivels up and, like
drought-stricken grass, I die down to the roots to wait it out. The
simplest acts demand a herculean effort, the pleasure I normally

take in people and the world itself is lost to me. I can be with people I love, and know that I love them, but feel nothing at all. I am observing my life more than living it.

I recognize in all of this the siege of what the desert monks termed the "noonday demon." It suggests that whatever I'm doing, indeed my entire life of "doings," is not only meaningless but utterly useless. This plunge into the chill waters of pure realism is incapacitating, and the demon likes me this way. It suggests sleep when what I need most is to take a walk. It insists that I shut myself away when what I probably need is to be with other people. It mocks the rituals, routines, and work that normally fill my day; why do them, why do anything at all, it says, in the face of so vast an emptiness. Worst of all, even though I know that the ancient remedies—prayer, psalmody, scripture reading—would help to pull me out of the morass, I find myself incapable of acting on this knowledge. The exhaustion that I'm convinced lies behind most suicides finds its seed in acedia; the rhythms of daily life, and of the universe itself, the everyday glory of sunrise and sunset and all the "present moments" in between seem a disgusting repetition that stretches on forever. It would be all too easy to feel that one wants no part of it any more.

The first experience of acedia that I recall (although I did not know to name it as such) occurred when I was fifteen years old, a scholarship student at a prep school in Honolulu. The job I held in partial payment of my scholarship was a pleasant one; during the noon hour, I answered the phone and did secretarial work at the Music School. Not being in the school cafeteria gave me a chance to diet, and my normal fare, in what now strikes me as a comical parody of the monastic desert, was a model of severity: Metrecal wafers, a low-cal soda, and an apple or an orange. (For readers who have never tasted Metrecal, allow me to suggest fresh asphalt with a hint of chocolate and the bitter afterglow of saccharin.) One day as I was unpacking my lunch, a lunch that my mother had faithfully packed for me, I suddenly saw the future stretch out before me: days and days of lunches that one day my mother would not be packing for me, that I would be responsible for myself. Day upon day of eating and excreting, of working at this job or that, of monotony, the futile round.

When, in my thirties, I encountered the monk Evagrius's classic description of the "noonday demon," I recognized my experience of many years before. He speaks of the depressing thought that suddenly "depicts life stretching out for a long period of time, and brings before the mind's eye the toil of the ascetic struggle, and . . . leaves no leaf unturned to induce the monk to forsake his cell and drop out of the fight." At fifteen I had no "cell" but a small bedroom in Navy housing near Pearl Harbor (which was luxurious to me because until recently I had been sharing a room with my two younger sisters). I had no knowledge of monks, or of ascetic practice. But I had been visited by the noonday demon and, in ways I was not to become fully aware of for many years, my life was changed forever. The fear of the daily had intruded into my consciousness at a time when it could do real harm. A shy, pudgy teenager, suffering from the loneliness that so many teenagers feel, I had just become more lonely. My fearful thoughts of the future seemed so absurd I could not speak of them to anyone.

Some thirty years later, I am back in Honolulu, in fragrant Manoa Valley, not far from that school. A letter-press book has come for me in the mail, exquisitely made by a friend, full of poems I wrote during a year at St. John's. The book, and the poems themselves, are a great gift, I know, but I can't bring myself to open the box. After a few days, when I finally do unpack it, the book's beauty seems remote. My mother and sister-in-law admire it—yes, it's lovely, I say, agreeing with them. But I can't feel it. They know this, and it troubles them. But they're tolerant; we share the hope that I'll soon snap out of it. Drugs, therapy, someone might suggest. The last time it got this bad I did consult with a doctor. We discussed many options, and what she suggested to me I treasure still: exercise, she said, and spiritual direction.

I have promised to go to services this Sunday, at the modest but spirited Disciples of Christ church where my brother is a pastor. I still feel half-dead but do my best to sing with the congregation. One of the verses of "Spirit of God, Descend Upon My Heart"—"I ask no dreams, no prophet ecstasies, no sudden rending of the veil of clay, no angel visitant, no opening skies; but take the dimness of my soul away"—makes me realize that I'm praying for the first time in days, and that it's working. The rest of that service is a giddy blur; I felt alive again, appropriately enough, on a Sunday morning. In his sermon, my brother says, "God's language is silence; how do we translate it?" He speaks of gifts differing, gifts of the Spirit coming to each of us, for the common good. The title of the closing hymn, "There Is Sunshine in My Heart Today," seems like icing on the cake. The melody is appropriately zippy, upbeat, the lyrics as thoroughly Protestant as the title would suggest, and I enjoy every bit of it.

When last I was home and attending church, the children's choir sang "Jesus Wants Me for a Sunbeam," a song I remember singing as a child. I suppose I loved it then. What made their song so marvelous in the context of our worship that day was that it was followed by a reading from Jeremiah 14 that made it clear that God did *not* want Jeremiah for a sunbeam. Gifts differing, I suppose. And I suppose that both of the hymns that have touched me today could be labeled "pietistic," not sufficiently concerned with the larger picture, the larger world. But it's acedia that made my world small, a self-centered hell—"Is there no way out of the mind?" Sylvia Plath once asked, anguished, in a poem—and these hymns that have released me to live in the real world again. In the context of this worship service, both hymns seem fine to me, not uncaring, not irresponsible, but merely a glad response to grace. I wonder if Christians might be permitted a certain gladness on Sunday morning. Even if the universe is mostly hydrogen atoms, and the few human beings who exist in it are continually at war with one another, even if time and space stretch out into the void. Here, in this ordinary church service, I have gained the strength to live this moment, the present moment, for the first time in days. I recall something that I read recently in a book on monastic practices: "A life of prayer," the monk Charles Cummings wrote, "is a life of beginning all over again." Ashamed of my own unsteadiness, my lack of courage and, in the words of another hymn, my heart so "prone to wander from the God I love," I have the strength to take it all up again. This is a day to begin.

PRIDE

Abba Elias said, "What can sin do where there is penitence? And of what use is love where there is pride?"—THE SAYINGS OF THE DESERT FATHERS

The young monk read from the Bible: "The Lord God called to the man, and said to him, 'Where are you?' He said, 'I heard the sound of you in the garden, and I was afraid, because I was naked; and I hid myself.' " I have always found that to be a poignant summary of the human response to evil: I was afraid, I tried to hide. I thought I knew where I was, at an everyday monastery Mass. But I was distracted for a moment by a thought that seemed absurdly out of place; I recalled that I'd forgotten to put on my favorite silver bracelet, the one I usually wear. It was handmade by the husband of an old friend, who gave it to me when I graduated from college. In the crazed atmosphere of Bennington in the 1960s, when so many faculty were having affairs with students that it was easy to become cynical about marriage, this couple had always seemed remarkably stable to me, still in love after more than twenty years, and good to be with.

I tried to concentrate on the gospel reading, a peculiar one: after Jesus began to preach, to cast out demons and heal the sick, some people had assumed that he'd gone mad. They tried to convince his family that Jesus himself was possessed by demons and should be restrained. "How do we respond to the good?" the monk asked in his homily. "How do we respond to the presence of the good?"

Suddenly I remembered another silver bracelet, lost in the shadows of my life, one my husband had given me, or had tried to give me, years before. It was beautiful lying in its box, but I was disappointed to find that it was a cuff bracelet, a kind I've never liked to wear. I had suggested to David that we replace it, or ask the silversmith, the woman who'd made his wedding band, if she could modify it. He said that he would, but I never heard any more about it. Now, for some reason, I remembered this event, and saw it clearly for the first time. The gift was good, and I had rejected it. I know my husband well enough to know that he would have taken it as a rejection and also that most likely he still had the bracelet buried among his things. I resolved to ask him, and also to apologize.

David was surprised, but he did remember, and after a few days found the bracelet in its original box. He polished it, and I now wear it. And all because I heard two questions: "Where are you?" and "How do we respond to the good?" The other reading at Mass that day was from Paul's second letter to the Corinthians: "We do not lose heart . . . our inner being is being renewed every day." My pride will resist any change I haven't chosen, but it's powerless against this force of which Paul speaks, the conversion that occurs without my even being aware of it, except when it erupts suddenly into my life. A statement of John Climacus, typically self-contained and bristling with certitude, suddenly made sense to me: "Men can heal the lustful. Angels can heal the malicious. Only God can heal the proud."

ANGER

His abba, taking a piece of dry wood, planted it and said to him,
"Water it every day with a bottle of water, until it bears
fruit."—THE SAYINGS OF THE DESERT FATHERS

If it is true that the Holy Spirit is peace of soul . . . and if anger is
disturbance of the heart . . . then there is no greater obstacle to
the presence of the Spirit in us than anger.—John Climacus,
THE LADDER OF DIVINE ASCENT

One night, many years ago, I was angry at my husband. He'd had good news—the galleys of his second book of poems were coming in the mail—but he'd responded to it by growing more distant and then driving off to God-knows-where. When he hadn't returned by evening, although I was worried about him, it was anger that woke me up in the middle of the night. Hoping I could get back to sleep, I lay in bed, my mind suddenly racing with all the things, great and small, that I held against my husband. As good as it felt to review this little catalogue of slights and injuries, it brought me no satisfaction; instead, I soon found that I was in a stew over someone else, a man who had treated me with contempt. Then it was someone else that I fussed and fumed over, a grudge I thought I'd forgotten. I was building an impressive storehouse of grievances, and I thought to myself, sleepily, *this could go on forever.*

I sat upright, suddenly wide awake. Of course it could go on forever; that was exactly the point. I'd recently come upon the writings of a monk named Evagrius and realized that I had rapidly moved beyond any justified frustration with my husband, and was becoming possessed by what Evagrius would have called the "bad thought" of anger. If my husband was in trouble, anger was the last thing either of us needed. I got out my breviary and prayed the compline psalms 4 and 91, with their talk of peaceful sleep and angelic protection. Despite all I'd read in the desert monks about how prayer causes demons to flee, I was amazed to discover how quickly the anger dissipated. In its place, I found that what I was really feeling for my husband was fear. Somewhere in my reading of monastic literature, I had found the statement that anger is the seed of compassion; I began to realize the truth of it.

The inner voice that had warned me—*this could go on forever*—now brought to my mind a poem I'd completely forgotten, one that I'd forsaken as hopelessly muddled years before. I wasn't even sure I could find that old manuscript, but the inner voice asked me to find it and work on it, and so I went. It was a love poem, of course, and if I ever needed proof of St. John's assertion that "love casts out fear," I had it. I spent the rest of the night reviving that dead stick of a poem (no doubt watering it as well; weeping is an ordinary but valuable part of the writing process). In the morning, when my husband telephoned—he was feeling better, he said, and would be home soon—I was ready to rejoice at the sound of his voice. I was able to welcome him instead of sniping at him. I'd been worried about him, I told him, and he said that he'd been worried about himself. "Say," I said, "remember that old poem I began years ago, when we first lived together in New York? I got it out last night and finished it. Want to hear it?"

NOON

As much of Noon as I could take
Between my finite eyes—Emily Dickinson

[The noonday demon] makes it seem that the sun barely moves, if
at all, and the day is fifty hours long.—Evagrius,
THE PRAKTIKOS

I quickly learned, at St. John's, that noon prayer, although it was the briefest of the daily liturgies, lasting only fifteen minutes, was often the most important of the Divine Offices for me to observe. The temptation not to go was strong; why interrupt my work? Why not just eat my lunch, and maybe take a brief nap afterward? Writing had filled the morning in satisfying ways, but in the harsh light of noon I saw what I'd done as busy work, signifying nothing, meaningless activity with a pretense to meaning. My words seemed like talk which I'd tried to use to shield myself from the awful silence of eternity stretching out forever before me.

Eternity is supposed to appeal to the monastic spirit, but when one is in the grip of the noonday demon, one wonders just how much of this "forever" our finite eyes can take. At St. John's, I found that the only cure was to go sit at noon, in the monastery choir, and let the bells of the Angelus wash over me.

Somehow, the abbreviated service, with two or three short psalms and a brief reading, would let me set aside my busy ideas and my words and sink into contemplation. A moment of rest, it became like a door opening into afternoon and evening, and I could welcome it all.

DEGENERATES

Not long ago I accompanied a Trappist abbot as he unlocked a door to the cloister and led me down a long corridor into a stone-walled room, the chapter house of the monastery, where some twenty monks were waiting for me to give a reading. Poetry does lead a person into some strange places. This wonderfully silent, hidden-away place was not as alien to me as it might have been, however, as I'd been living on the grounds of a Benedictine monastery for most of the last three years. Trappists are more silent than the Benedictines, far less likely to have work that draws them into the world outside the monastery. But the cumulative effect of the Liturgy of the Hours—at a bare minimum, morning, noon, and evening prayer, as well as the Eucharist—on one's psyche, the sense it gives a person of being immersed in the language of scripture, is much the same in any monastery. What has surprised me, in my time among monastic people, is how much their liturgy feeds my poetry; and also how much correspondence I've found between monastic practice and the discipline of writing.

Before I read a few poems of mine that had been inspired by the psalms (the mainstay of all monastic liturgy,) I discussed some of those connections. I told the monks that I had come to see both writing and monasticism as vocations that require periods of apprenticeship and formation. Prodigies are common in mathematics, but extremely rare in literature, and, I added, "As far as I know, there are no prodigies in monastic life." The monks nodded, obviously amused. (The formal process of entering a monastery takes at least five years, and usually longer, and even after monks have made final vows, they often defer to the older members of the community as more "fully formed" in monastic life.)

Related to this, I said, was recognizing the dynamic nature of both disciplines; they are not so much subjects to be mastered as ways of life that require continual conversion. For example, no matter how much I've written or published, I always return to the blank page; and even more important, from a monastic point of view, I return to the blankness within, the fears, laziness and cowardice that, without fail, will mess up whatever I'm currently writing and, in turn, require me to revise it. The spiritual dimension of this process is humility, not a quality often associated with writers, but lurking there, in our nagging sense of the need to revise, to weed out the lies you've told yourself and get real. As I put it to the monks, when you realize that anything good you write comes *despite* your weaknesses, writing becomes a profoundly humbling activity. At this point, one of the monks spoke up. "I find that there's a redemptive quality," he said, "just in sitting in front of that blank piece of paper."

This comment reflects an important aspect of monastic life, which has been described as "attentive waiting." I think it's also a fair description of the writing process. Once, when I was asked, "What is the main thing a poet does?" I was inspired to answer, "We wait." A spark is struck; an event inscribed with a message— *this is important, pay attention*—and a poet scatters a few words like seeds in a notebook. Months or even years later, those words bear fruit. The process requires both discipline and commitment, and its gifts come from both preparedness and grace, or what writers have traditionally called inspiration. As William Stafford wrote, with his usual simplicity, in a poem entitled "For People with Problems About How to Believe": "a quality of attention has been given to you: / when you turn your head the whole world / leans forward. It waits there thirsting / after its names, and you speak it all out / as it comes to you . . ."

Anyone who listens to the world, anyone who seeks the sacred in the ordinary events of life, has "problems about how to believe." Paradoxically, it helps that both prayer and poetry begin deep within a person, beyond the reach of language. The fourth-century desert monk St. Anthony said that perfect prayer is one you don't understand. Poets are used to discovering, years after a poem is written, what it's really about. And it's in the respect for the mystery and power of words that I find the most profound connections between the practice of writing and monastic life.

"Listen" is the first word of St. Benedict's Rule for monasteries, and listening for the eruptions of grace into one's life—often from unlikely sources—is a "quality of attention" that both monastic living and the practice of writing tend to cultivate. I'm trained to listen when words and images begin to converge. When I wake up at 3 A.M., suddenly convinced that I had better look into an old notebook, or get to work on a poem I'd abandoned years before, I do not turn over and go back to sleep. I obey, which is an active form of listening (the two words are etymologically related).

In fact, I tell the monks, when I first encountered the ancient desert story about obedience—a monastic disciple is ordered by his *abba* to water a dead stick—I laughed out loud. I know that abba's voice from those three A.M. encounters; I know the sinking, hopeless feeling that nothing could possibly come out of this writing I feel compelled to do. I also know that good things often come when I persevere. But it took me a long time to recognize that my discipline as a writer, some of it at least, could translate into the monastic realm.

The monastic practice of *lectio divina*—which literally means holy reading—seemed hopelessly esoteric to me for a long time. When I'd read descriptions of it, I'd figure that my mind was too restless, too impatient, too flighty to do it well. But then the monk who was my oblate director said, "What do you mean? You're *doing* it!" He explained that the poems I was writing in response to the scripture I'd encounter at the Divine Office with the monks, or in my private reading, were a form of *lectio*. He termed this writing active *lectio,* at least more active than the usual form of meditating on scripture. I had thought that because I was writing, because I was *doing* something, it couldn't be *lectio*. But writing was not what I'd set out to do; words came as if organically, often simply from hearing scripture read aloud. I was learning the truth of what the Orthodox monk Kallistos Ware has said about the monastic environment; that in itself it can be a guide, offering a kind of spiritual formation. Not all my poems are *lectio*—to believe that would be too easy, a form of self-indulgence—but the practice of *lectio* does strike me as similar to the practice of writing poetry, in that it is not an intellectual procedure so much as an existential one. Grounded in a meditative reading of scriptures, it soon becomes much more; a way of reading the world and one's place in it. To quote a fourth-century monk, it is a way of reading that "works the earth of the heart."

I should try telling my friends who have a hard time comprehending why I like to spend so much time going to church with Benedictines that I do so for the same reasons that I write: to let words work the earth of my heart. To sing, to read poetry aloud, and to have the poetry and the wild stories of scripture read to me. To respond with others, in blessed silence. That is a far more accurate description of morning or evening prayer in a monastery than what most people conjure up when they hear the word "church." Monks have always recognized reading as a bodily experience, primarily oral. The ancients spoke of masticating the words of scripture in order to fully digest them. Monastic "church" reflects a whole-body religion, still in touch with its orality, its music. In the midst of today's revolution in "instant communication," I find it a blessing that monks still respect the slow way that words work on the human psyche. They take the time to sing, chant, and read the psalms aloud, leaving plenty of room for silence, showing a respect for words that is remarkable in this culture, which goes for the fast talk of the hard sell, the deceptive masks of jargon, the chatter of television "personalities." Being with monks is more like imbibing language—often powerfully poetic language—at full strength. One night, when we ended a vespers reading with a passage from Job; "My lyre is turned to mourning, and my pipe to the voice of those who weep," I was awestruck, not only by the beauty of the words but also by the way those words gave a new dimension to watching the nightly news later that night, leading me to reflect on the communal role of the poet.

Poets and monks do have a communal role in American culture, which alternately ignores, romanticizes, and despises them. In our relentlessly utilitarian society, structuring a life around writing is as crazy as structuring a life around prayer, yet that is what writers and monks *do*. Deep down, people seem glad to know that monks are praying, that poets are writing poems. This is what others want and expect of us, because if we do our job right, we will express things that others may feel, or know, but can't or won't say.

At least this is what writers are told over and over again by their readers, and I suspect it's behind the boom in visits to monastic retreat houses. Maybe it is the useless silence of contemplation, that certain "quality of attention" that distinguishes both the poem and the prayer.

I regard monks and poets as the best degenerates in America. Both have a finely developed sense of the sacred potential in all things; both value image and symbol over utilitarian purpose or the bottom line; they recognize the transformative power hiding in the simplest things, and it leads them to commit absurd acts: the poem! the prayer! what nonsense! In a culture that excels at creating artificial, tightly controlled environments (shopping malls, amusement parks, chain motels), the art of monks and poets is useless, if not irresponsible, remaining out of reach of commercial manipulation and ideological justification.

Not long ago I viewed an exhibition at the New York Public Library entitled "Degenerate Art," which consisted of artworks approved by Hitler's regime, along with art the Nazis had denounced. As I walked the galleries it struck me that the real issue was one of control. The meaning of the approved art was superficial, in that its images (usually rigidly representational) served a clear commercial and/or political purpose. The "degenerate" artworks, many crucifixes among them, were more often abstract, with multiple meanings, or even no meaning at all, in the conventional sense. This art—like the best poetry, and also good liturgy—allowed for a wide freedom of response on the part of others; the viewer, the reader, the participant.

Pat Robertson once declared that modern art was a plot to strip America of its vital resources. Using an abstract sculpture by Henry Moore as an example, he said that the material used could more properly have been used for a statue of George Washington. What do poets mean? Who needs them? Of what possible use are monastic people in the modern world? Are their lives degenerate in the same sense that modern art is: having no easily perceptible meaning yet of ultimate value, concerned with ultimate meanings? Maybe monks and poets know, as Jesus did when a friend, in an extravagant, loving gesture, bathed his feet in nard, an expensive, fragrant oil, and wiped them with her hair, that the symbolic act *matters;* that those who know the exact price of things, as Judas did, often don't know the true cost or value of anything.

N E W
M E L L E R A Y
A B B E Y   L I T U R G Y
S C H E D U L E

3:30 A.M.—Vigils
6:30 A.M.—Lauds
9:15 A.M.—Tierce
11:45 A.M.—Sext
1:45 P.M.—None
5:30 P.M.—Vespers
7:30 P.M.—Compline

CHICAGO:
RELIGION
IN AMERICA

I have a deep affection for Chicago, although I don't know the city well. In the 1930s, when they were music majors at Northwestern, my parents courted along Michigan Avenue, at the Art Institute, Symphony Hall, the old Opera House. My own memories of the city come from the 1950s, when my father directed the band at the Great Lakes Naval Training Center in nearby Waukegan. For a time during the mid-fifties he hosted a variety show on WGN-TV called "Your Navy Show," which featured winners of regional Navy talent contests who sang, danced, did magic tricks, and unicycle stunts. Television was relatively new—my family had obtained its first set just a few years before—and it was cool to have a dad on TV. Best of all, I was sometimes allowed to accompany him to the studio in the Loop. Once, when I was nine years old, I sang a duet with another girl on the program, a piece of inspirational fluff entitled "Let the Sun Shine In."

The programs were done live, and I don't recall much about our performance, except that the producer had sternly warned us not to wipe our brows or scratch our noses under the hot lights. I do have memories of our rehearsals, of being in awe of the studio itself, the stage with its vast contraptions—banks of lights, pulleys, and sandbags, one of which fell, loudly and spectacularly, onto the floor where the stage crew had recently been standing. "They could have been killed instantly," someone said, and I had a new, terrifying concept to contend with.

I was also in awe of another new phrase, "stage mother," and the forceful, incarnational way that it had became a part of my vocabulary. My own mother was at home with a new baby, but the mother of my singing partner took up the slack, fussing furiously over my tendency to leave my sashes untied and my sock cuffs unrolled. Mostly she fussed at the producer and my father, making sure they fully appreciated her daughter's talent, and which side "favored her," another new concept for me. I had never met a mother like her and was appalled at the way her daughter caved in to her bullying. I tried to engage the girl in mild acts of rebellion, but to no avail.

I came to associate Chicago, the Loop especially, with new words and phrases: "child star" was another that came my way. I was fascinated by the Mouseketeers—the idea of a tribe of children appealed to me—and when my father took me into the city for what he promised would be a big surprise, it turned out to be the Mouseketeer Doreen signing copies of a book. I had a special affinity for Doreen—we both had buck teeth and braids—but the experience of meeting her disturbed me. She looked exhausted, her face greasy with makeup, her hands dirty. The signature on the book had been made with a rubber stamp. I mumbled something to her and she mumbled something in return, and then I took my book from the stack and pretended for my dad's sake that all of this had been wonderful. But I must have looked disappointed, because he began to explain to me what being a "child star" could mean.

My father's forays into the entertainment world supplied other startling words and concepts: "He'd sell his own mother down the river" was a comment he made about one star who'd been a guest on the television show, allowing me to ponder iniquity at a whole new level. My favorite of the new phrases was "killing time," which is what my father said we could do every time we missed the train back to Waukegan. The violence of the phrase puzzled me, but not for long, as "killing time" turned out to mean that we went to movies, concerts, the Art Institute, the Field Museum, Kroch & Brentano's bookstore, and the Marshall Fields department store, where one year my mother trusted us to pick out a new winter coat for me. We lunched in restaurants that seemed elegant to me, but were probably not.

I especially loved the sense that I had crossed over into the adult world. One of the places I felt this most keenly was the shop where my father took his cello for repairs; on a second story, its Old-World smell of resin and wood contrasted sharply, and most pleasantly, with the busy streets below. Time seemed to move more slowly there, and I always hated to leave.

One year, when I was six or seven, my father took my brother and me to the Loop for Christmas shopping. We'd saved our allowance money to buy presents, but on reflection, my dad must have subsidized those gifts for our mother, little sisters, cousins, and best friends. It was a bitterly cold day, and when we passed by a Salvation Army band my father, who was wearing his Navy greatcoat, stopped and offered to relieve the trumpeter for a few songs. A Methodist pastor's son, he knew all the hymns, and the Salvation Army coats looked so much like his own, he figured that no one would notice a Navy officer sitting—in this case, standing—in.

The bell-ringer asked if I'd like to ring the bell, which I did with great enthusiasm, beaming up at everyone who put in coins. On the rare occasions when someone put in folding money, I'd exclaim, "Wow—a whole dollar!" A few fives went into the bucket as well, and my boundless joy—buck teeth, pigtails, and all—made the passersby smile. My prepubescent brother, embarrassed by this display, hid in a store across the street.

I hadn't been to Chicago for many years when I received an invitation to give a reading in the Lenten lecture series at Fourth Presbyterian, a lively church in the heart of the Loop. The church had reserved a room for me in a hotel nearby, and when I arrived there, one night in early March, I was rattled from an hour spent in a cramped and noisy commuter plane and anxious to settle in, as the next day would be busy. When the bellhop opened the windowshades, I was surprised to find that I'd been given a corner room, the walls mostly glass. I had a stunning view of the city. There were the requisite bedside phone, mini-bar, and large television set. But the fax machine on the desk startled me, and I couldn't repress my giggles when the young man pointed out the phone and small television in the bathroom.

I apologized quickly when I saw his guarded look. Bellhops meet some exceedingly odd people in the course of a day; it was 9:30 at night and he had a woman on his hands who was laughing over nothing at all. "I'm sorry," I said, "but this is all too much. I've just spent the last few days in a Trappist monastery, and it's just too funny." "A monastery," he nodded, and asked, "What was it like?" "Well," I replied, looking around the hotel room, "it was more real, almost the opposite of this. It was a place you felt you could stay for ever."

He sighed, gazed out the window, and said, "One of my best friends just joined the Capuchins." Clearly bemused and with wonder in his voice, he added, "My friend, he says it's what he wants to do with his life." "It must be a hard life," I replied, "but maybe it's worth doing."

He nodded, and we both relaxed and stood for a few minutes, looking out at the brilliant skyline, thinking about the hidden worlds into which friends disappear, seeking God in ways more intense than we can imagine. I wondered at the odd ways religion surfaces in America, in such tender, unhurried conversations between strangers.

The hurry-up world was all around us, and all the iniquity that the human race can provide. A comment of Ambrose Bierce came unexpectedly to mind: "You can't stop the wicked from going to Chicago by killing them," as did the words from Deuteronomy that I'd heard that morning at the monastery: "The word is very near you; it is in your mouth and in your heart, so that you can do it."

THE WAR
ON METAPHOR

I once had the great pleasure of hearing the poet Diane Glancy astound a group of clergy. Mostly Protestant, mostly mainstream Lutherans. She began her poetry reading by saying that she loved Christianity because it was a blood religion. People gasped in shock; I was overjoyed, thinking, *Hit 'em, Diane; hit 'em where they live.* One man later told me that Diane's language had led him to believe she was some kind of fundamentalist, an impression that was rudely shattered when she read a marvelous poem about angels speaking to her through the carburetor of an old car as she drove down a rural highway at night. Diane told the clergy that she appreciated the relation of the Christian religion to words. "The creation came into being when God spoke," she said, reminding us of Paul's belief that "faith comes through hearing." Diane saw this regard for words as connected not only to writing but to living. "You build a world in what you say," she said. "Words—as I speak or write them—make a path on which I walk."

My experience with Diane and the clergy is one of many that confirms my suspicion that if you're looking for a belief in the power of words to change things, to come alive and make a path for you to walk on, you're better off with poets these days than with

Christians. It's ironic, because the scriptures of the Christian canon are full of strange metaphors that create their own reality—the "blood of the Lamb," the "throne of grace," the "sword of the Spirit"—and among the names for Jesus himself are "the Word" and "the Way."

Poets believe in metaphor, and that alone sets them apart from many Christians, particularly people educated to be pastors and church workers. As one pastor of Spencer Memorial—by no means a conservative on theological or social issues—once said in a sermon, many Christians can no longer recognize that the most significant part of the first line of "Onward Christian Soldiers, marching as to war" is the word "as." (The hymn has been censored out of our new hymnal by the literal-minded, but we sing it anyway.)

The gulf between poets and Christians has long struck me as one of the fine ironies of the late twentieth century, and I've noted with a mix of amusement and distress the way that the war on metaphor reveals itself in the new Presbyterian hymnal. Verses of hymns employing language that suggests that faith might require struggle, particularly anything that uses military metaphors to convey this, have been excised. The awesome sense of struggle and victory (and even exorcism) in "A Mighty Fortress" and "Let All Mortal Flesh Keep Silence" are still in, but I wonder for how long. This metaphoric impoverishment strikes me as ironic, partly because I'm well aware, thanks to a friend who's a Hebrew scholar, that for all of the military metaphors employed in the Old Testament, the command that Israel receives most often is to sing. I also know that the Benedictines have lived peaceably for 1500 years with a Rule that is full of terminology, imagery, and metaphors borrowed from the Roman army.

One difficulty that people seeking to modernize hymnals and the language of worship inevitably run into is that contemporaries are never the best judges of what works and what doesn't. This is something all poets know; that language is a living thing, beyond our control, and it simply takes time for the trendy to reveal itself, to become so obviously dated that it falls by the way, and for the truly innovative to take hold. I had great fun one afternoon going through the 1952 Presbyterian hymnal, looking for what would have seemed its most daringly modern hymns when it appeared. My favorite was "Remember All the People" by Percy Dearmer, a hymn I've never even heard; apparently it faded fast. In promoting Christian mission among the peoples of the world, Dearmer gives us "the endless plains / where children wade through rice fields / And watch the camel trains," and also, most memorably, those who "work in sultry forests, where apes swing to and fro." At least these images are vivid enough to have brightened up some youngster's Sunday morning; I can't say the same for a cutesy benediction I once found—"Go in peace, and not in pieces"—that I believe is from the 1970s, or the drearily abstract version of the Lord's Prayer that liturgical scholar Gail Ramshaw has dredged up from the 1960s, "Our Father, who is our deepest reality." God is merciful, and most of us can now grasp how vapid these prayers are.

Metaphor is valuable to us precisely because it is not vapid, not a blank word such as "reality" that has no grounding in the five senses. Metaphor draws on images from the natural world, from our senses, and from the world of human social structures, and yokes them to psychological and spiritual realities in such a way that we're often left gasping; we have no way to fully explain a metaphor's power, it simply *is*. What I find offensive about some new Bible translations is the way in which they veer toward abstraction and away from metaphor. The new *Inclusive Language*

New Testament and Psalms published by Oxford is an egregious example. The translation committee omitted metaphors of darkness
as being too close to "darkies," and therefore racist. Thus John 1:5
is rendered, dully, as "The light shines in the deepest night, and
the night did not overcome it." The question this new literalism
raises for me is what *time* of night? 1 A.M., or 3? The fact that the
translators imagine "night" to be an adequate substitute for "darkness" only proves that they have a seriously impoverished understanding of metaphor and the nature of language.

To abolish the metaphor of the treachery of darkness is to attempt to live in our heads, and not in the natural world. Darkness
is a pain; it causes us to trip and stumble over objects that would
be visible to us in the light. It is nature itself that these scholars
would deny, and the metaphors that human beings, over thousands
of years, have pulled out of the natural world in order to describe
their religious experience. To a poet, such an "inclusive" translation feels very much like exclusion.

A friend who is a Cistercian monk once said in a letter that he
had taken a book of contemporary poems with him on a hermitage
retreat because of "poetry's ability to draw together sacred and secular, back to the oneness of it all that we Westerners split. This
touches me where I live. Monks should not see divisions." This
monk does value abstract reasoning when it's appropriate and rec-
ognizes the human need to make distinctions. But when seeking
to be at home in himself and with God in solitude and silence, he
knows that metaphors, which insist on connecting disparate elements in ways that the reasoning mind resists, will be of more use
than any treatise. His remarks encouraged me but also reinforced
my sense of both poetry and monasticism as marginal enterprises,
existing on the fringes of the mainstream culture, which educates

us to think of metaphor as a lie. I sometimes get in trouble when I refer to the Incarnation as the ultimate metaphor, daring to yoke the human and the divine. To a literalist, I have just said that the Incarnation isn't "real." As a poet, I think I've said that it is reality at its most alive; it *is* the new creation.

March 18

MECHTILD OF MAGDEBURG

In a way, I imagined Mechtild before I learned of her existence. As I began reading feminist theology in the 1980s, I was haunted by the idea that women in the church's past might have been as critical and outspoken as those in the present, and conjured up a fierce medieval nun who had walked a fine line between orthodoxy and heterodoxy. When I began to read Mechtild, with her vision of bishops in the lowest circles of hell, her description of the corrupt clergy of her day as "goats [reeking] of impurity regarding Eternal Truth," I knew I had found the woman of my dreams.

It was a Benedictine sister who first turned me loose with Mechtild, and I'll always be grateful to her for introducing me to a lively, observant, and witty poet whose work I might never have encountered. Mechtild's praise of a soul "[that] has cast from her the apes of wordliness" is typical. My husband was a bartender for years, and I can assure you, the "apes of worldliness" is right on. I found Mechtild's imagery to be extraordinarily sensuous and evocative, as when she describes herself as "a dusty acre" in need of "the fruitful rain of [Christ's] humanity, and the gentle dew of the Holy Spirit." Another passage that endeared Mechtild to me is her description of herself as a mystic: "Of the heavenly things God has shown me, I can speak but a little word, no more than a honeybee can carry away on its foot from an overflowing jar."

But Mechtild, like many poets, both resists and transcends categories. More orthodox than not, she nevertheless was frequently put on the defensive by church officials, no doubt unamused by Mechtild's criticism of the deadwood clergy of her day: "Stupidity is sufficient unto itself," she wrote. "Wisdom can never learn enough."

When a theologian criticized one of Mechtild's early images of the Trinity ("I must to God—my Father through nature, my Brother through humanity, my Bridegroom through love") by protesting that all God does in us is through grace and not nature, she responded boldly, appropriating language that Jesus himself used when preaching to his disciples. "Thou art right and I, too, am right," she wrote. "Listen to a parable. However good a man's eyes may be, he cannot see over a mile away; however sharp his senses, he cannot grasp supernatural things, except through faith." She continues with a Pauline image of the Godhead "[pouring] His own Divine nature into [the soul]," and concludes humbly: "What we know is as nothing, if we do not love God properly in all things."

Mechtild had left the comforts of an upper-class home when she was in her twenties, joining a movement of women nicknamed Beguines who desired a religious life, but not in cloistered, contemplative communities. Living and praying in common, they worked among the poor and the sick in the burgeoning medieval cities. This was a dangerous life at a time when the church was becoming increasingly clerical, and the women were frequently attacked as heretics.

But Mechtild held on for nearly fifty years, sometimes protected by the Dominican friars who had become her confessors and friends. The story of the Benedictine women of Helfta, taking the aged, half-blind, and embattled Mechtild into their monastery, surely is one of the great stories of hospitality in monastic history. And when I began to study Mechtild's central eucharistic vision, "Of a poor maid and the Mass of John the Baptist," I began to see hospitality as its theme. The "poor maid" is Mechtild, and the image is not simply a literary device. In the vision, as often happened in her life, she has been denied communion by church authorities, and asks God, "Must I be without Mass this day?" Because of her desire, God "[brings] her wondrously into a great church" in which she sees several saints, among them John the Baptist, who is about to sing the Mass. Mechtild is dressed in rags and does not think she should remain. But the Blessed Virgin herself invites her into the choir, "to stand in front of St. Catherine," and Mechtild receives communion after all.

As church officials were becoming increasingly sensitive to any suggestion of anti-clericalism, Mechtild was attacked by a literal-minded churchman for suggesting that a "layman" such as John the Baptist could say Mass. Mechtild responded, typically, by referring to her critic as "My Pharisee" and raging: "No Pope or Bishop could speak the Word of God as John the Baptist spoke it, save in our supernatural Christian faith which cannot be grasped by the senses. Was he then a layman? Instruct me, ye blind!"

I first read Mechtild's vision on a Palm Sunday, at the abbey where I'm an oblate. By the world's standards, this was a most inappropriate place for me to be: as a woman, married, a Protestant, a doubter. It was my first experience of Palm Sunday in a monastery, and despite the hospitality of the monks, I was acutely aware of my otherness. Then the abbey's liturgy director asked me to participate in their reading of the gospel for that day, a group reading, in which the abbot took the part of Christ, another monk was the narrator, and so on. I had the part of the young servant woman who questions Peter following Jesus' arrest. By identifying him as a follower of Jesus, she precipitates Peter's denial of Christ.

The monks included me and a handful of other guests in the community's procession into church. In choir I sat in front of the abbey's farm manager, not St. Catherine, but small matter. Divine hospitality was at work, and it has the power to change everything. After that Mass, I found that my soul, to quote Mechtild, was "startled, but inwardly rejoicing." Later that day, when I got around to reading some articles about Mechtild, one scholar charitably pointed out that "theology was not her strong point." Thank God for small mercies, I thought.

Mechtild of Hackeborn, one of Mechtild of Magdeburg's sisters in the monastery at Helfta, once described the Order of St. Benedict as "standing in the middle of the church, holding it up like a column on which the whole house rests." While the sense of monasticism as the center of the church may be lost on many people today, I think it still holds true, and hospitality is at the center of it all. In a world in which we are so easily labeled and polarized by our differences: man/woman, Protestant/Catholic, gay/straight, feminist/chauvinist, monastic hospitality is a model of the kind of openness that we need if we are going to see and hear each other at all.

The radical, incarnational nature of that hospitality hasn't diminished at all since Mechtild's time, or St. Benedict's. It still has the power to effect conversion and to work miracles. In the nearly ten years that I have been a Benedictine oblate, I have become convinced that hospitality is at the center of the Christian faith—the bread of the Eucharist is called the "host," after all, and for good reason. But church hierarchies, in Mechtild's time as in our own, become inhospitable whenever they forget that they are not the center.

Mechtild's images of hospitality became more intimate as she aged. It does not surprise me that she grew impatient with the infirmities of old age, finding them "cold and without grace." But God comforts her with words both homey and profound: "Your childhood was a companion of the Holy Spirit; your youth was a bride of humanity; in your old age you are a humble housewife of the Godhead." In her last writings Mechtild reveals that the hospitality of the nuns of Helfta had helped her to transform what could be regret into thankfulness: "Lord!" she writes, "I thank Thee that since Thou hast taken from me the power of my hands . . . and the power of my heart, Thou now servest me with the hands and hearts of others." Mechtild entitled this section "How God Serves Humankind," and there is no better definition of hospitality than that.

April 2

MARY OF EGYPT

I once gave an icon of Mary of Egypt to a woman who counsels teenaged prostitutes. They range in age from ten—a girl who'd developed early, and whose stepfather and brothers had put her on the streets—to a world-weary eighteen. Many are runaways, most often from abusive homes, most have grown accustomed to being treated like trash. My friend's job is to convince them that they aren't trash. She works hard—sometimes enduring threats from pimps—to help these girls see that they are good for something besides being bought and sold.

Mary of Egypt lived in the fifth century, but her story is all too familiar in the twentieth. Running away from home at the age of twelve, she became a prostitute in Alexandria. At the age of twenty-nine, she grew curious about Jerusalem and joined a boatload of pilgrims by offering the crew her sexual services for the duration of the journey. She continued to work as a prostitute in Jerusalem. On hearing that a relic of the true cross was to be displayed at the Church of the Holy Sepulchre, her curiosity was aroused again, and she joined the feast-day crowds. But at the threshold of the church some invisible force held her back. Suddenly ashamed of the life she'd led, she began to weep. Kneeling before an icon of the Virgin Mary, she begged forgiveness and asked for help. A voice said to her, "If you cross over the Jordan, you will find rest." Mary spent the rest of her life, forty-seven years, as a hermit in the desert.

Late in her life, Mary encounters a monk who had come to the desert for a period of fasting, and she tells him her story. Touchingly, she relates that she had missed the fish she used to eat in Egypt, and the wine—"I had enjoyed wine very much," she says. The monk is amazed to discover that Mary knows many Bible verses by heart, for in the desert she has had no one but God to teach her. She asks him to bring communion to her, when next he comes to the desert, and this he does. On his third visit, however, he finds that Mary has died. A lion—which contemporary audiences would have recognized as a symbol of Christ, the lion of Judah—comes to help him dig her grave.

Monks have always told the story of Mary of Egypt to remind themselves not to grow complacent in their monastic observances, mistaking them for the salvation that comes from God alone. And in the Eastern Orthodox churches, Mary's life is read on the Fifth Sunday of Lent, presented, as the scholar Benedicta Ward tells us, "as an icon in words of the theological truths about repentance." Mary's story is an important one, but not because she seems particularly relevant to teenaged prostitutes, or because the world would be a better place if prostitutes thought better of things and headed for the nearest desert to live in caves. Repentance is not a popular word these days, but I believe that any of us recognize it when it strikes us in the gut. Repentance is coming to our senses, seeing, suddenly, what we've done that we might not have done, or recognizing, as Oscar Wilde says in his great religious meditation *De Profundis,* that the problem is not in what we do but in what we become.

Repentance is valuable because it opens in us the idea of

change. I've known several young women who've worked in the sex trade, and one of the worst problems they encounter is the sense that change isn't possible. They're in a business that will discard them as useless once they're past thirty, but they come to feel that this work is all they can do. Many, in fact, do not like what they become. The facile thinking of middle-class America—I'm OK, you're OK, your pimp is OK—isn't of much use to these women once they recognize that they need a change.

The story of Mary of Egypt opens the floodgates of change. It comes from a tradition of desert stories suggesting that if monks and whores can't talk to each other, who can? The monk who encounters Mary still has a lot to learn; his understanding of the spiritual life is facile in comparison to hers, and he knows it. Mary, for all her trials, is like one of those fortunate souls in the gospels to whom Jesus says, "Your faith has made you whole." Benedicta Ward has said that these stories are about deliverance from "despair of the soul, from the risk of the tragedy of refusing life, of calling death life," which may be one function of the slang term for prostitution: it is called "the life." But the story of Mary of Egypt is one any of us might turn to when we're frozen up inside, when we're in need of remorse, in need of the tears that will melt what Ward terms "the ultimate block within [us]; that deep and cold conviction that [we] cannot love or be loved." In this tradition, Ward says, virginity, defined as being whole, at one in oneself, and with God, can be restored by tears.

SAVED
BY A ROCKETTE:
EASTERS
I HAVE KNOWN

*Let us sing now, not in order to enjoy a life of leisure, but in
order to lighten your labors. You should sing as wayfarers do—
sing, but continue your journey. Do not be lazy, but sing to make
your journey more enjoyable. Sing, but keep going.*
—St. Augustine

A dark plaid, deep reds and browns. My favorite dress.
Soft cotton, no scratchy lace. Buster Brown shoes. An occasion; my mother has set my hair in rags overnight and in the
morning she lets me brush out the curls. Then we go to a department store in downtown Washington, D.C., where along with
other children, I have tea and cookies with the Easter Bunny. I have
the photograph to prove it.

I love singing in the cherub choir at the First Methodist
Church in Arlington, Virginia. In the picture I pose before the altar,
hands pressed together, eyes closed tight as if I am praying hard.
But I am thinking about the way I look, in the starched white collar and big black bow tie, my arms like angel wings in voluminous
pale blue sleeves.

. . .

Much is made of new things. The electric stove, on which I promptly burned the palm of my right hand. The television. There's a story on television that I like very much, because it is the same story I hear at Sunday school. I love Jesus; I love to sing about him. But now the story changes; something new, as dark as the clouds behind Jesus' face. He is nailed to a cross; he is going to die. I have never seen a movie in which someone dies, and I do not like it. Especially Jesus. How can I sing about him any more, if he dies? I run into the kitchen, where my grandmother Norris is cleaning a fish. I am in tears. It is Good Friday, she tells me, good because it's the day Jesus died, because he died to take away my sins. I don't know what this means; I am transfixed by the fish's eye. Something is wrong here, very wrong. I go to my room, climb inside my wardrobe, and shut the door. I am going to stay there a long time. I am not going to come out, ever. The grown-ups have gone crazy, or they've lied to me, they've kept it hidden, what a terrible world this is, where Jesus dies.

We each have a purse and matching hat. White gloves, socks with lace cuffs. Crinolines under stiff cotton skirts that make us feel important. Patent leather Mary Janes. My two little sisters and I pose for a photograph before leaving for church. We stand by the station wagon. "Robin's egg blue," my mother had called it. I like to think of the car as an egg, my family hatching through the doors. For my youngest sister, it is her first purse. It distracts her. She swings it back and forth, hitting us on the knees. *Quit it,* we say. *Shush. Stand still for the picture.*

Sunrise at Punchbowl cemetery. My father's band is here, the 7th Fleet Navy Band, and also the church choir he directs in downtown Honolulu. That's why I'm here, to sing in the choir. It feels odd to be singing so early, to be up before the sun. It is hard to imagine all this death; I have not lost anyone to death, except the collie we named Lady. Her death seemed so large, I felt the need to do something. I set my toy ironing board up in the back yard and covered it with one of mom's old tablecloths. Death was hungry, and I couldn't do enough. Not just dog biscuits and Lady's collar, but some of my things, my favorite marbles, and a Golden book—Scuffy the Tugboat—and a copper bracelet that I bought with my allowance on vacation the summer before; it all went on the makeshift altar. I couldn't do enough. Death was empty, and I tried to fill it.

I remember one morning when our neighbor came over as we were eating breakfast, still in her nightgown, her thin hair in rollers, gray at the roots. Out of breath, she said, *Harry's collapsed,* and my father ran next door and called the ambulance and missed a whole morning of work. After school that day, a new phrase, "dead on arrival."

I remember the front page of the newspaper on the day that the plane crashed in Rio de Janeiro with members of the U.S. Navy Band on board. Everyone died. My father's face turned ash-white; he looked old, not like my dad any more. He had known all the people on that plane. He cried, and my mother cried. She told me that if we had stayed in Washington, my father would have been on that plane and he would be dead. I could not imagine this.

The men's voices drone, I am sleepy and hungry. The soldiers' white crosses are beautiful in the morning light. Such a peaceful place, such terrible deaths, and so many. Easter Sunrise Service.

Spring break, spent with friends from college. My favorite was at Montauk, walking in cold sand, watching the sun come up. Easter is a blank space on the calendar, and I barely remember the Easters of my childhood. Once, though, my mother and I are visiting her parents in Lemmon, and we go to church on Easter Sunday with my grandmother. I grumble over having to dress up and deliberately sing flat on the hymns, until my mother jabs me with her elbow.

After college, Manhattan, my first apartment. My roommate and I furnish it mostly with hand-me-downs from her family's home on Long Island. The necessity of buying things—even salt and pepper shakers, or a small Oriental carpet—terrifies me. It seems risky, this pretense to adulthood. One Thursday night in spring, my roommate brings home some mescaline, a gift from another Juilliard student. I am not much for drugs, except for a little pot, but I agree to take it with her on Friday night after work. For a time, it is a giddy high, and pleasant; from our little balcony we watch the lights change along West End Avenue and are unaccountably amused. But then she says something that seems sharp to me, and I'm afraid to reply. The clouds rolling in from the west, along the Hudson River, come too fast. They roil, coiling like snakes about to strike. As if they would tell me something, but in a language I don't know.

I can't look at her face, or my own face in the mirror. I can't sleep; thoughts come too quickly, one on another. If I were a machine, I'd be a ticker-tape printing. I wonder if I am a ticker-tape; if everything about me, everything I thought I knew, is false. My life a pretense, an evasion—thoughts tick away, too fast—me as I want to be, not as I am. I get up, turn on a light, but don't dare go outside. I sit at the card table we use for meals. I sit, holding on. I know that if I let go, even once, I will go to the balcony and jump to my death. I don't know why this should be so, but it is so. I sit for hours.

When it grows light outside, I get up and go to the bathroom, clinging to the walls, still afraid to let go. I imagine that I am on a space walk, and my tether must not break. I am afraid to wake my roommate, afraid that she'll be angry. I lie down in bed but am afraid to sleep. Later, she wakes up and wonders if she should take me to a hospital. No, I say. She cuts a grapefruit and hands half of it to me. I begin to cry, because I think she hates me, but now she wants to feed me. Not like the Jimmy Cagney movie, I say, where he grinds the grapefruit into a woman's face, and I am crying. It's a bad trip, she says. And I say, I guess so, and for the rest of the day she mothers me, watching me and feeding me and not going out, because she's afraid to leave me alone. All that Saturday, we watch old movies. She makes popcorn and hot chocolate. We watch Kirk Douglas in *Ulysses,* which I think is the story of Jesus.

On Sunday I am better, but still shaky. You have to pull yourself together, she tells me. You can do it. We had planned to walk to a friend's apartment, a horn player who lives with a woman named Barbara, a Rockette. As frightened as I am, I am not going to pass up the chance to meet a Rockette. The windows of the building across the street from her apartment are blind eyes that spark with malice; watching us, and mocking. It is difficult to be with people; the words they use, everything they do, has too much meaning; inside the poem of their lives, I can't keep track of my own. I want to sleep. I am a graceless guest. I spill half a plate of food on the floor. No matter, she says. Barbara is a cheerful woman, and a good cook. She fills my plate again and says something that makes me smile for the first time in days. Happy Easter, she says. On Monday I am afraid to put on a pair of shoes. I stare at the shoes in my closet and am afraid of them all. I have to force myself to get dressed and take the bus to work. It is weeks before I can ride the subway without an offhand temptation to throw myself on the tracks. I write to a friend, "I think I need to *live* better, but I have to do things step by step. It is the journey of the embryo."

I am working for the South Dakota Arts Council in a junior high school. An irrepressible seventh-grade boy who has for days been writing passionate poems about motorcycles and TransAms says to me during last period on Friday afternoon: "This is the best week we ever had in school. You're here. At noon on Tuesday in the gym we had a guy from the L.A. Lakers. And on Thursday some convicts from the State Pen came to talk to us. And next week we're off, for Easter."

One bright Sunday morning, my husband and I are awakened by a knock on our bedroom door. It's a small town, and sometimes we wake to find a friend sound asleep on the living room sofa, having wandered in after the bars closed. But it's unusual for anyone to be knocking on our bedroom door. "Dave? Kathleen?" We recognize the voice, a cowboy friend, and we reply, sleepily, "Just a minute," as we untangle bedsheets and pull on bathrobes.

He's standing in our kitchen, a half-empty bottle of Canadian whiskey in one hand, a plastic bucket in the other. He says, "We had some yearling bulls that we had to cut to go to grass, and I thought, I sure would hate to see these big nuts go to waste. I cleaned 'em up; they're ready to cook." Our friends love my husband's cooking, but this is the first time he's been asked to prepare rocky mountain oysters for breakfast.

David decides to stir-fry them in the wok. I pour whiskey into

three glasses and toast some of my home-made bread. There's buffalo berry jam that my grandmother made, the last jar we have.
"Hey, it's Easter," I say, "let's celebrate," and we have ourselves a
feast.

It's Palm Sunday at the abbey. The monks have invited their guests
to join them in the procession into church. Four girls, their cate-
chism teachers, and myself. It's a rag-tag procession, and the children wave their palms self-consciously. No matter. It will have to
do. The hour is on us.

At Mass I stand alongside the youngest girl. She stares at the
celebrant as if at a flame, her eyes wander around the great candy
box of a church, its pretty angels and painted vines, lilies spinning
around the Christ Child. She seems to be too young for first communion, but she's careful to do what everyone else does, which is
mostly standing still.

Yet we move, and change. Her life crosses mine, and there is
no name for it. The quantum effect. Communion. At about her
age I refused to believe that Jesus dies; I wonder if I believe it yet.
I wonder what she knows of death, if she, too, will run from pain,
to a dark beyond telling, if she will find God there, for the touching and tasting.

The girl stares at her hands where bread has fallen as if from
heaven, and looks around wildly, face aflame. "Do I eat this?" she
wonders, half-aloud. "Yes," I whisper. "Yes."

It's been a rough winter. Medical, financial, emotional disaster
that somehow we've come through. After weeks on the road as an
artist-in-schools, I feel ready for a Holy Week, my first experience
of the Roman Catholic Easter liturgy. My husband is at home, writ-

ing; he'll be better off, he says, knowing that I'm here. My "I-survived-Catholic-school-and-won't-go-near-a-Mass-ever-again" husband thinks I'm where I belong. He may be right.

Good Friday is stark, solemn, final. But on Holy Saturday the world seems expectant again. I'm delighted to find that the long story-telling session of the Vigil contains some of my favorite images from childhood—the parting of the Red Sea, and passage through the desert, following a fire by night and a pillar of cloud by day.

The Vigil moves us through the night. I try to keep in mind what one monk has said to me, about not letting the self-voice take all the room inside me. Somewhere, Thomas Merton says that "simplicity is completely absorbed in listening to what it hears," and for much of the night, I am a simple-minded listener.

Another monk, a liturgist, has suggested that I sit in the choir loft so that I have a good view of everything. Two monks join me there, and as there are three bells, they say, and only two of them, would I take one bell at the Gloria? In the chilly tower, they give me the rope for the smallest bell, which is probably the only one I can handle. "Be careful not to tip it," one monk says, demonstrating. It is hard to see; his black habit merges with the shadows. There is no electricity in the bell tower, only the light of the full moon.

We return at the close of the Vigil, near midnight, and ring the bells for a long time. Through the frosty glass I can make out the lights of cars on the Interstate in the distance; I wonder if they can hear the racket we're making, if someone is wondering what the bells are for.

Afterwards, the abbot invites me to the Easter party—beer, popcorn, candy, and good conversation until one in the morning. True celebration; maybe these people can enjoy Easter because they also observe Lent well enough to be happy to see it go. I have such a good time that I spend the rest of the night dreaming it all over again. This time there's a monk at the party I've never seen before, and when I introduce myself, I'm surprised to see that he's wearing gold vestments. He seems amused to meet me, amused also at my confusion. "Oh, I'm here all the time," he says, waving his right hand as if this is of no consequence. "You just don't see me."

I wake refreshed, truly glad for the first time in months. At a late breakfast, the monks grumble over a full-page spread on the monastery in the local paper. "They make it look like we're spiritual all the time," one says. "Next time they come, we should make them take a picture of our pool table." "I could always have them help me check the pregnant cows," says the farm manager.

There is much teasing of one monk who's been misquoted, so that he seems to be denying the Resurrection; the theologians of the monastery busy themselves with determining exactly which heresy is implicit in his remark. The reporter has also garbled the monastery schedule, so that it sounds as if the monks sleep all day and go to church all night. "Whatever," says the liturgy director, glancing at his watch.

TRIDUUM:
THE THREE
DAYS

In a monastery, the Easter Triduum—which literally means "the three days," Maundy Thursday, Good Friday, and Holy Saturday—is a total surrender to worship. Time feels suspended, allowing for focus on the events commemorated: Jesus gathering with friends the night before his death, to share a last meal; Jesus' arrest and execution; and his resurrection. If you've become acclimated to the normal rhythms of the monastery, the daily round of prayer, meals, and work, the liturgies of the Triduum are guaranteed to throw you off.

One year at St. John's, I was invited to join a group of women who would be singing at all the Triduum liturgies as part of the monastery schola (or choir). When a friend wrote to me to ask what Easter in a monastery had been like, this is what I sent her:

MAUNDY THURSDAY
7 A.M.—Morning Prayer
10:30 A.M.—Schola rehearsal
Noon—Midday Prayer

NAP!!!

5:45 P.M.—Reception & Festal meal, Monastic refectory

7:30 P.M.—Schola rehearsal

8–9:30 P.M.—Mass of the Lord's Supper

9:30–11:45 P.M.—Vigil of Adoration (Silent meditation in the church)

11:45–Midnight—Prayer of Closing Adoration (Sacrament is removed from church)

GOOD FRIDAY

7 A.M.—Morning Prayer

Noon—Midday Prayer

2 P.M.—Schola rehearsal

3–4:30 P.M.—Liturgy of the Lord's Passion

NAP!!!—Also, baking bread for Sunday's Potluck

9:30 P.M.—Compline

HOLY SATURDAY

7 A.M.—Morning Prayer

10 A.M.—Rehearse for reading at Vigil

10:45 A.M.—Schola rehearsal

Noon—Midday Prayer

NAP!!!

5:30 P.M.—Vespers

9:45 P.M.—Schola rehearsal

10:45 P.M.–1:45 A.M.—Easter Vigil

1:45–2:15 A.M.—Reception, Great Hall

EASTER SUNDAY

9:30 A.M.—Morning Prayer

Coffee & informal hymn sing with theology students in graduate dorm

Noon—Midday Prayer
12:30–2:30 P.M.—Potluck at Ecumenical Institute
NAP!!!
5:30 P.M.—Vespers

EASTER MONDAY
Back to normal monastery schedule

TRIDUUM NOTES

If we are agnostics most of the time, we can believe at least during the liturgy.—Gail Ramshaw

THURSDAY

The Triduum begins with the singing of the "Ubi Caritas" in the monastic refectory; the words of the great medieval poem—"Where charity and love are found, there is God"—set the tone for our meal and the liturgy that follows. I know Benedictines who could transform a meal at McDonald's into a love feast, but this is ridiculous. "Love one another," the abbot reads from the Gospel of John. At this moment, at this table, it seems possible.

After the feast, I stand with the rest of the schola in the chilly cloister walk. As we'll lead the procession into church, we wait there for the community to line up behind us. This is the night Jesus spends in the garden of Gethsemane, praying by the vigil light of the stars. Near midnight, the abbot will wrap up the Eucharist in the cloth of the humeral veil and carry it out of the church.

FRIDAY

At morning prayer on Good Friday a monk sings one of the Lamentations of Jeremiah, and it hurts; it feels like a blow to the solar plexus. Jeremiah's images are strikingly contemporary: infants dying of thirst, children on the streets with no one to care for them, the wealthy facing sudden ruin, young women being raped in a city gone mad: "Jerusalem, Jerusalem, return to the Lord your God," the young monk sings, and then a terrible silence in the church. And in my heart.

I have finally come to Good Friday on its own terms. It is the morning after, the coming-to. Last night we feasted with our dearest friends, and now we wake to find that for the dearest of them, Jesus himself, death is imminent. We gather in the harsh light of morning, the harsh light of grief.

At lunch, in the guest dining room, leftovers from last night's feast. The world has changed sinced then. The church bells have been silenced, and I notice more than ever how disorienting this is. I've been here since early September, and the bells had come to make sense of the time for me, every quarter hour. Now time itself is absorbed in the flow of the Triduum liturgies.

Of all days for there to be a power outage! Foolish non-virgin that I am, I have left something I need in my study in the sub-basement of the library. I borrow a janitor's flashlight and descend. My familiar work space has become close, dark as a tomb, and as I climb the three flights back into sunlight I am as dazed as Lazarus.

On the afternoon of Good Friday, we wait in the cloister walk again; one woman carries on about the car trouble that has plagued her all semester. It is not an easy thing, silence. Not the silence of death. I wonder if the others are as tired as I am; I really will need a nap today, if I am to stay awake for vespers. I haven't been up past 10 P.M. in months. I'd better take a nap—but when?

The familiar gospel is hard to take—"Woman, there is your son," Jesus says from the cross, "and there, your mother." A friend buried his mother on Wednesday, and I don't know how he can bear this. I return to the apartment to find my husband sitting on the cold patio, reading the Gospel of Mark to a squirrel.

SATURDAY

On Holy Saturday, I walk up the hill to the cemetery and I meet old Fr. Gall walking stiffly toward me, dressed in a black suit, a narrow, European cut decades out of fashion. He twirls his walking stick and says, brightly, "Ah, you have come to visit those who are in heaven? You have come to seek the living among the dead!"

The air is full of the anticipation of snow, a howling wind. Words will not let me be: *in cold and silence you are born, from the womb of earth, the cloud of snow yet to fall.* And from somewhere in the liturgy: *What has been prepared for me?* Tonight I have a big responsibility; after the Service of Light, after the long story of the Exultet is sung—"This is the night, this is the night"—I will speak the first words of the Liturgy of the Word, the opening lines of Genesis: "In the beginning, God . . ."

My friend Columba and I share this first reading—here, they divide it between God and a narrator. Rehearsing in the abbey's chapter house, we had flipped a coin, and Columba won the part of God, which I didn't mind in the least. The narrator has better lines. Now, standing in the church full of people I can barely see, I say them slowly, as if I had all the time in the world. It is the creation of the world we are saying, and I'm surprised to find surprise in the lines: let there be . . . *and there was,* God waiting to see, and to call it good.

As my eyes grow accustomed to the light in the church, I can see my husband hunched in the balcony. I had warned him not to come, because the Mass usually puts him in such a bad mood. We make a comic spectacle, at least when it comes to religion: what makes me giddy with joy annoys or angers him. He said he had to come if I was singing in the choir; go figure, I said, shrugging, and dropped the subject.

I had wondered if being so much a part of this service would distance me from it—the liturgy director once told me that distraction had been a problem for him when he first took the job. I'm glad that I had the sense to take off my watch. This liturgy will carry us along in its own sweet time. But the music is demanding, and I have to pay attention. I'm glad to find that this does not distract me but makes me more focused. The truth of the old saying "The one who sings prays twice" is evident tonight.

Nearly three hours after we've begun, the abbot announces, just before the final blessing, that coffee and orange juice and light refreshments will be served in the Great Hall. I wonder if Benedictines can do anything without feeding people, without making it a party. And it's quite a party, full of stone-sober people who are drunk on liturgy. I look for my husband. He's been outside smoking, and when he comes up to us he puts his arm around me and says to the monks, "The last time I went to the Vigil it was still in Latin, but you guys do it up right." They laugh. "The choir sounded magnificent," David says to me. "You liked it?" I reply, amazed. "It was beautiful," he says, and he seems to mean it. "Abbot Timothy," I say, "we have an emergency. This is not the man I married." The abbot laughs, we all laugh, and visit until nearly 2 A.M.

SUNDAY MORNING
Somehow, I'm back at morning prayer at 9:30. The great week of singing, the Octave of Easter with its incessant "Alleluias," begins. Some of the women in the schola, myself included, have still not had enough singing, so we go to the grad school dorm and make

coffee and hold a hymn-sing in the lounge. Someone finds an old Methodist hymnal, and I teach these Catholics "I Love to Tell the Story," and "Softly and Tenderly, Jesus Is Calling." We revel in the schmaltzy harmonies.

EASTER MONDAY

On Easter Monday, I learn a great secret about monasteries. It's not the strenuous liturgies of the Triduum, not even the complex turns of the Vigil, that monks have to worry about getting through, but Easter Monday. At morning prayer, a man who has been a monk for nearly sixty years has suddenly forgotten how to begin morning prayer. A jump-start is required; then we're off and rolling, into forty days of Easter.

CINDERELLA
IN KALAMAZOO

In the spring of every year, a medieval congress is held in Kalamazoo, which attracts several thousand scholars from all over the world. Days are given over to presentations on every aspect of medieval culture—coins, games, weaponry, literature, theology, monasticism—and at night there are magnificent concerts of medieval music, and dances that provide a spectacle worthy of Chaucer—hundreds of tipsy medievalists, some of whom are evidently let out of the library once a year, abandoning themselves to a tape of "Born to Run." The first year that I attended, I fell in with a bunch of Cistercians and Trappists celebrating the 900th year of Bernard of Clairvaux's presence on earth, and had the time of my life. When I began attending vespers and compline with them, in part so that I could listen to their singing, the choir director boomed in a friendly but commanding voice, "This is not a spectator sport!" I got a crash course in church Latin and the chant, a wild ride. I wondered if Cinderella's journey in her pumpkin-turned-coach could have felt less momentous or strange.

On Saturday night, after we'd sung the "Salve Regina" to an oceanic stillness, and been blessed with holy water, we retired to the basement of the chapel for champagne and conversation. I walked back to the dorm that night in such a joyful state I hardly noticed it was raining. My shoes became soggy—so, Hawaiian that I am, I took them off and walked barefoot up the hill to the dorm. Holy ground.

In the harsh fluorescence of the lobby I found a Trappist monk with a worried expression, pacing the floor. The other monks he'd expected to help him move a table into place to serve as an altar for morning Mass had not appeared, and it was getting late. I said I'd be glad to help him, and he looked me over, doubtfully. We got the job done—I swear this is true—as the clock was striking midnight.

I knew that in a few hours I'd be on a plane, damp shoes and all, flying back through two time zones, to the man I love, to a dusty old house in a dusty little town on the Plains. I laughed and cried myself to sleep.

THE VIRGIN
MARTYRS:
BETWEEN
"POINT VIERGE"
AND THE
"USUAL SPRING"

For the birds there is not a time that they tell, but the point
vierge *between darkness and light, between nonbeing and being.*
You can tell yourself the time by their waking, if you are
experienced. But that is your folly, not theirs.
—Thomas Merton, CONJECTURES OF A GUILTY BYSTANDER

I first came to the virgin martyrs as an adult, and from a
thoroughly Protestant background, which may explain
why I have little trouble taking them seriously. I find them relevant, even important, but many Catholics I know so resent the way
they were taught about these saints that they've shoved them to the
back of the closet. "Why are you writing about the virgin martyrs?"
one Benedictine sister asked me, incredulous and angry: "They set
women back! As if in order to be holy, you had to be a virgin,
preferably a martyr. And that's not where most women are." The
current edition of the Roman breviary gives credence to the sister's
outburst, saying of St. Cecilia, Virgin and Martyr, that "she is
praised as the most perfect model of the Christian woman because

of her virginity and the martyrdom which she suffered for love of Christ." Married Christian women, then, and those who do not suffer enough, would seem doomed to be imperfect models of Christian faith.

For many Catholic women, the virgin martyrs are simply a mystery. A friend relates, "In parochial school, we were taught things like, 'She sacrificed her life to preserve her virginity,' and we thought, well, why didn't she just give it to him—like a handbag? The nuns never explained to us what virginity *was*. They didn't want you to know exactly *what* you weren't supposed to give up, so you were regularly confused by these cryptic narratives." In fact, the virgin martyrs make little sense unless you are willing to talk about what their virginity means, and are also willing to look at them in their historical context. The women who provoke such irritation and puzzlement, identified in the church's liturgical calendar as "virgin and martyr," were among the first women revered by Christians as saints. Most come from a time when there was no powerful Christian church, as we understand it; many Christians came from the Roman nobility, but to declare yourself a Christian was to relinquish social standing, and be executed as a rebel, a traitor to the Empire. Most of the virgin martyrs date from the persecution of Christians under the Roman Emperors Decius and Diocletian in the third and fourth centuries, but they range from second-century Rome to sixth-century Persia, where Christians were persecuted by both Persian emperors and Jewish kings.

The virgin martyrs were a source of inspiration to Christians through the Middle Ages, but today are maddeningly elusive. There is no entry for "virgin martyr" in *The Catholic Encyclopedia*, and one can search entries there, and in *The Encyclopedia of Early Christianity*, on both "virginity" and "martyrdom" without getting a picture of these women or their importance in church history. A secular reference, the *Women's Studies Encyclopedia,* reveals that while the tales of early women saints and martyrs (some of them virgins, some married with children) have largely been dismissed as legendary, historical sources do exist, notably the *Ecclesiastical History* of Eusebius, written in the early fourth century, and the third-century *Passion of Perpetua and Felicity,* especially valuable because "it includes the prison diary of Perpetua herself, one of only a handful of works by women authors to survive from antiquity."

Growing up as a Methodist, I envied Catholic girls their name days, holy cards, medals, and stories of women saints. I had few female images of holiness, except for the silent Mary of the crèche, and "girls of the Bible" stories sanitized for middle-class consumption. It was a far less textured and ambiguous world than that of a Benedictine sister I know who recalls two virgin martyrs among the many images of women in the windows of her childhood church. "There was Barbara, and Catherine, my namesake," she says, "which made me enormously proud. I found it inspiring that women could be saints. I also remember that my mother used to pray to Saint Barbara 'for a happy death,' which seemed a powerful thing." Like many girls of the 1950s, she was also invigorated by Ingrid Bergman in the film *Joan of Arc.* "After I saw that movie," she said, "I had my hair cut short, and walked around *being* Joan. I had no armor, of course. My uniform, all that summer, was a faded blue sweatshirt."

But for all their power to inspire a young girl, the virgin martyrs convey an uneasy message of power and powerlessness. They die, horribly, at the hands of imperial authorities. They are sanctified by church authorities, who eventually betray them by turning their struggle and witness into pious cliché, fudging the causes of their martyrdom to such an extent that many contemporary Catholics, if they're aware of the virgin martyrs at all, consider them an embarrassment, a throwback to nineteenth-century piety; the less said, the better. It's enough to make one wonder if the virgin martyrs merely witness to a sad truth: that whatever they do, or don't do, girls can't win. A book published in the early 1960s, *My Nameday—Come for Dessert,* is a perfect expression of this heady ambiguity. Offering both recipes and religious folklore, the book defines virgin martyrs as young women "who battled to maintain their integrity and faith." But the radical nature of this assertion— that girls could have such integrity as to suffer and be canonized for it—is lost in Betty Crocker land: "St. Dorothy was racked, scourged, and beheaded in Cappadocia. Her symbols are a basket of fruit and flowers, which may be incorporated in a copper mold for her nameday dessert."

A girl named Dorothy, reading such prose, might conclude that the world (or a part of it called Cappadocia) is a very dangerous place. At least until dessert. Eventually she might discover that, more than most saints, the virgin martyrs expose a nerve, a central paradox of Christian history: that while the religion has often justified the restricting of women to subservient roles, it has also inspired women to break through such restrictions, often in astonishingly radical ways. And the church, typically, has emphasized the former at the expense of the latter.

Dorothy's story is that of a young Roman noblewoman who has refused a lawyer's proposal of marriage and is mocked by him as she is being led away to her execution. Her crime, as with most of the virgin martyrs, was being a committed Christian who refused to marry or to worship idols as required under Roman law. The young man calls out to Dorothy from a crowd of his friends and asks her to be sure to send him fruits from the garden of paradise. This she agrees to do. When, after her death, an angel delivers three apples and three roses, the young man converts to Christianity and is also martyred. Dorothy, then, is a dangerous young rebel, a holy woman with the power to change a man and to subvert the Roman state, in which, as Gilbert Marcus has noted in *The Radical Tradition,* "marriage and the family were the basis of *imperium . . .* the guarantee of the gods that Rome would continue."

While the names of many of the young women martyrs of the early church are known to us (Agatha, Agnes, Barbara, Catherine, Cecilia, Dorothy, Lucy, Margaret), the political nature of their martyrdom has been obscured by the passage of time and by church teaching that glorifies only their virginity, which we erroneously conceive of as a passive and merely physical condition. For them, virginity was anything but passive; it was a state of being, of powerful potential, a *point vierge* from which they could act in radical resistance to authority.

One can trace the muting of these women by looking at the way the church has chosen to describe them. The early narratives about the virgin martyrs have a remarkable vigor that later theologizing about them lacks. An early account of the sixth-century slave Mahya, for example, has her running through the streets of her south Arabian town of Najran, after her owners and family have been put to death, shouting, "Men and women, Christians, now is the moment to pay back to Christ what you owe him. Come out and die for Christ, just as he died for you. . . . This is the time of battle!" But by the ninth century, Methodius of Sicily, preaching about the third-century martyr Agatha, said, "She wore the glow of a pure conscience and the crimson of the Lamb's blood for her cosmetics." While this imagery may have impressed Agatha's bravery upon Methodius's original congregation, to us it just seems sick.

We live at the end of a century sickened by violence. Any claim we make to an enlightened modernity must be weighed against the fact that child prostitution is big business on a global scale; that most marriages in the world are arranged, as they were in ancient Rome, for economic and/or social advantage (the most advantageous being the selling of a young daughter to an older, wealthier man); that female infanticide and genital mutilation are still commonly practiced in many cultures; that in more civilized countries, the stalking, rape and/or murder of young women are staples not only of the nightly news but of dramatic entertainment. Maybe it's time to reclaim a *point vierge* and try to hear what the virgin martyrs are saying.

The best-known twentieth-century virgin martyr to be officially sanctified by the church is Maria Goretti, an eleven-year-old who was stabbed to death during an attempted rape in 1902 by a man we would now term a "stalker." Maria Goretti was an Italian peasant from a town near Anzio, a girl in a vulnerable position, both economically and socially. Her father had died when she was ten, and reading between the lines of the Roman Breviary ("she spent a difficult childhood assisting her mother in domestic duties"), we can assume that both child and mother were at the extreme margins of a marginal culture. For a young man to take advantage of such a situation is not unusual, nor is his resorting to violence when he is rebuffed. We understand these facts all too well from similar events in our own day.

Maria Goretti, canonized in 1950, was the first virgin martyr declared such by the church for defending her chastity rather than her faith, and it's easy to see this development in a cynical light; a perfect expression of a sexually uptight era. Indeed, a popular pamphlet of the time, written by an American priest, dubbed her "the Cinderella Saint." But our cynicism blinds us to a deeper truth: a martyr is not a model to be imitated, but a witness, one who testifies to a new reality. And our own era's obsession with sexual "liberation" blinds us still further, making it difficult to see the true nature of Maria Goretti's witness, what it might mean for a peasant girl to "prefer death to dishonor." We may make fun of someone so foolish—a male friend recalls with shame how he and his schoolmates snickered over Maria Goretti in the playground of his parochial school, not long after she was canonized—but such joking is a middle-class luxury.

For Maria Goretti, the issue was not a roll in the hay. The loss of her virginity in a rigidly patriarchal peasant culture could have had economic and social consequences so dire that it might well have seemed a choice between being and nonbeing. And is it foolish for a girl to have such a strong sense of her self that she resists its violation, resists being asked to do, in the private spaces of her body, what she does not want to do? When I was fifteen, and extremely naive, I was attacked by a young man, a college student, who I'm sure remembers the evening as a failed attempt at seduction. What I remember is my anger, the ferocity of my determination to fight him off. I know now that I'm lucky that I was able to simply wear him out; another man might have beat me unconscious and then raped me. It happens more than we like to think, even to middle-class girls like me. But the poor are far more vulnerable; perhaps the scandal of Maria Goretti is the recognition that there can be bodily integrity, honor, and even holiness, among the poorest of the poor, that even a peasant girl of simple faith can claim an inner self, a soul that will make room for Christ but not a rapist. Not even a rapist with a knife.

What we resist seeing in late-twentieth-century America— where we are conditioned, relentlessly, by images of girls' and women's bodies as *available*—is the depth of that soul, and how fierce a young girl's sense of bodily and spiritual integrity can be. Prepubescent and adolescent girls often express, as Robert Bolt says of St. Thomas More in *A Man for All Seasons,* "an adamantine sense of self." This is not necessarily a sure sense of who they are—in girls, this is still developing—but rather a solid respect for their physical boundaries. In the early Christian martyrs, this expressed itself as an unshakable faith in Jesus Christ, which enabled them to defy worldly authority. And, as Andrea Dworkin states in a chapter on virginity in her book *Intercourse,* each of the virgin martyrs "viewed the integrity of her physical body as synonymous with the purity of her faith, her purpose, her self-determination, her honor."

The virgin martyrs make me wonder if the very idea of girls *having* honor is a scandal, and if this is a key to the power that their stories still have to shock us, and even more important, to subvert authority, which now, as in the ancient world, rests largely in the hands of males. The genocidal excesses of our century have not dulled our capacity to be appalled by the brutality of the tortures inflicted on these young women. If anything, our era has made us more fully aware of the psychological dynamic of sexual violence against women that these stories express so unconsciously, in raw form.

The story of the fourth-century martyr St. Lucy of Syracuse is typical of the genre. At the age of fourteen (the median age for marriage in a culture that expected women to bear five children on average and die young, often in childbirth), Lucy was betrothed to a young pagan nobleman. Inspired by an earlier virgin martyr, St. Agatha, Lucy refused him and gave her goods to the poor. Both acts marked her as a Christian, and as Agnes Dunbar's *A Dictionary of Saintly Women* recounts: "The young man to whom she was betrothed denounced her as a Christian before the governor, Pascasius, who spoke insultingly to her. As she openly defied him, he ordered her to be dragged away [to a brothel, that she might be raped there], but it was found that neither strong men with ropes nor magicians with their spells could move her an inch; so Pascasius had a fire lighted to burn her where she stood; but as the flames had no power against her, one of the servants killed her by plunging a dagger into her throat."

Other versions of Lucy's story, like so many of these tales, provide detailed accounts of the verbal give-and-take between the martyr and the governing authorities, who are both enraged and frightened by the claim of the martyrs to an inviolable, divinely grounded sense of self. Saints Barbara, Catherine, Irene, and Margaret, among others, give speeches so replete with scriptural allusions that they amount to a form of preaching. Here is Mahya again, as Sebastian Brock and Susan Ashbrook Harvey describe her in *Holy Women of the Syrian Orient,* "castigating her torturers with a mighty freedom in the Spirit . . . Publically stripped naked at the orders of the king, Mahya yet holds to her dignity, boldly stating, 'It is to your shame . . . that you have done this; I am not ashamed myself . . . for I am a woman—such as created by God.' Had she finished her scriptural allusion," the authors note, "Mahya would have added, 'created by God in his own image,' " male and female. Typically, such speech angers male rulers; an account of the Syrian martyr Euphemia states that "Priscus the proconsul was troubled in his mind that he was overcome by a woman." And typically, the more the martyrs talk back, the more they mock those in power by their allegiance to Christ and his invincible power, the more frenzied is the male response, and the more the violence escalates. It's not pleasant reading, but it is good psychology.

It should come as no surprise that the virgin martyrs are both admired and feared for their intelligence, and for their articulate tongues; Catherine of Alexandria, for example, is the patron saint of philosophers because she converted the fifty philosophers who were sent to explain to her the error of her ways. No surprise, either, that they are often tortured by having their tongues torn out;

it's one way to silence a woman. But a theme of many of the stories is the martyr's miraculous ability to remain lucid, even eloquent, throughout her tortures; to retain even the capacity for worship (expressed best in these memorable words: "plunged into a cauldron of burning pitch, she lived for three days, singing praises"). While this outrages the modern consciousness, it also demonstrates that the silencing of holy women is not easily accomplished.

Accounts of virgin martyrs are so full of what one critic has termed "imaginative chaff" that they've typically been dismissed by church historians, labeled "dubious," "spurious," "a farrago of impossibilities." To appreciate the relevance of the virgin martyrs for our own time, we need to ask not whether or not the saint existed but why it might have been necessary to invent her; we need not get hung up on determining to what extent her story has been embellished by hagiographers but rather ask why the stories were so popular in the early church, and also what we have lost in dismissing them. A case in point is Thecla, a virgin and, by some accounts, a martyr of the second century. Her cult was officially suppressed by the Catholic Church in 1969—she is thought never to have existed—and few but scholars are aware of her today. But for many years in the early church she was the most well-known and beloved of female saints.

One can easily see how Thecla's story would have appealed to women in a church that had begun to consolidate power in its male clergy. Converted to Christianity by the apostle Paul, she becomes an apostle herself. When Paul refuses to baptize her, fearing that because of her youth and beauty she will not remain celibate, Thecla baptizes herself. Paul, having learned his lesson, commissions her to preach. Thecla is one of several miracle-working women mentioned in apocryphal acts of the apostles, and as scholar Gail

Paterson Corrington writes in *Women in Early Christianity,* "the equality of the female convert to the male apostle is frequently demonstrated both by her assumption of his role and functions (teaching, baptizing, preaching) and by the continuity of her apostolic work without his assistance."

Surely it is significant that the books of "acts" of these young women, which had wide circulation in the early church, were based on the "acts" of the apostles, which in turn were based on the gospel accounts of the ministry of Jesus. All of these stories served to incorporate the hopes of an embattled and vulnerable Christian minority. Their stories often strike me as Christianity of the most radical sort; these seemingly powerless girls were able to do what Jesus did, and change the world around them. Irene, for example, a first-century martyr, raises her father from the dead after his attempt to kill her (by having her dragged by wild horses—a typical grotesquerie) results in his own death. She brings back a child from the dead, and later raises *herself* from the dead, an event which results in the conversion to Christianity of many thousands.

Popular devotion to the saints has often been a kind of shadow religion, more or less ignored by the official church, by theologians and scholars. In studying the relevance of the virgin martyrs for our own time, we might note that belief in their power shows up in this "folk religion" in surprising ways. As a Benedictine historian wrote to me, "I have always been struck by the inverse ratio of historical knowledge about a saint and the oral tradition. We know nothing about Agatha other than the tradition of her death during Decius's persecution in the east coast of Sicily." The monk continues, "But when I ran across a statue of Agatha in a Chicago fire station and a year later saw people in Catania, Sicily, invoking Agatha's intercession to keep Mt. Etna's lava at bay, I had to admit to an incredibly deep and broad current of tradition at work."

What may be most valuable for modern people in the accounts of virgin martyrs is the depth of psychological truth that they contain. An account of the second-century virgin martyr Saint Barbara states that her father, a wealthy man, built "a strong, two-windowed tower in which he did keep and close her so that no man should see her great beauty." When Barbara escapes his control—surreptitiously baptized a Christian, she convinces the workmen to add a third window, so that she may meditate on the Trinity—her father's rage is without bounds. It is he who betrays her to government authorities for refusing to worship pagan gods. When their tortures, including a scourging and burning, do not work, but only seem to strengthen Barbara's resolve to pray, the men beat her with hammers and lop off her breasts. Finally, it is her father who drags her up a mountain by her hair and beheads her. He is then struck dead by lightning. A dysfunctional relationship, to say the least. In our day, Barbara and her dad might end up on the front pages, fodder for the "true crime" market.

And where is Barbara's power in all this? The oddly satisfying logic of hagiographical construction makes her the patron saint not only of stonemasons, architects, and prisoners but of electricians and artillery gunners—anyone, in fact, in danger of sudden death. Here the depth of Barbara's radical subversion is made clear. While she is most commonly depicted holding her tower, she is also one of the very few women saints who is sometimes pictured holding the eucharistic elements, a chalice and host. A person in danger of dying without receiving the last rites from a priest may pray for Barbara's intercession, and it's taken care of; she substitutes for the priest and the sacrament itself.

One would think that Barbara's priestly attributes, or those of Petronilla, a first-century martyr whose "usual emblem," according to the *Oxford Dictionary of Saints,* is "a set of keys, presumably borrowed from St. Peter," would make them favorites of Catholic feminists; instead, like the other virgin martyrs, they are largely forgotten, considered an embarrassment by women still smarting from the prayers of the old Roman Missal, which managed to be both sappy and insulting in giving thanks that God "didst bestow the victory of martyrdom on the weaker sex." But to forget a martyr is to put her through another martyrdom. Eric Partridge's *Origins* gives as the origins of our English word "martyr" both the Latin *memor* (mindfulness) and the Greek *martys* (witness); which suggests that when we are no longer mindful of a martyr, we lose her witness, we render her suffering meaningless.

I believe that the relevance of the virgin martyrs for today may rest in what one scholar of the early church, Francine Cardman, terms their "defiance of the conventions of female behavior," a defiance that their belief in Christ made possible. Knowing that they were loved by Christ gave them the strength to risk a way of life that was punishable by death (under Roman law, both a soldier's refusal to fight, and a woman's refusal to marry and breed for the Empire, were treasonous offenses). That the virgin martyrs have been in a sense betrayed by the very church that sanctified them may be clearly seen in the fact that, although they were executed for rejecting marriage, by the time of the Victorian Age, when Christianity had long been the dominant religion in the West, a scholar translating stories of the virgin martyrs could label as "unchristian" that which had made them Christian martyrs in the first place.

In a classic case of blame-the-victim, Agnes Smith Lewis, writing in 1900 on the subject of Syrian virgin martyrs, seems shocked by their unladylike behavior, stating that they "made themselves unduly obnoxious to the heathen, and brought upon themselves and their friends a bitter persecution, not only by their steadfastness in the faith of the Christ, but also by their *unchristian* renunciation of the marriage bond; a teaching which, if successful, would have upset all respectable society, and put an end to civilization." (Italics mine.) Exactly what the Romans had feared; what most offended their sense of family values. Lewis does express some sympathy for the martyrs, recognizing that "their alternative was to have been forced into loveless marriages with unsympathetic, and perhaps godless men."

One facet of the psychological realism in these stories that I find compelling is that the virgin martyrs are usually betrayed by those closest to them: fathers, suitors, mothers. And over the centuries they have been betrayed by their biographers, who sneer at the loveliest of their symbols. Take the tale of Juthwara, an English virgin martyr listed in *The Oxford Dictionary of Saints*. A young girl who becomes gravely ill when her beloved father dies, she is duped by a conniving stepmother who offers a remedy (for some no doubt thoroughly British reason, cheeses applied to the breasts) and then suggests to her son that Juthwara is pregnant. In the telescoped drama typical of these tales, when the young man finds Juthwara's underclothes moist, he immediately beheads her, and, the narrator notes, dryly, "The usual spring of water then appeared."

Juthwara patiently carries her head back to the church—the virgin martyrs are nothing if not persistent—shocking the young man into repentance. He eventually founds a monastery on a former battleground. The narrator reports, saucily, that Juthwara's "usual emblem is a cream cheese or a sword." Once our laughter subsides, we might ask what message this tale carried to its original audience. We might look beyond the fairy-tale elements to a story of familial betrayal transformed into love, of a witness given that has the power to change lives, to transform a battlefield into a house of prayer.

Ironically, it is often by taking the preposterous virgin martyr stories at face value that we can best see the kernel of meaning that they contain, their wealth of possibility. Once again (or, as usual), a virgin martyr gives witness to a wild power in women that disrupts the power of male authority, of business as usual. Is this a *point vierge*? Do we need to speak now about the power of virginity? Current dictionary definitions of "virginity" are of little use in helping us to discover why, in legends of the Christian West, virginity has so consistently been associated with the power to heal, why the virgin spring is a place of healing.

The 1992 *American Heritage Dictionary* defines a virgin in terms of incompleteness, as "a person who has not experienced sexual intercourse." The adjective *virgin* is defined in a more revealing way, as a "pure, natural, unsullied state, unused, uncultivated, unexplored, as in virgin territory," a definition that allows for, and anticipates, use, exploration, exploitation. In *Intercourse,* Andrea Dworkin correctly sees such definitions as coming from a male frame of reference, in which "virginity is a state of passive waiting or vulnerability; it precedes and is antithetical to wholeness." But "in the woman's frame," she writes, "virginity is a fuller experience of selfhood and identity. In the male frame, virginity is virtually synonymous with ignorance; in the woman's frame, it is recovery of the capacity to know by direct experience of the world."

We so seldom hear virginity defined from a woman's point of view that it is shocking, and difficult to fathom. Here are the words of a Benedictine sister, startled to be asked about the power of virginity. "This is something I carry very deep within," she writes, "that I carry very secretly . . . virginity is centered in the heart and could be named 'singleness of heart.' " Now we are far indeed from our dictionary definition, now we are hearing virginity described not in terms of physicality but as a state of being. The sister continues, "Virginity is a state that returns to God in whole-ness. This wholeness is not that of having experienced all experi-ences, but of something reserved, preserved, or reclaimed for what it was made for. Virginity is the ability to stay centered, with one-ness of purpose."

And now I am doing what I've often longed to do, what my education and cultural conditioning have trained me *not* to do: to bring the nun and the whore together, only to find that they agree. The designation might seem brutal: Andrea Dworkin is not a whore, nor am I. But we were both formed sexually in the mael-strom of the 1960s, at Bennington College, and the point I am making is that the great lie (or lay) of sexual liberation expected us, conditioned us, to play the whore. This is not an idle metaphor. I knew a Williams boy—no doubt destined for great things in the corporate world—who regularly solicited at Bennington for his thriving business as a pimp. And a few years ago, when the movie *Pretty Woman* was a hit, a bright and gifted fourteen-year-old girl I know attended a school Halloween party as the "pretty woman" character—a prostitute—and her parents, teachers, and friends considered it cute, not worthy of discussion.

I am grieving now for the girl I was back in the 1960s, who struggled with cultural definitions of a woman as someone at-tached to a man; who had to contend with a newly "liberated" de-finition of sexual freedom as that which made me more sexually available to men. My response was to cloister myself—at Ben-nington, in the mid-1960s, this was no mean feat—to keep to my-self and read a lot of books. Some of my friends responded by throwing themselves at men, often throwing themselves away. I grieve for the suicides, and for the girl I knew who survived, but with mutilated genitals. She had cut herself with a razor blade in a desperate attempt to rid herself of an exceptionally cruel and manipulative boyfriend. It took me a long time to see that with the peculiar logic of the mad, she had done something powerful (from the Latin "to be able to do things," to achieve a desired end). By damaging the only part of herself that was valuable to her boyfriend, she managed to break with him, and also received the psychiatric help she needed to become her own person.

I think of this girl as a virgin martyr, although she was not a virgin by the dictionary's definition. And she did not die, not literally. She may represent another kind of virginity, what Dworkin has termed "the new virginity, a twentieth-century nightmare," based on the belief that "sex is freedom." Now, Dworkin writes, the blood demanded of us is "not the blood of the first time [but] the blood of every time," expressed in increasingly violent images in both pornography and the fashion industry, and in bodily mutilation as fashion, with eleven-year-olds asking their mothers if they can pierce their belly-buttons, a practice that until just a few years ago was one of the more arcane forms of sado-masochism.

What might it mean for a girl today to be as the early virgin martyrs were and defy the conventions of female behavior? She would presume to have a life, a body, an identity apart from male definitions of what constitutes her femininity, or her humanity. Her life would articulate the love of the community (be it a family, a religious tradition, Christian or otherwise) that had formed her, and would continue to strengthen her. And she would be virgin, in the strongest possible sense, the sense Methodius had in mind when he said of St. Agatha: "She was a virgin, for she was born of the divine word."

What about the virgin martyrs? Do they set women back? Do they make room for the majority of women who are not virgins but mothers? The Benedictine sister spoke of virginity as something "reserved, preserved, or reclaimed for what it was made for."

In reclaiming our virginity, women can reclaim our first selves. We can allow the fierce, holy little girls we were to cast judgment on the ways our adult lives do and do not reflect what we were made for. If the Catholic church chose, for its own purposes, to suggest that a holy woman need be a virgin, preferably a martyr, that is not our concern. As Thomas Merton observed, birds do not tell the time.

We can reclaim our own saints. Wilgefortis (or Uncumber), for example, a virgin martyr who just may be an example of earthy, female humor. To avoid an arranged marriage, she grew a beard, a crime for which her father had her crucified, and now she serves to help married women become unencumbered of evil husbands. All you need is a prayer, and a peck of oats. And there is St. Perpetua, a martyr of early-third-century Carthage, breast-feeding her child in prison before being fed to the lions; and the aged deaconess Apollonia, probably a widow, who is seized by a crowd that beats her, breaks her jaw, and tears out her teeth. Physical virginity is not the issue, and it never was. Reading between the lines of the tortures the virgin martyrs endured, it seems obvious that they were raped. Scholars of the early church now confirm this. The real issue is that these unprotected women dare to make an outrageous claim—that as Christians, they have been made in the image of God—and are thus greatly feared by governing authorities and punished to the full extent of the law.

We can use these stories to remember the extent to which women have always been feared by male authorities, and to better recognize the ways that this fear translates into violence against women. We can remember that no woman is safe, or respectable, once she claims for herself the full psychic power of virginity. The noblewoman Ruhm responds to news of the massacre of her husband and other Christians in her town by walking bareheaded with her daughter and granddaughter into a public square: "She, a woman whose face no one had ever seen outside the gate of her house," gives a speech so powerful that the king is shaken by it. He wants to execute all the townspeople "for letting her go on at such length and thus lead the town astray." When Ruhm refuses to deny Christ, the king has her put to death, but not before he has killed her daughter and granddaughter and poured their blood into her mouth.

That story comes from sixth-century Syria; a witness to a horror closer to us may be found in Mark Danner's book about a massacre that occurred in December of 1981 in El Salvador, in the hamlet of El Mozote. Most of the peasants killed were evangelical Christians, and among the stories the soldiers told, years later, was that of a young girl, a story remarkably similar to accounts of the virgin martyrs:

> *There was one in particular the soldiers talked about that evening (she is mentioned in the Tutela Legal report as well), a girl on La Cruz whom they had raped many times during the course of the afternoon, and through it all, while the other women of El Mozote had screamed and cried . . . this girl had sung hymns, strange evangelical songs, and she had kept right on singing, even after they had done what had to be done, and shot her in the chest. She had lain there on La Cruz with the blood flowing from her chest, and had kept on singing—a bit weaker than before, but still singing. And the soldiers, stupefied, had watched and pointed. Then they had grown tired of the game and shot her again, and she sang still, and their wonder began to turn to fear—until finally they had unsheathed their machetes and hacked through her neck, and at last the singing stopped.*

One wonders: will the "usual spring" appear on the site where she died? Will this strange story of a powerless young girl who has the power to make soldiers afraid be embellished over the years, as the soldiers try to live with the horror of what they have done? This nameless girl has made her witness: it began when the soldiers' wonder began to turn to fear, and continued as they argued afterwards about her death. She had brought them to the *point vierge*, where conversion begins in the human heart.

"Some declared that the girl's strange power proved that God existed," Danner writes. "And that brought them back to the killing of the children. There were a lot of differences among the soldiers about whether this had been a good thing or whether they shouldn't have done it." Sometimes it takes a death to make us see the obvious. Sometimes it is a fierce little girl who is hard to kill, who gives witness to a mystery beyond our understanding and control. And in the wild center of that young girl's heart, we glimpse love stronger than death, a love that shames us all.

MINNEAPOLIS:
COCKTAILS WITH
SIMON TUGWELL

I have never met Simon Tugwell; I'm merely a fan. He's on my short list of contemporary theologians with a lively prose style—never a whiff of jargon or academic aridity. As a poet, I appreciate his compression of profound ideas into plain English. And I owe to him my first taste of laughter in a monastery choir. At noon prayer one day, the community was listening soberly, with grumbling stomachs, to Tugwell's *Ways of Imperfection,* a book about saints. Hearing that St. Thérèse of Lisieux "detested the pious trivialities which find their way into religious life" seemed to cheer people, and Thérèse's own description of her convent sisters as "a fine bunch of old maids" broke everyone up.

I appreciated, too, being led to the discovery that it is through our failings and weaknesses, our "ways of imperfection," that we find God, and God finds us, the God who can turn any mess we've made to the good. I hadn't thought much about the saints; they seemed a Catholic thing, impossibly holy people. But I was learning to see them as witnesses to our limitations and God's vast possibilities (as well as sense of humor), as Christian theology torn from the page and brought to life.

Years after I first encountered him, Simon Tugwell was a godsend in another way, late one April evening in Minneapolis. I'd had dinner with faculty of the Luther Northwestern Seminary in St. Paul, and then gave a reading in the imposing seminary chapel. Over four hundred people, mostly Lutherans, many with roots in the Dakotas, were in attendance, and we ended the reading with a lively discussion. Lutherans are great discussers. When it came time for me to sign books, I sat down at a tiny table at exactly 9 P.M. and didn't stand up again until over an hour later. I don't know how many people I spoke with during that time, but it must have been over a hundred. When I got back to the hotel at 10:45, I felt as if I'd been hit by a truck.

My husband was sound asleep; we'd planned to have a nightcap together, and I was disappointed, too wound up to sleep. After engaging as best I could with all those people, my throat was dry, my limbs ached, my brain was numb. I felt the need for *something*—a long walk, a swim, chocolates, champagne, strawberries, or even chicken soup—and I wasn't going to get it. Room service had shut down for the night; the pool was closed.

I'd noticed on my return that the hotel bar was still open, a respectable-looking place, and almost empty, which told me that I probably wouldn't have unwelcome attention from drunks. Earlier that day, I had bought a book edited by Simon Tugwell, entitled *Early Dominicans: Selected Writings.* There was no jacket photo, which I felt was a shame; another of Tugwell's books has an engaging photograph of him looking both angelic and impish in his Dominican habit.

Even without the impish countenance, I felt that Simon Tugwell would be a suitable companion for a drink or two, and I carried the book with me to a booth in the bar, where, fortunately, there was just enough light to read by. Gin gimlet in hand, I soon found myself immersed in the world of thirteenth-century Dominicans, an era and an order I know very little about. To my surprise, I discovered that it was exactly where I wanted to be.

"The Dominican Order exists in order to be useful to other people," Tugwell said, which I found refreshing. It's always good to meet people who understand that religion is about saving lives. None of us can understand what possible use we are in this world; it's one of the deeper mysteries. Rarely, grace comes to us in the form of another person who tells us we have been of help. But usefulness is not something we can know, or claim, for ourselves; I suspect that to have it as a goal of one's religious life would engage a person with mystery in tantalizing ways. Simon Tugwell seems to agree.

The gentle wit and formidable erudition of Tugwell's introduction to a group of people who had found a way, in difficult times, to go where they were needed made a peculiar bedtime story, but adequate. It nudged me back into myself. It was Tuesday of the fourth week of Easter, and for a month my head had been filled with stories from the Book of Acts, tales of the fervent camaraderie of the apostles. Lately, they'd scattered after the martyrdom of Stephen. Barnabas went to Antioch, and then up to Tarsus in search of Paul. Together, they founded a church at Antioch, and it was there that the disciples were for the first time called Christians. I had marveled at the fragile human agency of it all.

Tugwell's quotation from Humbert of Romans' "On the Formation of Preachers" was the last passage I read before I went back upstairs and hit the pillow. It seemed a good thing to sleep on. Glossing both Ezekiel 1 and Philippians 3, Humbert describes the contemplative preacher as one who has "eyes to the rear, to see whether they are being enticed back to the things they have abandoned, and eyes in front, to see if they are, like the apostle, surpassing themselves in what lies ahead of them, namely spiritual things, and eyes to the left, to see that they do not lose heart when things are difficult, and eyes to the right, to see that they do not become proud when things are going well." Angelic contemplation—the seraphim are all eyes—but also the kind of attentiveness that anyone might pursue who seeks to work in this world in a wholly human way.

A STORY
WITH DRAGONS:
THE BOOK OF
REVELATION

As we had read Jeremiah at St. John's during the fall, we read straight through the Book of Revelation at morning prayer during Easter, and oddly enough it came as a relief. We had been reading through the Book of Hebrews, and I'd had trouble staying awake. My good friend Susan, a systematic theologian, had the opposite reaction. She felt swamped by the incessant imagery of Revelation and missed the ideas that thread their way, laboriously, through Hebrews. I was happy not to be asked to think so hard at seven in the morning.

The Apocalypse, or Revelation, of John begins sweetly, blessing both "the one who reads aloud" and "those who listen to this prophetic message and heed what is written in it" (1:3). This presumes a communal context, in which a reader reads and others listen and respond, a context similar to the one in which I found myself in the monastery choir. Benedictines practice *lectio* both privately and in common. Benedict considered private reading so important that he allowed several hours a day for it in a monastery's daily routine. As *lectio* is not a matter of literacy so much as a disposition of the heart toward prayer, however, Benedict expected illiterate monks to participate by contemplating the words of psalms and the gospels they had memorized.

In communal *lectio,* I found that it helped to listen to the Book of Revelation *as* an illiterate; to keep in mind that its primary impact is visual. The Cherokee writer Diane Glancy once told me that she liked Revelation because there was so much to look at, so much that resonated with Indian culture. The colors, the horses, the eagles. The four directions, the four winds. The Book of Revelation does not make for easy listening, but Diane's comments reminded me that I could simply shut my eyes and let the pictures unfold. To my surprise, I found it a relief to listen to John's baffling, wild, beautiful, and often frightening images without resisting, without always seeking to make sense of them. Slowly, I began to grasp the consoling and even healing power of apocalypse. Most important of all, I saw the need to reclaim it as poetic turf.

The word "apocalypse" comes from the Greek for "uncovering" or "revealing," which makes it a word about possibilities. And possibilities are poetic territory. Both poetry and apocalyptic writing explore the limits of speech and thus must rely on intensely metaphoric language, as well as visual imagery. Revelation was Emily Dickinson's favorite book of the Bible for a good reason. "Uncovering" and "revealing" appeals to poets; it's the reason we write.

I'll stake a claim to Revelation simply by saying that I like any story with dragons in it. But this is a somewhat guilty pleasure; in some circles you can be labeled a fundamentalist just by admitting that you like the Book of Revelation. I suspect that this attitude is evidence of the extreme literalism, the fear of metaphor that in some ways defines American culture. But it also reflects a curious symbiosis of fundamentalists and liberals within American Christianity, in which the liberals have tended to cede to fundamentalists the literature of apocalyptic vision.

The Book of Revelation confronts our literalism by assaulting our fear of metaphor head-on, defying our denial of whatever is unpleasant or uncontrollable. As a writer, I know how unpleasant, even scary, metaphor can be. It doesn't surprise me that people try to control it in whatever way they can, the fundamentalists with literal interpretations of prophetic and apocalyptic texts that deny the import of its metaphorical language, the liberals by attempting to eliminate metaphoric images of plague, punishment, the heavenly courts, martyrdom, and even the cross—that might be deemed offensive, depressing, or judgmental.

Ironically, it was hearing Revelation read aloud that allowed me to re-examine the way I'd always stereotyped the book as "hellfire and damnation." Engaging the book as a listener forced me to consider the awesome power of metaphor, and how thoroughly it defeats our attempts to contain it. We do not value it for what it is, a unique form of truth-telling, and that is precisely what John's Apocalypse seemed to be: uniquely true, true in its own terms, and indefinable—or just plain weird—outside them. Its images radically subvert our desire to literalize them, and also expose the flimsiness of our attempts to do so. Mainstream and liberal Christians may denounce apocalyptic imagery as negative thinking, and fundamentalists may try to defuse them by interpreting them as simple prediction. But the Book of Revelation comes with a built-in irony. Whether one believes that John wrote the book, or regards God as the true author of all scripture, to interpret its images so literally is to show a strange disregard for the method its author employs.

There is no denying that metaphoric language, the language

of revelation, can be dangerous, especially when one attempts to force it back into the literal. Literal interpretations of apocalyptic metaphors have often led Christians to construct a boogey-man God who acts suspiciously like an idol, confirming our own prejudices. All too often, it has tempted Christians to pass judgment on other people. But hearing John's Apocalypse read aloud, I was astonished to find how little support there is for such a position. Judgment comes, and it's a terrifying spectacle. Judgment is up to God, and that's the good news. All evil is vanquished, and justice is done. The story reflects what we know from experience: that the point of our crises and calamities is not to frighten us or beat us into submission but to encourage us to change, to allow us to heal and grow.

We often use the word "apocalypse" to mean catastrophic destruction, and cosmic upheaval is evoked in Daniel, in the Book of Revelation, and several gospel passages, in images of earthquake, fire, and plague, of the sun and moon darkening, the sea turning to blood, and stars falling from the sky. But destruction is not what the word "apocalypse" means, and it is certainly not the heart of its message, which is hope for persecuted or oppressed communities in crisis, hope for those on the losing end. As I listened to the Book of Revelation over several weeks I found in it a healing vision, a journey through the heart of pain and despair, and into hope. And I was consistently reminded of how subtly this vision works on us. It asserts that the evils of this world are not incurable, that injustice does not have the last word. And that can be terrifying or consoling, depending on your point of view, your place within the world.

Like prophetic language, the images of apocalypse are meant to make us uncomfortable. That is their value to us, especially in a culture that has come to worship comfort. Using an apocalyptic lens, one might say that the desolation of a slum reveals who we are as a nation, a people, far better than the gleaming stores of a shopping mall. We are forced to look at what remains when pretense, including our pretense to affluence, is taken away. But apocalypse as a form of prophecy not only reveals the fault lines of the status quo, it takes our true measure with regard to it: the discomfort we feel when the boundaries shift is the measure of our allegiance to the way things are.

Apocalypse takes us far beyond the usual bounds of language and custom. If you've ever experienced the strangeness of being a healthy person in an Intensive Care Unit, or a hospice or nursing home, then you have experienced apocalypse in this sense. The world turned inside out, revealed as radically different from what we thought we knew, all the things we value so highly—productivity, control of mind and body, the illusion of personal autonomy—suddenly swept away. And our response to this revelation—whether it depresses us and makes us want to run, or whether we can discern hope, and love, and grace in this strange, new place—is a measure of our true condition. It reveals us to ourselves.

And isn't this one of the goals of writing? Contemporary writers live at a far remove from John of Patmos, whose identity as a writer was inextricably bound to that of his community. Artists in the late twentieth century have come to lament the loss of a communal role. Yet it has not entirely eluded us; in times of crisis, apocalyptic times, people still look to artists for *something,* maybe even hope. There is the story about the Russian poet Anna Akhmatova standing in the long lines outside the prison in—I'll call it St. Petersburg—waiting to leave letters and packages for loved ones caught up in Stalin's purges, not even knowing whether they were dead or alive. Recognizing the poet, a woman approached her and asked, "Can you describe this?" Akhmatova replied, "I can," and notes that "something like a smile passed fleetingly over what once had been her face." Akhmatova at that moment fulfilled a prophetic role, as well as an apocalyptic one: *I can describe this.* Just the act of describing can be defiance, in the face of terror; it allows the powerless a glimpse into another reality, one in which words and images (not guns and prisons) have power.

Akhmatova's story suggests that writing is an inescapably communal act, as it depends on both writer and reader (or listener). The writer must be willing to see, the reader to hear. Listening to John's Apocalypse day in, day out, I began to notice how much of it is concerned with the acts of seeing and writing. In the very first chapter a voice like a trumpet says to John: "Write on a scroll what you see" (1:11). When John turns to face the voice, he sees a figure that he describes, memorably, as holding seven stars, with a sword coming out of his mouth, and a face as bright as the sun. On touching John, the figure says: "Do not be afraid. I am the first and the last, the one who lives. Once I was dead but now I am alive forever and ever. I hold the keys to death and the netherworld. Write down, therefore"—I love that "therefore"—"what you have seen, and what is happening, and what will happen afterwards."

Moving with the unfathomable logic of a dream, which requires only that you give yourself up to it, the book continues, giving us angels who direct John to write, to not write, and even to eat the words of a little scroll. The angel who offers John the scroll warns him that "it will turn your stomach sour, but in your mouth it will taste as sweet as honey" (10:9). This passage echoes both Isaiah and Ezekiel, and serves to remind the listener of John's prophetic call. The transition that follows, the word "then" sounding clear as a bell when one hears the passage read aloud, is a further reinforcement of John's authority as a prophet. He says: "I took the small scroll from the angel's hand and swallowed it. In my mouth it was like sweet honey, but when I had eaten it my stomach turned sour. Then someone said to me, 'You must prophesy again about many peoples, nations, tongues and kings' " (10:10–11).

The Book of Revelation concludes as it begins, with a blessing invoked on those who hear it. This time, a warning is also given, against anyone who would add or take away from the words of the prophecy. The passage concludes: "The Spirit and the bride say, 'Come.' Let the hearer say, 'Come,' let the one who thirsts come forward, and the one who wants it receive the gift of life-giving water" (22:17).

It seems to me that the crux of this passage is the invitation given to the one who *hears* the book, which echoes an earlier invitation to John to come and witness the endless praise and worship that takes place in heaven, around God's throne. Now the listener is asked to become an active participant in the continuing process of revelation, to speak up and invite others to receive the words of the book. As John was an evangelist, exiled to the island of Patmos, he tells us, for "giving testimony to Jesus" (1:9), this is not surprising. What might be surprising to people conditioned by cultural literalism is the way that the apocalypse of John functions as a radical act of biblical interpretation, or, as the *Oxford Companion to the Bible* puts it, "a rereading of biblical tradition in the light of the death of Jesus."

Visionaries like John are at the mercy of what they see, and their visions bring them to the boundaries of language itself. But John is also a writer working out of a tradition. He tells us that his book is a record of what he has seen and heard, but clearly it is also a fruit of his own *lectio,* his imbibing of the Hebrew scriptures, and probably the literature of the gospel traditions as well. The *Oxford*

Companion tells us that the Revelation may be seen as "a scriptural meditation, based perhaps on the Sabbath readings from the Law and the Prophets which has been cast in visionary form. Probably it is a mixture of genuine experience and literary elaboration. Biblical metaphors and images—dragon, lamb, harlot, bride—come to new life in his imagination."

Isn't "new life" the point of the religion? And don't we get there by a mixture of experience and metaphoric exploration? Not by "adding" or "taking away," but by continually reinterpreting what we've been given? And aren't metaphors part of that given, allowing Jesus to describe the kingdom of God in terms of mustard seed and yeast? The nineteenth-century mathematician Bernhard Riemann once said, "I did not invent those pairs of differential equations. I found them in the world, where God had hidden them." When I stumble across metaphors in the course of writing, it feels much more like discovery than creating; the words and images seem to be choosing me, and not the other way around. And when I manipulate them in the interest of hospitality, in order to make a comprehensible work of art, I have to give up any notion of control.

For a long time I had no idea why I was so attracted to the Benedictines, why I keep returning to their choirs. Now I believe it's because of the hospitality I've encountered in their communal *lectio,* a hospitality so vast that it invites all present into communion with the text being read. I encounter there not a God who rejects me because I can't pass some dogmatic litmus test but one who invites me to become part of a process, the continuing revelation of holy word. Heard aloud, the metaphors of scripture are roomy indeed; they allow me to relax, and listen, and roam. I take them in, to my "specific strength," as Emily Dickinson put it in her poem "A Word made Flesh is seldom." And I hope to give something back.

Toward the beginning of the Book of Revelation, John is called to say to the church at Ephesus that God "[has] this against you, that you have abandoned the love you had at first. Remember from what you have fallen . . ." (2:4–5). These are words of conversion; taking hold, they can change a life. When I first heard them in the monks' choir, tears welled up in me, unexpected and unwelcome. I remembered how completely I had loved God, and church, as a child, and how easily I had drifted away as a young adult.

I realized suddenly that I'd been most fortunate in being given another chance to encounter worship, in middle age, in a context that restored to me the true religion of my childhood, which was song. For me, participating in monastic *lectio* has meant rediscovering a religion that consists not so much of ideas or doctrines but of song and breath. It's encountering the words of scripture in such a way that they become as alive as the people around me. As Emily Dickinson put it, words that "breathe."

And listening is the key. Isaiah 52, which echoes throughout Revelation 21, the "gemstone chapter" that is known to be Dickinson's favorite in the Bible, says simply, "listen, that you may live." Listening to the hard stuff, the words of Jeremiah and John of Patmos, I was able to return without fear to that other childhood god, the one my fundamentalist grandmother Norris had unwittingly imposed on me, and hear a different message in the metaphors of judgment and terror. "Who can stand?" (6:17) John asks, in a grim passage depicting the world's powerful scrambling into caves and behind rocks to hide from the wrath of God. *No one,* is the answer, and it's a comforting one—at the end of human power, of human control, we find a God of love, who desires to dwell with humanity, and "wipe every tear from [our] eyes" (21:4).

Somehow, the simple magic of hearing the Bible read aloud

opened my eyes to recognize the extent to which I had, in the words of Teilhard de Chardin, allowed "the resistance of the world to good [to shake] my faith in the kingdom of God." A secular worldview, terribly sophisticated but of little use to me in the long run, had taken hold of me in my early twenties, and in Teilhard's words, I had come "to regard the world as radically and incurably corrupt. Consequently [I had] allowed the fire to die down in [my] heart." Writing kept the fires of hope alive in me during the twenty years I never went near a church. But in the Benedictine choir, as I allowed the words of John's revelation to wash over me—to be repulsed, offended, attracted, and moved to tears of grief and anger, joy and wonder—my full sense of the sacredness of the world revived. I had begun to learn to listen as a child again.

The radiant faith of childhood demonstrates that the opposite of faith is not doubt but fear. Children don't doubt; they fear. Throughout John's Apocalypse, as the frightening images unfold, all the angels and the figure of Christ himself continually tell John: "Do not fear." I find the angels of Revelation refreshingly terrifying—calmly they stand at the four corners of the earth, holding the four winds; they plant one foot on land, one on the sea and, roaring like lions, invoke seven thunders. No warm, fuzzy gift-shop angels, nothing for the New Age or "personal spirituality" markets. I love the story of the red dragon with seven heads and ten horns, and his defeat at the hands of the archangel Michael, and wonder if this story would interest children much more than Barney the dinosaur. (In a children's sermon, in a mainstream Protestant church, I once heard Christianity described as a version of the Barney song, and all I could think was: Where is John of Patmos when we need him?)

At the moment when the new heaven and earth are revealed to John, Christ speaks from a great throne: " 'Behold, I make all things new.' Then he said, 'Write these words down' " (21:5). Hearing this in the monk's choir, I gasped. No wonder this chapter is Dickinson's favorite. Christ's commission may well have helped her define her calling, her vocation as a poet (and I would claim, one of the great biblical interpreters of the nineteenth century). I gasped again, as a phrase entered my mind: "Ezra Pound thundered, 'make it new,' and Jesus said, 'I will.' "

I had just experienced a healing, a joining together of what had been pulled apart in me for many years, when I thought I had to choose *between* literature and religion. It was my encounter with the Benedictines, after I had apprenticed as a writer for many years, that taught me otherwise. Much to my surprise, their daily liturgy and *lectio* profoundly intensified my sense of metaphor as essential to our capacity to hope, and to dream (not to mention to transcend the banalities of the Barney song). And it was free for the asking.

Dragons within, dragons without. Evil so pervasive that only the poetry of apocalypse can imagine its defeat. And to do that it takes us to the limits of metaphor, of human sense, the limits of imagining and understanding. It pushes us against all our boundaries and suggests that the end of our control—our ideologies, our plans, our competence, our expertise, our professionalism, our power—is the beginning of God's reign. It asks us to believe that only the good remains, at the end, and directs us toward carefully tending it here and now. We will sing a new song. Singing and praise will be all that remains. As a poet, that's a vision, and a promise, I can live with.

May 15

EMILY DICKINSON

"Called back," carried, as she had requested, out the back door and through the garden to the cemetery, past her beloved flowers in high bloom. A believer in synchronicity, one who reveled in its glorious irony, she'd taken the title of a ghost story she was reading and made it the text of her last letter: "Little Cousins, Called back. Emily." Her brother had "Called Back" carved on her tombstone, along with the dates of her birth, December 10, 1830, and her death, May 15, 1886.

"You think my gait 'spasmodic," she wrote to Higginson at the *Atlantic Monthly.* "I am in danger—Sir—You think me 'uncontrolled'—I have no Tribunal." "Perhaps you smile at me," she wrote. "I could not stop for that. My Business is Circumference." To friends she had refused to see, she wrote, "In all the circumference of Expression, those guileless words of Adam and Eve never were surpassed, 'I was ashamed and hid myself.' "

Like Hildegard of Bingen, Emily Dickinson is one of those pivotal, original poets who emerge from time to time in literary history; steeped in one tradition, they come to transcend it, acting as a bridge between the poetry of the past and that which is to come. Both are poets who emerged from a culture in which the words of scripture were read aloud daily, left to resonate in the poet's ear. Both come from a tradition in which biblical allusion is a commonplace; both stood the traditional mode of expressing such allusions on its head.

Both women were well-educated by the standards of their time, but as they were less grounded in logic and rhetoric than their male counterparts, they were not immersed in a learned culture so much as an oral one, and I suspect that this contributed greatly to their astonishing freedom to engage in serious play with the words of scripture. Both women, for example, freely assume the identity of biblical characters, male and female. Jacob was a favorite of Dickinson's; the idea of wrestling with God appealed to her. Both women boldly lay claim to a prophetic voice, Hildegard couching the story of her calling in the language of Ezekiel and Jeremiah, Emily Dickinson appropriating the words of Isaiah 43:2 when writing to a friend whose engagement had been broken: "When thou goest through the Waters, I will go with thee." On occasion, Dickinson even claimed a thoroughly divine prerogative, making a striking inversion in several letters to friends when quoting Jacob's statement to the angel (Gen. 32:26); "I will not let thee go except *I* bless thee," and also Psalm 91, writing "I give *my* Angels charge over thee." (Emphases mine.)

I believe that references to scripture may be found in every one of her poems and letters. I can never read Psalm 33's "Sing unto him a new song; play skilfully with a loud noise" without hearing her plaintive: "Why—do they shut me out of Heaven? Did I sing too loud?" Emily Dickinson is the patron saint of biblical commentary in the poetic mode. "I believe the love of God may be taught not to seem like bears," she once wrote, wryly refuting the prophet Elisha. "Consider the lilies," she wrote to her cousins late in her life, "is the only commandment I ever obeyed."

MARIA GORETTI:
CIPHER OR SAINT?

Exploitation is at the heart of Maria Goretti's story, so much so that I wonder if it is possible to write about her in the late twentieth century without exploiting her further. In a curious way she reminds me of Marilyn Monroe. A virginal peasant girl canonized as a "martyr of purity" by the Roman Catholic church and a Hollywood sex goddess martyred on the altar of celebrity would seem to have little in common. Yet both make a witness to the perils of being female in life *and* in death. Their lives, their deaths, have been appropriated, squeezed for every drop of meaning by those who've not necessarily had their best interests at heart. Very little is known about Maria Goretti, and all too much about Marilyn Monroe, but each in her own way has become a perfect cipher, a blank page on which others write to suit their own purposes. Both have been so consistently ill-used that they make us cry out, "Enough, already; let her rest in peace."

The bare facts of Goretti's story sound familiar to anyone who reads a newspaper. In 1902, at nearly twelve years of age, she was knifed to death in an attempted rape. Her murderer, who had threatened her in the past, was Alessandro Serenelli, the son of her father's partner in tenant farming, a boy she'd known for much of her life. When Maria was younger her destitute parents had moved, with their seven children, to a farm in the Pontine marshes of Italy in a desperate but futile attempt to better their circumstances. It was there that the father died of a fever, leaving his wife and children vulnerable to increased economic exploitation. It was there that Maria Goretti received her first communion, and also took on considerable domestic labor while her mother and older siblings worked in the fields. She was murdered in the kitchen of the rented house that her family shared with Alessandro and his father Giovanni.

The apparatus of hagiography so quickly entered into the telling of Goretti's story that one must proceed with caution in interpreting even the simplest facts concerning her life and death. In an article entitled "Maria Goretti: Rape and the Politics of Sainthood," Eileen J. Stenzel has written, "To read the lives of the saints literally is to misunderstand the polemics and politics of sainthood." Stenzel discovered, in teaching an undergraduate course on Catholicism, that the story of St. Maria Goretti inevitably polarized her students. "Some," she writes, "would claim that the rationale for [her] canonization was understandable given the social climate of the 1950s. Others were outraged that the Roman Catholic church would ever have said that a woman is better dead than raped."

But the literalism that would hear that as the church's message obscures the complexities of Goretti's story and ignores the economic and social realities of her time and place, a rural Italian village of the early twentieth century. As Stenzel points out, it was "the world in which Maria struggled to survive [that] promoted the belief that a woman was better dead than raped." And by canonizing her, the church has seemed to many to agree. Ironically, it is the church's own eagerness to promote Goretti as a model of chastity that has fostered such cynicism and obscured the most profoundly religious elements of her story.

Hagiography is one of humankind's more strange endeavors. That a child, an illiterate peasant at that, should become of such importance to the Roman Catholic church in the mid-twentieth century that it expanded its official definition of martyrdom in order to canonize her seems ironic to skeptics but to the faithful is evidence of grace. Thomas Aquinas had opened the door back in the thirteenth century, writing that "human good can become divine good if it is referred to God: therefore, any human good can be a cause for martyrdom, in so far as it refers to God," but until Maria Goretti's canonization in 1950, martyrs were considered by the church to be those who had clearly died for their faith. As Kenneth Woodward explains in *Making Saints,* the church decided that "technically, [Goretti] did not die for her faith. Rather, she died in defense of Christian virtue—a significant though by now routine expansion of the grounds on which a candidate can be declared a martyr."

Goretti thus earned herself a place in the history of hagiography, paving the way for other twentieth-century martyrs such as Maximilian Kolbe, who died at Auschwitz. She also exposed a fault line in the church's historical treatment of the virgin martyrs, young girls who were executed during the persecutions of Christians in the second to sixth centuries. That they had died because they were Christians was never in dispute, but in accounts of their martyrdoms from the fifth century on, it is their commitment to preserving their virginity that is emphasized. Many of the stories relate the miraculous interventions that occurred when Roman officials sentenced the girls to be sent to brothels. Butler's 1880 edition of *Lives of the Saints* typically praises St. Agnes for her "voluntary chastity," for "purity," and for "joyfully preferring death to the violation of her integrity."

That "joyfully" rankles these days, and maybe always did. But in terming Goretti "the St. Agnes of the twentieth century," and in expanding the definition of martyrdom to include Goretti as a "martyr of purity," Pope Pius XII laid to rest the old ambiguity surrounding the virgin martyrs. His use of Goretti proved not ambiguous at all; as Woodward relates, the church immediately set about to make her "the heroic embodiment of the church's sexual ethics." And, as Scott Hoffman notes in a recent essay on Goretti, the church intended this concept of purity to embrace "not only chastity, but [many] other virtues in opposition to the modern world."

Maria Goretti's canonization process was remarkably swift. Her canonization was, in the words of one hagiographer, "unique in the history of the church," because her mother, brothers, and sisters were able to be present. To the modern mind, Goretti seems suspiciously convenient. The Catholic church had need of a young saint who could promote traditional values in the wake of post-war modernism, and as Kenneth Woodward relates, Goretti soon became, in Italy, at least, "the church's most popular icon of holy virginity after the Virgin herself . . . a saint whose story had become symbiotic with the church's teachings on sexual purity." The purposes to which the Catholic church wished to put Goretti are made abundantly clear in the address given by Pius XII at her beatification in 1947, when he criticized the press, the fashion and entertainment industries, and the military (which had begun to conscript women) and termed Goretti "a ripe fruit of the domestic hearth where one prays, where children are educated in the fear of the Lord, in obedience of parents, in the love of truth, and in purity and chastity."

Maria Goretti, cipher, was well on her way toward becoming a media event. The sermon preached in Union City, New Jersey, on the day after she was canonized, and covered by the *New York Times,* sounds eerily familiar in mid-1990s America. The priest, echoing Pope Pius XII, called Goretti "a saint of the Christian home" who stood for divinely ordained family values and against "parental absenteeism and juvenile delinquency." He blasted Hollywood movies, and the popular press in general, for "lurid descriptions of sex crimes and of the lives of notorious murderers," and even took a stab at comic books, which he termed "the marijuana of the nursery." As Scott Hoffman notes, dryly, "St. Maria Goretti had arrived on the Jersey shore." Maria Goretti comics were apparently all right; they were a staple of the small industry that Goretti became in America during the 1950s. She was promoted with such fervor by the American church, held up so insistently as a model for the first generation of post-war baby-boomers and their parents, that Hoffman wonders, "Did [Goretti] die for Christ, or the middle class?"

Reading the devotional literature about Goretti that was aimed at American Catholics in the 1950s, one is tempted to say that she died for whatever purpose one wanted her to. In Helen Walker Homan's smarmy *Letters to the Martyrs,* for example, Goretti becomes a beacon of anti-Communism. As the martyred St. Agnes stood against the Roman Empire, Homan finds that Maria Goretti represents the "Christian principles not compatible with those of a totalitarian State." Another of Goretti's hagiographers, Monsignor James Morelli, makes Goretti an American patriot. In his book about Goretti, entitled *Teenager's Saint,* he writes that now that the world is "drawing itself into two enemy camps, Communism and Christianity. . . . Our church and our country have no use for weak, lukewarm souls who are always ready to give in to evil. . . . The hour has come for hardy, tough fighters who loyally and openly live a fully Christian life under the banner of the Church."

Several writers stop just short of praising Goretti for her illiteracy. "Heaven forbid that anyone think . . . that the key to sanctity is illiteracy," Mary Reed Newland writes in *The Saints and Our Children:* "What God is showing us . . . with the life of this saint is that He alone *can* be quite enough." While this has interesting theological implications, particularly for liberation theology, such subtleties are lost on the hagiographers of the 1950s. Devotional pamphlets, such as "The Cinderella Saint," tended to romanticize Goretti's poverty. And Monsignor Morelli, in a chapter entitled "The Little Madonna," takes the opportunity, over Goretti's dead body, to complain about educated women. "Look at all the 'career girls,' " he writes, "who can't even mend a torn dress, or cook a simple meal, let alone manage a household." (Goretti's selfless dedication to domestic responsibilities, especially after her father died, is much praised in all the accounts of her life.) The career girls, the monsignor finds, "don't compare to the little unlettered Italian girl who had a better way of writing."

Taking a quick turn into the darker corners of 1950s Catholic spirituality, Morelli continues: "With her way of writing, Saint Maria Goretti wrote in letters of blood a page of history which is her undying glory. Perhaps some of our modern educated girls, who seem to have spent all their wisdom attending to trifles and serving self, could reflect on the great lesson of Maria Goretti." One must ask: *What* lesson? Better unread, *and* dead?

Several of Goretti's hagiographers found the saint useful for teaching children about chastity in an age in which, as Mary Reed Newland writes, "the devil [has so] successfully convinced the world that God made [sex] for pleasure alone." Writing of Goretti as a "model of chastity," Newland finds her murderer to "stand for all the boys and girls whose minds and souls have been ravished by dirty literature, pornographic pictures, suggestive movies," and the like. "Like so many young people," she writes, "he became preoccupied more and more with passion and lust because no one had turned his mind in a different direction." This, of course, is the role of the Catholic parent, and Newland challenges them all to do as Goretti's parents did, "parents *who knew they were supposed to raise saints but had no way of knowing they would.* They knew little else but that to do God's will in all things is the secret of sanctity. How well they taught this child!" (Emphasis Newland's.)

The passage that follows, a dizzy mixture of sanctimonious prudery and sound practical advice on sex education, culminates, predictably, by reminding girls that they must be careful to dress modestly and explaining that the pain of menstruation is "part of the great privilege that goes with being a girl, whom God has given the gift of life-bearing." The grain of truth in all of this—that the ability to bear a child is wondrous and mysterious, not to be taken lightly—is overshadowed by the sheer bizarreness of Newman's prose. Her essay typifies what is wrong with the standard hagiography of St. Maria Goretti; its excesses of masochistic piety cloud whatever genuine religious value the work might have for the reader.

Newland speaks, for instance, of the considerable insults that Maria and her mother, Assunta, suffered at the hands of the more well-to-do Serenellis, father and son, as "the means by which [the women] died their daily death to self . . . the purification . . . that God permitted in order that these two souls be prepared for the gift of martyrdom." To the modern reader this suggests nothing more than the woman-as-doormat school of theology, which is still used in the most conservative Christian churches to keep women from leaving abusive marriages. Appallingly, Newman continues: "The mother must willingly surrender the child who would wear the crown."

Newland even projects onto Goretti a sophisticated awareness of her upcoming death. Given that her assailant had threatened her in the past, the terror of his presence in that household should not be minimized. But what Newman does with it is obscene, an unappealing blend of Jansenism and gnosticism. She suggests that what Goretti knew of the sacraments—a priest preparing himself to "give his body to God to do His holy will," or a married couple planning "to beget with God's help the souls He has known forever"—helped Maria Goretti prepare for her own martyrdom, being "willing to die rather than sin, [even] willing to die rather than permit her neighbor to sin." This is a lot of weight to put on an innocent eleven-year-old, but where Maria Goretti is concerned, the hagiographers have shown no shame.

The sickest use of Maria Goretti is found in Monsignor Morelli's *Teenager's Saint,* in which he gives a clinical description of the cause of her death, telling his young readers that Serenelli's knife had "penetrated the thorax and penetrated the pericardium, the left auricle of the heart and the left lung . . . the abdomen, the small intestine and the iliac." He follows this with a strangely enthusiastic description of each of the eighteen stab wounds and its location on Goretti's body, adding that "victory was hers. Doctors testified in their statement that her virginity emerged from the fight absolutely unsullied." Morelli here does violence to the tradition of the early virgin martyrs, for whom virginity was not centered in their genitals but in their souls.

Presumably, Morelli's visceral overkill was designed to take a teenager's mind off sex. Unless, of course, that teenager were a budding sexual psychopath; then the passage would have the opposite effect, appealing to the worst prurient interests. The appalling mix of sexual repression and fascination with Goretti's wounded body makes her not only a cipher but a version of the *Story of O,* a perfect model of pornographic surrender. A Catholic friend recalls that a statue of Goretti was placed at the foot of the stairs at his boys' school. "I guess on our way out the door every day," he says, "she was supposed to remind us where sex could lead."

Girls often got a milder version of Goretti's significance. One friend recalls, "If you had an impious thought, you were supposed to pray to her, but I never understood why. Somehow she was supposed to help you to be good." She comments that a picture of Goretti, "looking demure, crouched in a corner while a man in the foreground held a knife," was merely confusing to her. "I never understood just *why* he was attacking her. It was never explained to us." The real girl, of course, was as lost in all of this as any rape victim caught in the system between a politically ambitious D.A. and a media-savvy defense attorney determined to make a saint of the assailant by castigating his victim. It comes as no surprise that Giordano Guerri, the Italian journalist who in 1985 published a book accusing the church of having invented Goretti's martyrdom, suggested that Goretti was not so innocent, that she had intended to give in to Serenelli all along.

What possible relevance does Maria Goretti have today? I was pleased to find Eileen Stenzel's article about her in a book about violence against women, less pleased by its densely ideological prose, its air of preaching to the converted. At first glance, Stenzel seemed to be just one more person using Goretti to promote her own political agenda, identifying Goretti as "a challenge to the current position of Rome that women cannot be ordained because women cannot represent Christ on earth." But the delicious irony in Stenzel's calling Goretti a "pastoral testimony to the priesthood of women" is that she is concentrating, far more than Goretti's conventional hagiographers, on the truly religious elements of her sanctity, which is centered on forgiveness.

Witnesses have testified that as Maria Goretti lay dying, she forgave her assailant and expressed the desire to see him in paradise. Several years later, when he was in prison, she appeared to him in a dream, and caused him, finally, to repent. That a mere girl could have the power to so change a man is a challenge to the patriarchal status quo. And as Stenzel points out, there is considerable theological significance to this aspect of Goretti's story. "Maria did not urge [Serenelli] to seek out a priest for forgiveness," Stenzel writes. "She forgave him. God did not send angels to a sleeping prisoner; Maria appeared to him and forgave him." Goretti, then, may be seen to represent Christ, much as St. Barbara, a virgin martyr of the second century, the saint one invokes when in danger of sudden death.

Much of our difficulty with Maria Goretti comes from the fact that her hagiography is of the nineteenth century, but she is a twentieth-century martyr, one with great significance in an age when violence against women is increasingly rejected as a norm, and properly named as criminal violence. Ironically, it is the overload of devotional material and sappy titles such as "Lily of the marshes" or "Lily of Corinaldo," designed to prove Goretti's sanctity, that make it so difficult for people to take her seriously today. The real child, whoever she was, was quickly and thoroughly encased in the stereotypes of conventional hagiography. Like almost all young saints, she is said to have been "without whims, a saint, an angel," whose "unusual piety had an almost adult quality," and who, despite her destitute circumstances, had "a natural grace and a certain inborn refinement" and practiced "the everyday virtues with perfection."

Unfortunately, it is precisely this kind of language that obscures for modern people what is most believable about Maria Goretti: that as a pious child of a peasant culture she may well have resisted rape in religious terms ("No, it's a sin! God does not want it!" is what her would-be rapist reported that she had said to him). It is also conceivable that she would have forgiven him on her deathbed, again for religious reasons.

Something about Maria Goretti must have struck a spark with the women of the village who tried in vain to stop her bleeding, the ambulance drivers who carried her by horse-drawn cart to the nearest hospital, the doctors, nurses, and priests who attended her on her deathbed. In the traditional manner of saint-making, it was local acclamation that brought Maria's case to the attention of the Vatican. I like to think that somehow she touched hard people in a hard time and place: her innocence; the radical fact that a young girl had dared to resist a man, the appalling consequences she faced as a result. Apparently there was something in the child's recounting of the attack, and in her mother's grief, that compelled her neighbors, the police, the nurses, to keep retelling the story.

Maybe it was no more than the need to believe that a brutal, needless death might be somehow useful, and have religious meaning. Who can blame them, if they exaggerated? Or if Maria Goretti's mother in her grief declared that her daughter, "in all her short life had never been disobedient," and suddenly recalled that Maria had responded to her first communion by promising, "I shall always be better." Maybe those around Maria Goretti as she died were struck by the courage of someone deemed by society to have no significance at all. Peasant cultures are notorious for not valuing girls, except as cheap labor with a potential for motherhood.

In his book *On the Theology of Death* Karl Rahner speaks of martyrdom in terms of Jesus' declaration in John 10:18: "I have the power to lay down my life and to take it up again." Rahner remarks, "This is particularly true at that moment when we seem most fully under the domination of external forces: 'nobody takes my life; I myself lay it down.' And this is exactly what happens in the martyr's death; it is a free death." Rahner emphasizes that he is speaking of an extreme situation, and a liberty that cannot be obtained by any other means: "In that death which is violent," he writes, "which could have been avoided, and which is, nevertheless, accepted in freedom, the whole of life is gathered in one moment of ultimate freedom."

I don't find it hard to believe that Maria Goretti is a martyr in the classic sense, that she died for her faith, after all. To say anything less is, I believe, to continue to relegate her to the status of a cipher. In our age, virginity seems little enough to make a fuss over; many girls see it as a burden to be shed as soon as possible. It is difficult for us to conceive of a girl refusing to allow a violation of what she surely saw as her God-given bodily integrity, even though it cost her life.

Why should Maria Goretti be so hard for us to understand, and accept? A recent *Newsweek* contains a grim account of a married couple in Canada who habitually kidnapped, tortured, raped, and sometimes murdered teenage girls. Because they videotaped their victims, the defiance of one fifteen-year-old, Kirsten French, is on record. "Ordered to perform a particular sex act," the article notes, "she refused, insisting, 'Some things are worth dying for.' " The girl never gave in, even when her tormenters showed her the videotaped death of another of their victims.

I am not suggesting that this young girl is better off "pure" and dead than raped and alive. I am stating emphatically that in this extreme situation, no doubt having realized that her death was inevitable, she had every right to act as she did. To choose a free death. Of course it's sad to think of this as freedom, to imagine an adolescent having to make such a choice. But the wisdom of the world tells us that girls are targets. In several countries in Asia girl infants are sold to brothels to be raised as prostitutes. In the civilized West, they're stalked, raped, and murdered, if not on the streets, in the movies and on television. If one dares say to her attacker, "Some things are worth dying for," there is nothing joyful about it, except possibly deep within, some inner defiance, some inner purity and strength that defies the sadist, and the power of his weapons.

The mystery of holiness infuses such defiance. I am haunted by the idea that Kirsten French's killers may have responded to this spark of holiness in her. They had dismembered the corpse of a fourteen-year-old girl they'd killed the year before. It was a videotape of her death that they showed to Kirsten French in an attempt to intimidate her into submission. This may signify nothing at all, but it is the stuff of hagiography. The body of Kirsten French they buried intact.

I am haunted also by the countless women whose names we'll never know, who have faced their rapists with a holy resistance, and possibly even forgiveness, known only to themselves and God. Rapes reported and unreported in so many societies such as our own, which paint themselves as respectable and deny the commonplace, daily reality of rape. It is always something that happens to "someone else." It is always something she did, or didn't do: she wore blue jeans, or a skirt, she took a walk through the woods behind her house, she walked down a city sidewalk, she had the wrong uncle, or boyfriend, clergyman, or neighbor. Maria Goretti as cipher allows us to cling to our lies, our illusion of goodness. But Maria Goretti as saint can free us, a symbol of resistance to evil tempered by forgiveness, a symbol of the grace of healing that we long for, for those wounded by rape and sexual abuse, both rapist and victim.

But convenient untruths die hard. In a world in which some cultures still believe that a woman is better off dead than raped, we are wary of accepting the resistance of a Maria Goretti, a Kirsten French. As we read of them, sitting in our comfortable chairs, we think, surely, they had another way. Maybe not. It is not a cipher, but a real girl who says the "no," who becomes a warrior in the face of death, insisting, "Some things are worth dying for." Maybe only those who have faced that moment of terrible freedom have the right to agree. Maybe only a saint's example can bring us to forgive.

EVENING

Fairer through Fading—as the Day
Into the Darkness dips away"—Emily Dickinson

Abba Poemen was asked for whom this saying is suitable, "Do not be anxious about tomorrow" (Matt. 6:34). The old man said, "It is for the man who is tempted and has not much strength, so that he should not be worried, saying to himself, 'How long must I suffer this temptation?' He should rather say every day to himself, 'Today.' "—THE SAYINGS OF THE DESERT FATHERS

At St. John's I discovered the true purpose of vespers, which is to let my body tell me, at the end of a workday, just how tired I am. Often I'd come to vespers after dinner, and in the middle of a psalm, or in the silence between psalms, I'd find that my great plans for the evening—to attend a concert, lecture, or a film—were falling by the way. I'd sometimes notice monks who seemed as tired as I, and recall the maternal mercy of Abba Poemen, who when he was asked about the problem of monks falling asleep during communal prayers, had said, "For my part, when I see a brother who is dozing, I put his head on my knees and let him rest."

Sitting in the choir, in the wooden seats that hadn't seemed so hard at morning prayer, or at noon or at Mass, I would realize that I'd been running for hours on nervous energy. Grateful for the quiet flow of vespers that had nudged me into acknowledging my weary state, I'd become more willing to do what my body asked of me: let the day suffice, with all its joys and failings, its little triumphs and defeats. I'd happily, if sleepily, welcome evening as a time of rest, and let it slip away, losing nothing.

GENESIS

I have been too depressed to go to the Liturgy of the Hours, and I could kick myself. I only have a few weeks left at St. John's; why, when the liturgy has meant so much to me over the last nine months, am I shutting down inside, unable to embrace it in my last days here?

I force myself to go to vespers but feel so dead inside that not even the poetry of the psalms can penetrate my despair. A few words seem to spark—"You are close to all who call you, who call on you from their hearts"—but the flame I know is in them soon dies down. Still, I'm glad to be here, where I belong. Then the reading comes; the first words of Genesis, words I read aloud in this church over a month ago, at the Easter Vigil: "In the beginning, God." I am shocked to recall how full of life I was that night, shocked to now find myself taken back, against my will, to the garden of creation.

The words are like the cool voice of rain after heat lightning. I resolve to walk tomorrow through the wetlands and prairie grass restoration areas, and the oak savannah. The monks are engaged in establishing a native habitat arboretum on their land, and I need to drink it in, to say good-bye. Spring has been slow in coming, but now the new pine cones, aglow with pollen, push aside their blood-red cauls. Now the oak buds' embryonic, waxy fingers begin to open in the sun.

ROAD TRIP

It was hard to leave Minnesota: oak trees, birch, and maple; the loons and blue herons and snowy egrets. I will miss them, and the snapping turtles sunning themselves on the log at lakeshore. I was surprised to feel relieved, as if a weight had been lifted from me, at the Mobridge crossing of the Missouri River. It felt good to leave behind the glacial drift prairie and come onto the high, near-treeless plateau of western Dakota: the moonscape, the miracle, of shortgrass country. And when I walked into a truck stop where a young man who looked as if he was born wearing his cowboy hat was saying into the phone: "I'm jes' now gettin' me some lunch," I knew I was home. "Language is the only homeland," says the poet Czeslaw Milosz, and here on the range, where there are many more antelope than people, if a discouraging word is ever heard, at least it isn't "deconstructionism."

It was hard to leave the monastery, with its dignified liturgical rhythms, hard to face that moment of truth when—wonder of wonders—I filled out the weekly attendance pad at Spencer truthfully, checking the box marked "Member of this church." Pentecost Sunday.

It is bone-dry here, and people tell us it's been like that for much of the spring. Yesterday we had one of our rare, quiet, straight-falling-down rains, and today, at my first Presbyterian worship service in ten months, the lay preacher, a farmer, gave a rousing call to worship: "Good morning," he said. "I guess the first order of business is to thank God for all the rain we got last night. Out at my place, we got just forty-hundredths, but maybe some of you got more—Praise the Lord!' " Inspired, indigenous, from the heart. Home, home, in the wild West.

PLACES AND DISPLACEMENT: RATTLESNAKES IN CYBERSPACE

Place can stick to us in western South Dakota. Walking past the high school on a wet day, it is easy to tell which of the cars belong to the country kids. They're caked with mud up to the windows, having come the twenty or more miles to town on slick gumbo and gravel roads. It's easy to lose track of place, too. My friend Alvie in the nursing home talks often of her ranch house on the Grand River. She says, in a tone of wonder: "I can't remember if we sold it, or if it's standing there empty. But I sure like to picture it, and the wild plums in spring. I remember it all the time." Periodically, she'll ask me, "Is this Lemmon or Morristown?" the town some twenty-five miles to the east, which is where she lived as a child, where she moved when she and her husband retired. Alvie has misplaced her place, but in the far reaches of her mind it still comforts her.

Alvie tells me that her father always told her she was my grandfather Totten's first patient when he got off the train in Morristown in 1909. Of course the town knew a doctor was coming, and her father had been lying in wait. He grabbed him and took him straight to the apartment above their hardware store, where Alvie lay ill with both measles and pneumonia. I have no idea how much of this is true, how much is family legend. But it's good to see Alvie so alert; telling this story always perks her up. My grandfather stayed with the family for three days, she tells me, and her dad never forgot it. Stories like this place me here, as do the graves of the two small boys in our family plot in the Lemmon cemetery. My grandfather had been unable to save his own sons in the influenza epidemics of the teens and early twenties. Somewhere in the dusty shelves of the house are their photographs, toddlers playing in the yard, being dandled on my grandmother Totten's knee.

To be an American is to move on, as if we could outrun change. To attach oneself to place is to surrender to it, and suffer with it. The space I was born into in Washington, D.C., is now a parking garage; the hospital, like most urban medical centers, has for years been following its Manifest Destiny, building bigger and better buildings surrounded by a wasteland of parking lots. Miraculously, the field across from our house in Beach Park, Illinois, between Waukegan and Zion, where we lived until I was eleven, is still being farmed. Chicago's development seems to have gone more to the south and west. That field once gave me an uneasy taste of earth. Bigger kids, the ones with more daring, used to sneak through the field to a grove of trees at its center, and one day in spring I decided to go by there myself. I must have been seven or eight years old. I had no idea how steep the furrows would be, how far down my feet would sink into the rich, moist earth.

All I could think of was the folk tale about the girl who trod on a loaf, being too vain to soil her new shoes. I wasn't wearing new shoes—I wasn't that foolish—but I couldn't get the illustration from my book out of my mind: the peevish girl sinking deep underground, pretty new shoes and all. With great fear and trembling I got out of that field, and never went back. I contented myself with visiting the pussy willows in the ditch, and the small pond behind our house.

Hawaii is the next place I remember well, as my family moved there in 1959, just before statehood, and has remained ever since. I graduated from high school in Honolulu. It doesn't take long, in Hawaii, to register the dramatic, usually dreadful impact of change, and experience a discontinuity with the past. I remember when the Honolulu airport was one room, a hanger open on both ends. You went in the front door to buy your ticket and a flower lei, and walked out the back onto the tarmac to board your plane. I remember when the site of the vast Ala Moana shopping center was a lovely swamp, full of birds whose names I never knew. When Robert Louis Stevenson lived in a hut in Waikiki, he used to walk through this swamp on his way to and from downtown Honolulu.

I once had a job in the library of the Bishop Museum. There, under the vigilant eye of Miss Margaret C. Titcomb, I labeled glass negatives of Honolulu that had been taken around the turn of the century. I knew the city well by then and was shocked to discover that many busy, downtown intersections had once been stream beds with flower-laden banks. The streams had been paved, or made to run underground. I gained a new respect for the power of money, of business interests, to simply sweep place away.

Like many young writers from other places I lived for a time in New York City. The hothouse atmosphere of its literary world was not necessarily good for my writing at the time—my poetry then was hopelessly cerebral, as was the fashion—but there have been residual benefits. Most important is the respect I gained for poetry as an oral art form, listening to readings by poets as diverse as W. H. Auden, Richard Howard, Denise Levertov, Robert Lowell, Adrienne Rich, Tomas Tranströmer, Diane Wakoski, Richard Wilbur, and James Wright.

I won a first-book competition during those years; a book full of strange music and promise as well as some dreadful, sophomoric verse. I was sophisticated in the shallow way that only a person in her twenties can be, and both I and my poetry suffered for it. It wasn't until I had moved to the place of my childhood summers, my grandparents' house, where my mother grew up, that my voice as a writer emerged. A friend, reading the new poems I began writing there, commented, "When you moved to South Dakota, it's like you discovered gravity."

This is a journey many writers have made. Feeling a call to go back to the matrix of the family stories, we place ourselves in their landscape. For me that is the western Dakotas, which has shaped my work for over twenty years. I am placed here, maybe not the way my friend Tom Lyman is, who in his late seventies still lives on the ranch he was born on, but deep enough. Yet, even though I have not followed the college teaching route of many writers—I live one hundred miles from the nearest small college, over four hundred from a university of any size—I am also a person of the literary culture, and it places me here in a distinct way. If you will, it displaces me.

The fact that so much of my work is directed outward, to publications, colleges, and organizations in the urban areas of the nation, can't help but set me apart from the people I live with in an agriculturally based society. And my perceptions of them, and the place in which we live, can't help but be altered by links with the world outside that are a necessary part of surviving as a writer in isolated circumstances—modem, fax, FedEx, and my preferred "snail mail." Often I am a stunned observer of the ways in which my worlds collide. The first time I had a poem printed in the *New Yorker,* I was startled to hear the pastor at Spencer Presbyterian announce it in church on Sunday, as one of the "joys of the congregation." His gesture made me more a part of the Lemmon community, even as it separated me from it.

Having to frequently come and go from Lemmon, as most of my paying work is elsewhere, has reinforced my sense both of rootedness and displacement. It's because I'm acclimated to the relative calm of my small town that I usually enjoy (at least for a few days) the sound of traffic in the charged-up, urban intensity of midtown Minneapolis or Manhattan. I enjoy the feel of being an anonymous one among many on a crowded sidewalk or subway platform. And sometimes I am enlarged by unexpected connections that surface between my rural place and the city. During the Gulf War in 1991, I happened to be in New York City, and my conversations with cab drivers centered on the young people we knew who'd been sent to fight. Urban poor, rural poor, for whom the military represents opportunity. One cab driver, a pleasant Jamaican immigrant, had picked me up at a ritzy address and had a hard time believing that I knew people who were in the war. He told me he had a nephew and several cousins in the Gulf.

One summer day, not long after I'd returned from St. John's, I took part in a conference call among writers scattered across America. To begin, our chair had asked us to "go around the room," a cyberspace room, stretching from California and Oregon all the way to Connecticut and upstate New York. I stretched out in a favorite rocker to take the call. Just a few days before, near the crest of a butte some forty miles from Lemmon, a place with a view of nearly sixty miles to the south and west, my body had been totally absorbed in giving a rattlesnake enough room. I'd scared him up at dusk, after a spectacular sunset, and while I couldn't see the snake at all, instinct told me where his rattling had come from and I quickly backed off.

It was a good night, all in all, and even the rattlesnake's presence felt like a blessing, a West River welcome after I'd spent nearly a year in Minnesota, writing up a storm and consorting with trees and lakes, blue herons and loons. *All is forgiven,* the rattlesnake said; *watch your step.* I received another kind of welcome at a social and hymn-sing held at Hope Church, a country church I love. It sits in the middle of a pasture, and as the pickup trucks were arriving I was hugging everyone in sight—people I hadn't seen for many months, ranch men and women in their best jeans and snakeskin cowboy boots, some moving stiffly, seemingly suddenly older, little kids who seemed to have grown about a mile, new babies. We were also keeping an eye on the sky. It was overcast, and it didn't seem as if the sunset would amount to much. Wait a few minutes, one of the old-timers said. Soon the eastern sky turned pink, bathing our faces in rosy light. I had my back to the west when I *felt* the light change, as if I'd been nudged on the shoulder by an unseen hand. It was as if the light had spoken. I turned to a horizon ablaze with deep scarlet; the upper sky had turned to fine-spun gold. When the night settled in and mosquitoes came out, we went inside the church and sang with gusto the hymns of our childhoods: "Amazing Grace," "I Would Be True," "I Love to Tell the Story." Welcome home.

LEARNING TO LOVE: BENEDICTINE WOMEN ON CELIBACY AND RELATIONSHIP

It is the union with God that is the original, and the human union that is the imitation, just as the marital union of Adam and Eve was an image of the creative act whereby God created each one of them, body and soul, and created them in relationship to himself.—Maximilian Marnau, O.S.B., GERTRUDE OF HELFTA: REVELATIONS OF DIVINE LOVE

So dare to be as once he was, who came to live, and love, and die. Gaudeamus Domino . . .—Dolores Dufner, O.S.B., THE WORD OF GOD

During each of the four semesters that I was at St. John's, I took brief retreats at St. Benedict's, a neighboring community of Benedictine women. It was my first experience of "directed" retreats, which entailed meeting with a sister once or twice a day. As we were planning one such retreat, I said I'd like to focus on my marriage, and asked if I might prepare a brief paper for her

249

to read in advance. She agreed, and when we met our discussions soon became very frank.

The sister began to speak of her own life as a celibate woman. She had entered the convent in her late teens and a few years later, when she was still in formation—that is, she had not yet made life-long vows as a Benedictine—she'd become infatuated with a priest. "I quickly learned," she said, "the truth of Psalm 32; I was miserable as long as I tried to keep it hidden. But as soon as I admitted to myself, and then to my novice mistress, what was going on, I felt an enormous release from guilt." She'd been corresponding with the priest, "an innocent correspondence on his part, I think," she told me, "but I was truly infatuated, for the first time in my life." The advice she got from the novice mistress was "to just put it away, break off all contact, and let it work its way out." While she found this painfully difficult at the time, she obeyed, sneaking off just a few cards to the man during the course of a year. Not long after she'd finally thrown out the last of his letters that she'd kept hidden, she attended a workshop where she ran into him by accident. "I realized then," she said, "that my obedience had dispelled the mental image that I'd built up of him. My infatuation hadn't taken the real person into account. I found that love starts," she added, "when you see the real person, not the one you've invented." She and the priest have now been friends for many years.

The sister said, "I learned from this experience that it isn't 'how good you are' that matters—I was still full of a romantic desire to be a 'good nun,' but my image for that didn't have much to do with reality. What matters," she said, "is not that you're good but that you trust. I had trusted God, and I had trusted my novice mistress, to see me through this. It was the obedience that did it. However," she added, "I also learned something about myself. Infatuation is a part of me; I like to fall in love, I like to be in love."

I teased her a bit; "Sister," I said, "that sounds a lot like me. Maybe we're just a couple of floozies." Her astonishment—never in her life had anyone come close to calling her a "floozie"—soon turned to laughter. "It was quite an experience," she said, "to discover that I was a floozie at heart, *after* having entered the convent.

"I learned to accept my need for love," she said, "and my ability to love, as great gifts from God. And I decided that, yes, I did want to remain in the monastery, to express my love within a celibate context. It was not difficult to see falling in love as a part of seeking God. But it was also good to realize that while infatuation might be an impetus to seek God, it puts you out of balance, and therefore is something to be treated with care." Then she said something that has stayed with me for years, that seemed utterly mysterious, but that I knew I'd have to try to grasp if I were ever to understand my monastic friends. "I finally realized," she explained, "that I had to keep in mind that my primary relationship is with God. My vows were made to another person, the person of Christ. And all of my decisions about love had to be made in the light of that person."

I was stunned. I could not conceive of Christ being so alive for me, or myself that intimate with him, but couldn't deny what this sane, mature, and gracious woman was saying to me. It turned out that her expressing the unimaginable is what made the retreat for me; later that day I was thinking about my marriage—the sister's remarks, after all, had been made in a discussion of marriage, and the fidelity it requires—and wondered if I had been coming at things the wrong way round. The problem did not start with theology—with my inability to grasp Christ as a living person—but might have more to do with my resistance to accepting the full mystery of the Christ present in any person, but most particularly, for me, in my husband. The great commandment, to love God with all your heart and soul, and your neighbor as yourself, seemed more subtle than ever. I began to see the three elements as a kind of trinity, always in motion, and the three loves as interdependent. It would be impossible to love God without loving others; impossible to love others unless one were grounded in a healthy self-respect; and, maybe, impossible to truly love at all in a totally secular way, without participating in the holy.

When the sister said, "It takes time to love," she was reflecting on her more than thirty years' experience in a Benedictine convent. And when I nodded my assent, I was responding in the light of nearly twenty years of marriage. I wonder if the lyrics by Dolores Dufner, quoted above, do in fact convey the great human task—to learn to live, and love, and die. Perhaps to take on one is to accept all three. These are, of course, the classic questions of human psychological development. And it may be that growing to mature adulthood requires us to reject much popular mythology: that life is simply handed to us, that love is easy, quick, fated, romantic, and death a subject to be avoided altogether. My conversation with the sister encouraged me to ask other Benedictine women what the task of learning to love has been like for them. It seemed to me that women who have committed themselves to celibacy might have a great deal to say about how the practice has formed them spiritually, and also helped them develop their capacity for love.

I soon discovered that the sister's experience of infatuation was not uncommon, and not surprising, given the sexual repression in convents during the 1950s. "We were taught to avoid the thought of anything remotely sexual," one friend wrote me. "We certainly never used the word 'sex.' Even deep friendships with other women in the community were discouraged. We sublimated all our energies into work. I think," she added, "that's why we worked so hard!" In a scenario that seems typical for many religious, it wasn't until she was in her mid-thirties that a crisis developed, the first real test of her vow as a celibate. "I fell in love with a priest," she says, "and that's when I realized what celibacy is all about."

She, like many of my Benedictine friends, feels that falling in love is a normal, necessary but painful part of one's formation as a celibate. "It's a part of human development that can't be denied," one sister wrote to me, "and if we deny or repress it in the name of holiness we end up with a false religion, we end up hurting ourselves and our communities." Another sister said, "To fall in love is to experience ego collapse. The other person completes something in your own personality." Citing the philosopher Ernest Becker, she said, "There are two basic ways to experience a radical change: to undergo a nervous breakdown, and to fall in love. And love is preferable. Love, if we can move beyond projecting onto another person and see them as they really are, also makes us more aware of who we are."

It was clear to me that when the sisters spoke about "falling in love," they did not mean engaging in sexual intimacy but rather coping with the emotional onslaught that infatuation brings. Several women spoke of the goal of celibacy in terms of "having an undivided heart" and said that they'd learned to be wary of any relationship that seemed out of balance with their goal of seeking God in a religious community. Sally Cline, in her book *Women, Passion and Celibacy,* relates a story about a nun who had once been romantically involved with another nun, who told Cline that the worst thing about the relationship "(though at the time it seemed the best) [was] the intense focus on each other." I suspect that many monastics would agree with Cline's conclusion that "the difference between sexual intimacy and social celibacy is less a matter of genital contact than that matter of *focus.*" (Emphasis Cline's.)

One prioress sent me a tape of a talk she'd delivered to her community, and when she spoke of what she termed "sins against celibacy" it was not sexual acts that concerned her so much as emotions. "Celibacy is not an excuse for being unhappy or uncharitable, to stuff feelings down, to become angry, or an iceberg," she said. "The worst sin against celibacy," she told the sisters, "is to pretend to not have any affections at all. To fall in love is celibacy at work," she said, adding, in a remark that drew a knowing laughter from the women present, that "most of us should have fallen in love twenty times or so by now." Her remark was by no means a license for the sisters to run out and have affairs. It was an honest, realistic assessment of human sexuality as celibates experience it. As was clear from what she said next, she was confirming the religious context in which monastics seek to place their affective experience. "Celibacy is not a vow to repress our feelings," the sister told the group. "It is a vow to put all our feelings, acceptable or not, close to our hearts and bring them into consciousness through prayer."

When celibacy goes wrong with men, it often makes headlines. Although women's religious communities have had sexual abuse suits brought against them in recent years, their failures at celibacy have generally not been as public. Several sisters told me they felt this is in part because men and women celibates define their celibacy in different ways. "The men," one said, "tend to define it as not having sex; they want to use that energy to serve the church. They're more clinically oriented. And when they overcompensate for being celibate, it's through food, alcohol, sports, or work." She felt that women tended to see celibacy as more an issue of communal living, and would discuss it more in terms of "a way to govern affective relationships." She said, "We women can also lose ourselves in work." But, she added, "the worst thing that we do is to deny our true feelings and become rigid, afraid to relate. We distance ourselves from both men and women."

Several sisters spoke to me about emotional frigidity as a maladaptation that celibate women especially are prone to. "It seems a distorted image," one sister said, "of the nurturing quality that to me is so much at the heart of our identities as women." I suspect that many of the horror stories people tell about nuns in the parochial schools of the 1950s are about women who adapted to celibacy by closing up their emotions and refusing to love. As one sister said to me, "I'm always so sad to experience women who are not loving people, but they've been celibate their entire life. To be celibate, it seems to me," she added, "means first of all being a loving person in a way that frees you to serve others. Otherwise celibacy has no point."

For the women I talked with, deep and enduring friendships seemed to provide a healthy channel for their affections. They saw friendship not merely as a safety valve, however, but as having a profoundly religious dimension. One sister said, "Unless we're open to the gift of friendship, allowing ourselves to be loved and to really love in return, only then can we know what it might be to have God love us and to love God. I really believe that the experience of love is the only teacher of love." Although being open to friendships and to "falling in love" has obvious danger for celibates, and most of the women felt that wrong moves and mistakes were inevitable, one said that "I am less inclined to name them mistakes and believe that they are genuine experiences of growth, of learning how to be a celibate."

Monastic women do sometimes suffer from their own naivete, and from the fact that most monastic formation programs, at least until recently, gave short shrift to the issue of celibacy. The remark of one sister is typical: "We were pretty much left on our own to work it out, because sexual matters simply were not discussed." A former prioress who said much the same thing about her own days as a novice, added, "I now see that this was utterly foolish, considering that celibacy is something that has to be formed in us. It is not a simple part of our monastic vow, but a part of the long conversion process that lasts a lifetime."

Loneliness is one of the issues that all the women said had to be faced in learning to be a celibate. A sister who works in formation said, "That's a big part of adjusting to life in a monastic community, to sit and face your loneliness, your emptiness, and not let distractions turn you from the task. If a young sister comes to me and says that she's been masturbating, the question I want her to address is: Why? Why now? Is she lonely? Is this a pattern she's establishing? Has there been some major event in her life—the death of a friend or family member, or an experience in the monastery that's left her feeling alienated? Is she infatuated with someone, and using this as a way to find sexual release?" The latter situation, the sister said, "makes me rejoice. If she's falling in love, then she has an opportunity to grow past the romantic image of what it means to be a nun. I know this from my own experience. The questions she'll need to ask herself, if she wants to remain a nun, are: How does Christ's love show through this person she loves? How can she best show her love in return—for the person, for the community, for Christ? Chances are it's not by masturbating."

Many sisters have said that they felt it was important for them "to be able to talk about and learn about our bodies and how they function. I do not think that ignorance is any kind of holiness." But in the years before Vatican II, sexual ignorance was often accepted as a given for monastic woman. One sister who worked for years as an obstetrics nurse said that she chose that specialty in part because she was appalled that so many sisters had no knowledge of their own anatomy. "So much of Catholic moral teaching has to do with knowledge, intention, and consent of the will," she said, "and these women had so little knowledge, I felt that they had no way to grasp the basics of sexual morality as their own church understood it."

Sisters have told me of pathetic attitudes toward sex that were largely the result of such ignorance. Several mentioned being disturbed as young sisters to hear older women say things like, "Babies are so beautiful; it's too bad they come into the world in such a disgusting way." Such an attitude would be incomprehensible to most parents, and serve only to reinforce the idea that nuns are otherworldly. It also reflects, in a most unpleasant way, the notion that virginity is equated with divinity, and that on the scale of holiness married people are inferior to those who have taken religious vows. I once heard a Benedictine woman say that gynecological exams made her feel violated, as if she'd been raped. It was not a casual remark; her whole body tensed as she said it, her disgust became physically apparent. I was stunned to think that a grown woman might not comprehend the difference between a medical exam, rape, and sexual intercourse. While she would never learn this from experience, I began to wonder if there weren't some way for her to accept on faith that sexuality could be something other than an object of fear and loathing. It seemed especially important as the sister was working as a pastoral minister, which of course meant that she was engaged on a daily basis with married people and their families. I wondered if her sexual attitudes had something to do with the fact that several parishioners had told me that they found her ineffectual as a minister, distant and cold.

As more and more sisters work as pastoral assistants and hospital chaplains, I sense a tension between the ignorance that once insulated them from the world and the demands of these new ministries. A prostitute beaten half to death by a customer should not have to explain to a hospital chaplain what a "blow job" is; it's something the chaplain should know. (Even if the chaplain's job is mainly to listen, it helps to understand the language being spoken.) When a sister working in Minneapolis, long a center of child pornography and prostitution in America, sees a copy of *Playboy* for the first time and says in shock, "Why—those are real women posing in those photographs!" she reveals a naivete that borders on the criminal. I wonder if "criminal naivete" might not be a good term to add to the lexicon of moral theology, to apply to false innocence, the ignorance of people who should know better.

I am not one of those people who think that monastics are a bunch of escapists who should all become activists in the world. I believe that a contemplative who is being with God, praying with and for the world, is doing something that is invaluable in part because it transcends utility. And my experience of praying the psalms with the Benedictines has taught me that a contemplative who knows the psalms by heart is keeping up-to-date on the evils in this world—the record of human evil and violence in the psalms will make sure of that. But when monastic people are engaged in active ministries, as some have been throughout monastic history, they can't afford a drastic ignorance of the people they teach and serve.

Benedictine women know that such ignorance can cause considerable strain for them and their own communities. "We women have not been able to avoid the hard sexual issues," a former prioress told me. She related a story about a young sister whom she described as "terribly naive," who was befriended by an older woman who invited her on pilgrimages to several Marian shrines. "She had no idea that anything sexual could happen," the sister said, "and she was torn apart when it did." The prioress added, "For us, the question is the same whether sisters are having affairs with men, or with other women. Pairing off does violence to the group. It's a little like a marriage; a good community, like a good marriage, can survive an affair, one big shock to the system. But we can't survive a lifestyle of infidelity. We have to ask sisters to discern their choices and decide: Do they want that person, or the community?"

She asked the young woman to see a counselor to help her make a decision. "But," she told me, "the counselors saw their purpose as helping people to grow emotionally, so they promoted the relationship. They seemed to feel that it was better for her to grow through a sexual relationship than to remain a childish nun." This raised a dilemma for the prioress. While she herself recognized the need for the woman to grow up—like many Benedictines I've talked to, men and women, she felt that monasteries have all too often provided a refuge for immature people—she was disturbed that the counselors seemed to be implying that one *can't* grow emotionally in the monastery, in celibate relationships. The prioress knew from experience that this was not true, but she felt at a loss when dealing with the counselors. I suspect she'd run up against a classic conflict between a psychology that emphasizes individual development, and the Benedictine charism of life lived in community. She was also contending with a strong cultural prejudice against celibacy. To channel one's sexuality into anything besides being sexually active is seen as highly suspect; it leaves celibates vulnerable to being automatically labeled as infantile or repressed.

One of the first things I noticed about monastic people, when I first encountered them, was that most of them were not noticeably repressed, and certainly not infantile. Over the years that I've gotten to know the Benedictines better, this first impression has been strongly reinforced. Often their struggles with celibacy have

259

given them a truly sophisticated outlook on the subject of human sexuality, and many of their observations—for instance, that sexual stability and spiritual growth work together as a person matures—are of as much use to non-celibates as to monastics. In giving a conference on celibacy to her community, one woman said that it was extremely foolish to take celibacy, or any other aspect of sexuality, for granted. "As monastic people," she said, "we do need to sublimate our sexual energies, but we need to be conscious about it. Otherwise we run the risk of giving in to compulsions and addictions." She depicted the celibate as extremely vulnerable in American culture, which promotes addictive behaviors. "Celibacy, like so much in the monastic life," she said, "is mostly a matter of paying attention. We have to be wary of anything that dulls conscious awareness, such as alcohol, or even television commercials."

"The object of celibacy is consciousness," she said, "taking our unconscious feelings and sexual urges and placing them where we think God wants them. Our goal is to be celibate, conscious, passionate people." When it works, the celibate is, in the words of another sister, "stretching the ability to love, and particularly, to love non-exclusively." The students taught by sisters have often been the beneficiaries of this. More than one sister spoke to me about the joy of being able to draw on maternal instincts, particularly with their younger students. But I believe it goes beyond that. As Sally Cline, who as a child had the odd experience of being the only Jewish girl in a British convent school, has written, "I [understood] that one of the greatest gifts the nuns gave to us, their girls, the gift of passionate attention, came from their celibate philosophy that 'loves all' and 'loves all well.' "

Realizing that this was love, Cline says, was helpful in her teenage years. The nuns helped her see, she says, "that a non-sexually active love can be just as passionate and just as absorbing as a genitally rooted one, and that such a love has as its center the idea of being fully focused and intentional." According to all the sisters I spoke with, intentionality is a major part of celibacy. But for many of them, this was not at all clear when they first sought the monastic life. "I don't think that celibacy was much on my mind at all," one sister said. "It was certainly not what I was pursuing when I asked to join the community. It just came along as part of the deal." Eventually, however, she realized that "it did have to become a conscious choice, and one that has to be made time and time again. It is a daily choice," she said, "to live as a celibate."

The same might be said about a commitment to monogamy. But what distinguished all the Benedictine women that I spoke with from most of the married people I know is how consistently they spoke of celibacy as being rooted in the religious, as "having gospel value," or of "being a sign of the kingdom." It may be that the churches, both Protestant and Catholic, do not adequately convey to married people the sacredness of a lifelong commitment to another person, whereas for sisters the religious nature of their vows is an everyday reality. As one sister said, "One needs a deep prayer life to maintain a celibate life. It is only through prayer that the hard choices get made, over time, only prayer that can give me the self-transcendence that celibacy requires."

Self-transcendence is required in marriage as well, or in any lifelong commitment to another. But the culture does not encourage self-transcendence; just the opposite. Our cultural myths about love give witness to a comment Sören Kierkegaard once made about the "self-love of erotic love"; too many young people grow up understanding that "true love" means possessing and being possessed. Both are incompatible with celibacy, which seeks to love non-exclusively, non-possessively. This can be a healthy witness against the consumer model of love—the "If I can't have her, nobody will" psychology that spurs so many men to acts of violence. Nearly half of the murders in North Dakota, for example, are "domestic" in origin. Judging from the newspaper headlines, it seems that many men, and some women, can't give up the illusion of possessing another person. They can't allow a former boyfriend or ex-wife to be an independent human being.

When mature celibates talk about the value of celibacy, "freedom" is a word they commonly use. Freedom to keep their energies focused on ministry and communal living, freedom to love many people without being unfaithful to any of them. As celibates grow older, they tend to speak in terms of the "generative" qualities of celibacy. "We're not making babies," one sister says, "but we can make relationships." One reason so many celibates find satisfaction in working as teachers, spiritual directors, and pastoral ministers may be that it provides ample opportunity to help others grow. "To donate the self as a gift to others; that's the vow of celibacy," one sister told me.

Sisters are keenly aware that for years church teaching emphasized celibate religious life as the most holy of responses to God, with marriage as a distant second, and they resent that as deeply as anyone. They're often quick to point out similarities between a celibate commitment and fidelity in marriage. "Both are a discipline," one sister said. "Both can be a form of asceticism." Still, they also feel the need to define their monastic call in its own terms. "Celibacy is just one of the ways God calls us," one sister said. "It's another way, but not a better way."

When one sister described to me what she considered a healthy celibacy, she said, "First of all, it means not focusing on 'what I gave up,' but on what being freed by what I gave up has allowed me to do in terms of service to the church and other people." She said that she'd learned the need for balance in her life. "For me, the discipline of celibacy means a commitment to grow, intellectually and in my prayer life, to engage in regular prayer, both privately and with my community, to engage in some form of meaningful ministry, to take care of my body, to seek out solitude at regular intervals"—this, she admitted she often felt too busy to do—"and to take pleasure in beauty." Many sisters spoke to me of celibacy as something that had encouraged them to be sensitive to the many guises of beauty. "When I can enjoy a sunset, or a music concert, or a work of art, or people of all ages," one sister said, "then I know that celibacy is working." Having experienced the pleasure of friendships with many celibate men and women, it did not surprise me that all of the women connected the practice of celibacy with their ability to relate to others. "Celibacy," one sister said, "has given me a good way to integrate my sexuality with my spirituality; I've come to realize that the goal of both is union with God and with others." One woman put it very simply. "The fruit of celibacy," she said, "is hospitality."

THE CLOISTER
WALK

Love is intensity, that second in which the doors of time and space
open just a crack... —Octavio Paz

How but in custom and in ceremony
Are innocence and beauty born?
—William Butler Yeats, "A Prayer for
My Daughter"

I know exactly what I was doing at 10:30 A.M. on Sunday, May 31, 1992, but have no idea where I was. The enormous church of St. John's Abbey in Collegeville, Minnesota, designed by Marcel Breuer, was familiar to me, as I'd gone there nearly every day for the previous nine months to join the monks in their Liturgy of the Hours. On that Sunday morning I learned how little I knew about the place.

I was walking down the center aisle, trying to keep to the slow, deliberate pace the liturgy director had established as we proceeded down the cloister walk into the church. But it was hard, because I was alone now, and had little to gauge myself by. As instructed, I was holding the scriptures, a big book of lectionary readings, out in front of me at a little more than shoulder height. Following me, walking two by two, were nearly two hundred monks in black habits, and bringing up the rear, two acolytes and a priest who would preside at this Mass on the Seventh Sunday of Easter. The congregation of several hundred had risen for the first hymn as I started slowly down the aisle.

An incongruous thought danced through my mind: even Mae West never entered a room followed by this many men. I seemed incongruous, too, someone with a checkered past, who until the last few years hadn't been to church much since high school. Breathing deeply, to get my bearings, I found that I was walking a path with a downward tilt much more steep than I had realized. By contrast, the altar loomed before me, brilliant white, a simple but powerful shape. The magnificent folds of concrete holding up the roof seemed weightless, and the expanse above me limitless, the ceiling lifted clean off by the sound of the pipe organ.

It was the reverse of an experience most adults have had, of returning to a place that had seemed vast in childhood, and finding it pathetically small. This church was a place I thought I knew, a big space I'd tamed by my daily presence there. Now I was discovering that it was wild after all, and could roar like the sea. Walking on the terrazzo floor, I was reminded of a recurring dream, in which I move through the galaxy, stepping delicately (and sometimes leaping) from star to star. This sunlit room now seemed such an expanse, my every step daring an enormous distance.

My mind chugged along: don't stumble on the steps, remember to bow at the altar and put the lectionary on the ambo. Take the first choir stall on the left but don't sit down, because the monks will enter there. They swept past me like small black clouds to take their places with me in the front row, and I found the voice to sing the last verse of the hymn as the liturgy began to flow in all directions around me. The quantum effect.

I did my reading, a text from the Book of Acts about the stoning of Stephen. "I see an opening in the sky," Stephen said, and I thought, "Amen." Good liturgy can act like an icon, a window into a world in which our concepts of space, time, and even stone are pleasurably bent out of shape. Good liturgy is a living poem, and ceremony is the key.

Any outsider writing about monastic life runs the risk of romanticizing it. I've simply described what I experienced one Sunday morning at St. John's. I'm assuming, hoping even, that some of the monks were wondering what was for dinner, or thinking dark thoughts about a confrere who had annoyed them at breakfast, or regretting a sharp remark they'd made over the pool table the night before. Good ceremony makes room for all the dimensions of human experience in the hope that, together, we will discover something that transforms us. This is why I suspect that individuals can't create true ceremony for themselves alone. Ceremony requires that we work with others in the humbling give-and-take of communal existence.

Monastic people seek to weave ceremony through every mundane part of life: how one eats, how one dresses, how one treats tools, or enters a church are not left to whim. Ceremony is so large a part of what Benedictines do that it becomes second nature to many of them. The monastic life has this in common with the artistic one: both are attempts to pay close attention to objects, events, and natural phenomena that otherwise would get chewed up in the daily grind. One of the things I like most about monastic people is the respect they show for the holy hours of sunrise and sunset, and in these days when the horrors of sexual warfare fill the news, I find it nothing short of miraculous to be with a group of grown men who will sing at close of day: "Day is done, but love unfailing / dwells ever here." The fact that Christian monastics, men and women both, have been singing such gentle hymns at dusk for seventeen hundred years makes me realize that ceremony and tradition, things I've been raised to distrust as largely irrelevant, can be food for the soul.

Ceremony forces a person to slow down, and as many of us live at a frenzied pace, encountering monastic prayer, or a traditional monastic meal—eaten in silence while a passage from scripture or a religious book is read aloud—can feel like skidding to a halt. My nine months' immersion in the slow, steady rhythms of monastic life was a kind of gestation. But now that I'm back "in the world," now that my husband and I have come home from Minnesota, I'm not sure what I'm giving birth to. At times I'm homesick for a place that isn't mine, homesick for two hundred monks and their liturgy. Most people have the sense not to get themselves into such a predicament. What do I do now for ceremony, and community?

My instinct is to keep as much of the monastery in me as possible. Now I honor the coming of dawn with a long walk instead of going to church, but small difference, if I can turn it toward prayer. I keep some Benedictine practices, as best as I can: reading psalms daily, singing hymns, and also doing *lectio,* a meditative reading of scripture. Otherwise I suspect my world would go flat. And sometimes it does: sometimes I'm closed off from both beauty and pain, suffering from what the world calls "depression" but the ancient monks would call listlessness or *acedia.* Drought times, when I have to hunker down and wait for rain, for hope.

I keep in touch with my monastic friends at St. John's, and at other, smaller communities in the Dakotas that I visit frequently. Above all, I try to remember where I am: a small town on the Great Plains that may not be here in fifty years. But even in this hamlet of 1600 souls, considered insignificant by the rest of the world, there is much that people need to tell. I became more reclusive over the last year, but when I'm with people I try to listen to them. Alice, for one. When the Presbyterian church recently held its Sunday service in the park, the minister sharing a flatbed truck with a local country-western band, Alice and I were standing over to the side. A country woman, the wife of a retired rancher in poor health, she was someone I'd missed when I was away. Her only child, a young man of thirty-five, had died unexpectedly the year before. She stood there, swaying to the music, the steel guitar whining through "What a Friend We Have in Jesus," and said, "I haven't danced in three years." "Well, it's time, then, Alice," I said. And so we danced.

THE GARDEN

My garden, even more than most, is an exercise in faith. And in failure. I inherited it when I moved to my grandmother's house but scarcely knew what I had. Her perennial flowers were up and in bud in the wet spring when we moved into the house. I had memories of the garden as a child, of weeding and thinning the leaf lettuce that we would eat sprinkled with vinegar and sugar, of helping my grandmother pick tomatoes and string beans. Visiting her flowers, admiring the day lilies, lily-of-the-valley, painted daisies, columbines, and other flowers whose names I forget, was one of the joys of summer when I was a child.

In the first years I was in the house, I felt that I should care for the flowers but didn't know how. Advice from neighbors helped, but not enough. Advice from books was sometimes of use, but often it only reinforced my sense of myself as a hopeless gardener. I'd weed around the flowers and usually pull some flowers by mistake. Often, in the spring, I was working away from home, and the weeds got away from me. I was mightily impressed that the columbines and painted daisies never failed to come back up, no matter how I neglected them. They came to seem like unlosable friends.

My grandmother had a small stand of mint that she used for making her own mint jelly. I recall that she used to call mint "near a weed," and she was careful to keep it within bounds. In my twenty-one years of struggling with the garden, I've let the mint take over. It keeps the real weeds down. I use it in sun tea all summer and often send it, fresh or dried, to my urban friends, for whom it is a luxury. I do try to keep it from overrunning the columbines, my grandmother's favorite flower, and mine, a flower that can withstand both bitter cold winters and the wild storms of summer. The delicate whimsy of the columbine is deceiving. After violent hail and wind, I've seen the flowers, long spikes intact, blooming in the mud, the long stems bowed down but not broken.

In the half of the garden where my grandmother grew her vegetables, I've given up on tomatoes—end rot, no matter what I tried—and in some years have simply let the weeds take over. When I manage to be at home in the early spring, I have a friend till the ground and plant basil, lettuce, and snow peas. In a recent fit of optimism, I've tried to establish parsley (having killed off my grandmother's patch years ago), chives, sorrel, rosemary, and thyme. The thyme died before the summer was out, as did much of the tarragon patch a friend helped me establish years ago. Some of it seemed to have survived, and I hope it will be up next spring, along with the rosemary, parsley, sorrel, and chives. I wouldn't put money on any of it.

My parents were never much for gardening, and oddly enough, it was when I lived in New York City as a young adult that I first felt compelled to work with the earth. I had friends with a country place in Rhode Island, and I looked forward each spring to getting my hands into the warm soil and doing whatever job they had for me to do. I'd visit several times a summer and on into fall, shoveling manure and compost, gathering seaweed at a nearby beach for the compost pile, hoeing, weeding, picking potato bugs and re-leasing lady bugs, picking the ripened corn and tomatoes and egg-plant just before we were to cook them.

In the medieval era gardens were designed to suffice for the loss of Eden. The garden I've grown into, in my middle age, seems more a kind of Purgatory, but I love it. It's a ratty little garden, not much at all. But I can call it mine.

THE CHURCH
AND THE
SERMON

Sometimes I feel that the small, isolated town I live in is as much a mystery to the outside world as any monastery. Here, churches help to define the community in ways that urban people might find incomprehensible. They are the only local institutions, for instance, that could have generated enough local support to establish and maintain a domestic violence hot line (and now a safe house), a community food pantry, and services to destitute transients. My husband, who grew up in New York, said that it wasn't until he moved here that he realized how much ministers do.

The Sunday morning service is a social highlight of the week for many people. Especially for the elderly, it's one of the few times all week that they get out. But for them, and for many younger people, church is much more than visiting with friends over coffee before the service; worship has been important to them all their lives, so they go. If a guy skips church now and then, it has much more to do with his love of fishing, or the need to get a hay crop in, than with existential angst. For many families here, church is both a serious commitment and a joy.

When I'm asked to preach I try to take advantage of my role as both an insider—the granddaughter of a woman who was a member of the church for most of its existence, over sixty years—and an outsider, someone who did not grow up in the town and has lived for much of her life in cities. Sometimes, especially when I've preached just before a new pastor is due to arrive, I've said things about us as a congregation, and our history as a church, that no salaried clergyperson could say; whatever I think might help us drop some of the old baggage that accumulates in any institution so that we might better welcome the new person with our hands free.

I've also taken great pleasure in the times I've been able to yoke my disparate worlds together in such a way that the congregation can benefit. I've found that the practical wisdom of the desert fathers and mothers, for example, is something that people here can appreciate. It's biblically based enough for any Protestant, and it's also great storytelling, which keeps people awake in the pews. People enjoyed the story about the monk who decided that he was making no spiritual progress in the monastery. He told the other monks that they were holding him back, constantly doing things that made him angry, which of course interfered with his prayer. But when the monk had left and was settling in a cave of his own, looking forward to perfect peace, he became frustrated over some trifle and threw a water jug against a wall, breaking it in pieces. Realizing that his anger was within him, and that it would be with him wherever he went, he returned to the monastery, apologized, and was taken back.

Dorotheus of Gaza has been a big hit; in fact it was people's responses to quotes from him in my sermons that first led me to suspect that there might be a good many connections between monasteries and small towns. Anyone who has endured the pain of gossip at close quarters, the petty squabbles that erupt in church congregations, can appreciate the honesty of Dorotheus: "We remain all the time against one another," he says, "grinding one another down . . . Each considers himself right and excuses himself . . . all the while keeping none of the Commandments, yet expecting his neighbor to keep the lot!" When I read this at Hope, the country church, people nodded; they saw themselves in it, even though Dorotheus had said it about monks living in sixth-century Egypt.

Only those who know how long resentments can smolder in the living memory of a congregation can best savor Dorotheus's advice that prayer is the only remedy, particularly a difficult and humbling prayer such as, "O God, help my brother, and help me through his prayers." In this prayer, Dorotheus says, we show sympathy and love for those with whom we're in conflict, and also acknowledge our need for compassion in return. "Where there is sympathy and love and humility," Dorotheus asks, how can anger continue to develop? He compares the ability to pray for our enemies to learning a trade such as carpentry. "Always [we have to] start by doing," he says, "and doing it wrong, making and unmaking, until, little by little, patiently and persevering, [we] learn the trade while God looks on at [our] labor and humility, and works with [us.]" These words might make no sense at all in the world as most of us know it, but people who are committed for the long haul to either a monastery or a small-town church know how true they are. The Hope and Spencer congregations have also appreciated the pithy definition of anger by another monk, Abba Isaiah, who summarized it as quarreling, lying, and ignorance. And also, John Climacus's evocative bodily image in his statement that "the man who claims to love the Lord but is angry with his neighbor is like a man who dreams he is running."

I seldom quote from modern theologians in my sermons, although I'm often indebted to their scholarship, because I often find their language too theoretical to be of much use. The language of the theologians of the early church, however, is remarkably vivid, energized by metaphors so grounded in earthy reality as to still be effective after more than a thousand years. John Chrysostom, for example, one of the most learned men of the fourth century, often speaks in a way that is thoroughly accessible to country people today. "Pride is a rock," he said, "where wild beasts lurk that would tear you to pieces every day." In coyote country, that image has real meaning.

I have fun giving Chrysostom, old "Golden Mouth" himself, a good run in western South Dakota, but it's also serious business. After the accidental death of a young man that grieved the whole community, the kind of death that can test anyone's faith in God, I read in a sermon a portion of one of Chrysostom's sermons on Divine Providence. Imagine someone without the least notion of agriculture, he says, "observing a farmer collecting grain and shutting it in a barn to protect it from damp. Then he sees the same farmer take the same grain and cast it to the winds, spreading it on the ground, maybe even in the mud, without worrying any more about the dampness. Surely he will think that the farmer has ruined the grain, and reprove the farmer." The reproof comes from ignorance and impatience, Chrysostom says; only waiting until the end of the summer, he would see the farmer harvest that grain, and be astonished at how it has multiplied. So much the more, he adds, ever the consummate theologian, should "we await the final outcome of events, remembering who it is who ploughs the earth of our souls." I hoped it helped just a bit, to remind people that when the tragic, inexplicable events come, one of the hardest things to accept is that we don't have answers or explanations enough to cover the way they tear us up inside.

Chrysostom's metaphor of the soil of our souls made sense to the people in the congregations I was addressing, but to many in the world it might seem a contradiction. The popular mythology of our day, the one-sentence stereotype of Christians that you encounter everywhere, is that Christians are people who have always despised the earth. Most of us, Christians or not, were brought up to believe that "earth" and "soul" are distinct categories, thoroughly separate, and not to be mixed. All I can say is, many things were looser in the fourth century than they are in our uptight, narrow-minded age. And they're a lot looser now, out in western South Dakota, than in either the academy or the city.

June 9

EPHREM THE SYRIAN

The metaphoric poverty of the contemporary churches sends me back to an earlier time in Christian history, when Ephrem, the great theologian of the early Syrian church, wrote theology *as* poetry. The Incarnation was everything to him; frequently, Ephrem prays in a way made possible by the doctrine itself:

> *Have mercy, O Lord, on my children.*
> *In my children,*
> *Call to mind your childhood,*
> *You who were a child.*
> *Let them that are like your childhood*
> *Be saved by your grace.*

Ephrem's Christianity, as the contemporary scholar Sebastian Brock has remarked, is much more Semitic than Greek. A man after my own heart, Ephrem "avoids—indeed abhors—definitions, which he regards as boundaries that impose limit; his own method, by contrast," Brock says, "is to proceed by way of paradox and symbol."

Ephrem is a serious and orthodox Christian theologian—officially, a Doctor of the Church—but he does lead his readers into strange places. One of his hymns on faith includes a passage on God's efforts "to [clothe] Himself in our language, so that He might clothe us in His way of Life." Ephrem compares this, memorably, with a person trying to teach a parrot to talk by the use of a mirror.

In his own time, Ephrem had such a reputation for holy tranquility that one story told about him in *The Sayings of the Desert Fathers* concerns a prostitute who solicited him, mostly to see if she could tempt him to anger, for, we are told, no one had ever seen him angry! He asks her to follow him and, when they reach a crowded place, tells her that she may now do what she desires with him. Ashamed, she departs. We hear nothing more of the woman, though in many monastic stories concerning prostitutes, the tremor of shame that the woman feels at the monk's gentle rebuke proves to be the means by which she is able to change her life. This story gives us a glimpse into the ancient monastic attitude toward sexual honesty; or, as a later monk, John Cassian, put it, the goal of having anger subdued by chastity so that a monk "is found the same, day and night, the same in bed as in prayer, quite the same alone as surrounded by men," with absolutely nothing to hide.

That utter transparency was evident to Ephrem's contemporaries; they found in him a sage who had sensed the interconnectedness of all things and was gifted with the language to articulate it. I'm grateful to Brock for making available another ancient story about Ephrem. A venerable monk had a vision in which angels sent by God with a scroll full of writing were discussing who on earth to give it to. They finally said, "No one can be entrusted with it except Ephrem." The tale concludes: "It is said of Ephrem that when he was a boy he saw a dream, or a vision, in which a vine shoot sprang up from his tongue; it grew, and everywhere under the heaven was filled by it. It bore bunches of grapes in proliferation, and all the birds of the sky came and ate of its fruits; the more they ate, the more the bunches multiplied and grew."

Ephrem died at nearly seventy years of age in the city of Edessa, while caring for people during a plague.

SMALL TOWN
SUNDAY MORNING

At the worship services of Hope and Spencer there's a time after the sermon, and before the Lord's Prayer, in which people are asked to speak of any particular joys they wish to share with the congregation, or concerns they want us to address in our communal prayer on that Sunday, and also to pray over during the coming week. It's an invaluable part of our worship, a chance to discover things you didn't know: that the young woman sitting in the pew in front of you is desperately worried about her gravely ill brother in Oregon, that the widower in his eighties sitting across the aisle is overjoyed at the birth of his first great-grandchild.

All of this pleases the gossips; I've been told that on Sunday afternoons the phone lines in town are hot with news that's been picked up in church. For the most part, it's a good kind of gossip, its main effect being to widen the prayer circle. It's useful news as well; I'm one of many who make notes on my church bulletin; so-and-so's in the hospital; send a card, plan a visit. Our worship sometimes goes into a kind of suspended animation, as people speak in great detail about the medical condition of their friends or relatives.

We wince; we squirm; we sigh; and it's good for us. Moments like this are when the congregation is reminded of something that all pastors know; that listening is often the major part of ministry, that people in a crisis need to tell their story, from beginning to end, and the best thing—often the only thing—that you can do is to sit there and take it in.

And we do that pretty well. I sometimes feel that these moments are the heart of our worship. What I think of as the vertical dimension of Presbyterian worship—the hymns in exalted language that bolster our faith, the Bible readings, the sermon that may help us through the coming week—finds a strong (and necessary) complement in the localized, horizontal dimension of these simple statements of "joys and concerns."

For many years this aspect of our worship has also been strongly ecumenical. If your neighbor who's a Catholic, or a member of the Church of God, had a heart attack the day before and was flown to Bismarck in the air ambulance, you ask for people's prayers for him and his family. Our prayers also extend to those who seldom darken a church door. Not long ago, the congregation learned from one of his longtime friends that Bill O'Rourke had died. (Wild Bill to his friends, way back in his drinking days.) Most of us knew that he'd been failing in the Veterans Hospital in Sturgis for some time. I knew him casually, but missed him. An old-time cowboy—he broke horses for the U.S. Cavalry between the world wars—he was permanently bow-legged. In retirement he'd become a fixture at the cafe on Main Street; you could nearly always find him there, holding court. More rarely, I'd run into him outside. Bill would wait for someone to come by who would stop and admire one of the Ford pickup trucks from the early 1950s that he kept polished and in running condition. When his death was announced, a sigh ran through the congregation. All but the youngest members, and our pastor, had known him for years, and had their own Bill stories.

It was an odd moment. Bill's death felt like a loss, to me, to many people, but we also knew that our young minister would know nothing of him. The pastor was about to begin the intercessory prayer that follows this part of worship, when one of Bill's oldest friends couldn't resist saying, "You know, Bill paid me the first fifty cents I ever made, back in 1930." The minister smiled, but looked a bit nonplussed. He took a breath, as if to start the prayer. From a pew in the back of the church came a voice, "And I'll bet you still have it."

Of course we laughed for a good long time, before continuing with our worship; it was the kind of story Bill would have enjoyed. He didn't care much for church decorum, but he took some aspects of religion seriously enough. The last time I saw him was at the Lutheran church, where he'd come for the funeral of an old friend. Bill sat alone at the back of the church. "I wanted to make sure they gave him a good sendoff," is all he said to me, after the service. He was apparently satisfied.

When the minister finally got to say his "Let us pray," we were ready. We had been praying, all along. We had been being ourselves before God.

AT LAST, HER
LAUNDRY'S DONE

Laundry seems to have an almost religious importance for many women. We groan about the drudgery but seldom talk about the secret pleasure we feel at being able to make dirty things clean, especially the clothes of our loved ones, which possess an intimacy all their own. Laundry is one of the very few tasks in life that offers instant results, and this is nothing to sneer at. It's also democratic; everyone has to do it, or figure out a way to get it done. When I picture Honolulu's Chinatown, circa 1960, which I passed through daily on a school bus, what I smell is the open-air fish market, but what I see are the signs, mysterious to me then, that read "Taxi Dance Hall: Girls Wanted," and all the colorful laundry strung up between tenements. There was never a day without it. In any city slum, it's laundry—neat lines of babies' T-shirts, kids' underwear and jeans—that announces that families live here, and that someone cares. For some people, laundry seems to satisfy a need for ritual. A television commentator with a hectic schedule once told me that the best, most contemplative part of his day was early morning, a time he set aside for laundering and ironing his shirts.

My images of laundry abound. One that I've never seen but

love to imagine is that of Benedictine nuns in the Dakotas, in the days before Vatican II, when many of them worked in elementary schools, beating their black serge habits on snow banks to get the dust out. They tell me that the snow was good for removing stains. I picture the small clothesline that a friend has put up in her penthouse garden in Manhattan. For her, laundry is a triumph of hope over experience. "I grew up in the suburbs," she explains, "and my mother hung clothes on the line. This is not ideal," she admits, "but on a nice windy day, the soot doesn't fall."

Of course an attachment to laundry can be pathetic, even pathological, in a woman who feels that it's one of the few areas in her life over which she has control. More often, though, it's an affectionate throwback to the world of our mothers and grandmothers. We may be businesswomen or professors, but it's hard to shake that urge to do laundry "the right way," just like mama did. The sense that "laundry must not be done casually," as an arts administrator once told me, is something that seems lost on most men. She and her husband had reached an armed truce: he could do his own laundry but was to leave hers alone. She had grown tired of picking lint from his red sweatpants off her good blouses.

Many women have a "system" that is not to be trifled with. "You're hanging the underwear wrong" I was solemnly informed by a woman minister one day as we rushed to get her laundry on the line so that we could get to a meeting. She had a Master of Divinity degree from Princeton Seminary, but that's not where she learned that only a slouch would dare to use a dryer on a fine, windy summer day such as this in Lemmon, South Dakota, or that the fact was so obvious it could remain unspoken between us. She relegated me to the simple stuff, pillowcases and towels, but she kept an eye on me.

At St. John's, we had been housed in a block of small, elegant, but very livable apartments designed by Marcel Breuer, and clothes-lines were not permitted. The great architect found them "tacky," we were told, and visually distracting. It is good to be home, where I can hang clothes and air bedding on the line, and be as tacky as I like. I come by my attachment to laundry honestly. One of my first visual memories is of my mother pulling clothes from the sky; she had a line on a pulley that ran from a window in our row house near the Naval gunnery in Washington, D.C. These days, my mother lives in a neighborhood in Honolulu where her backyard clothesline is something of a scandal. But she's a Plainswoman at heart, and a clothesline is simple necessity.

Living in the house where she grew up, I've become pleasantly haunted by laundry. I'm grateful that I no longer have to pull clothes through a wringer, as my grandmother did for years. Her bottles of blueing gather dust in the basement; I haven't used them, but can't throw them out. But, like her, I wouldn't dream of using the electric dryer unless I have to. In March or April I begin to long for the day when I can hang clothes on the line again. Our winters are so long and severe in western South Dakota that we bank on the slightest summer joys; the scent of clothes dried out of doors, the sweet smell of sun on them.

I must be vigilant; sudden thunderstorms march across the prairie in late afternoon, making a mockery of clothes hung out to dry. Our winds can be so strong that clothes go flying. And during times of drought, there is sometimes so much dust in the air that line drying is impractical. Old-timers who recall the "Dirty Thirties" speak of seeing grasshoppers eat clothes right off the line, a sight I never hope to see, although I've thought about it in the springs and summers when we've waited months for rain.

My youngest sister once had a dream about a tornado that seemed an astute portrait of our parents: as the storm approached,

Dad wandered off to get a better look at the twister and Mom ran to get the clothes off the line. I recall running into my clergy friend one evening at a church supper. She'd been frantically busy with meetings all day and the next night would be conducting a wedding rehearsal. News of a death in the congregation meant that she now also had a funeral to prepare for, and this led us to talk of epitaphs. "I know what I want on my tombstone," she said. "At last, her laundry's done."

DREAMING
OF TREES

I have noticed in my life that all men have a liking for some
special animal, tree, plant, or spot of earth. If men would pay
more attention to these preferences and seek what is best to do
in order to make themselves worthy . . . they might have
dreams which would purify their lives . . . —Brave Buffalo,
Sioux, By THE POWER OF THEIR DREAMS

Jim Burden, the narrator of Willa Cather's *My Antonia,*
says of the Nebraska prairie to which he has moved from
Virginia that "trees were so rare in that country, and they had to
make such a hard fight to grow, that we used to feel anxious about
them, and visit them as if they were persons." He adds, "It must
have been the scarcity of detail in that tawny landscape that made
detail so precious."

Burden is speaking of the American frontier at the end of the
nineteenth century, but his words ring true for a prairie dweller one
hundred years later. The small town where I live, like most towns
in the western Dakotas, was plunked down on a treeless plain. Set-
tlement followed the path of railroad lines, not rivers, and nearly
all of the trees, like all the buildings, had to be planted. Photographs of our backyard taken in the 1920s, when my mother was
a child, offer a view of buttes, a stark horizon. No houses. No trees.
Even now, standing in the dirt alley to the east of our house, I can

look north, down a three-block length of hedges and trees, to open country.

My mother can remember when most of the trees on our street, and in the town itself, were mere saplings. My husband and I had to take down a lovely cottonwood a few years ago—it was crowding a basement wall—and a neighbor came by to mourn with us. He was five years old when that tree was planted; he's now in his seventies. It was strange to think that we were erasing a part of his childhood. My husband says that destroying that tree still makes him sad, that he imagined it to be like killing an elephant, something larger, wiser, and more mysterious than himself. I miss the tree for the marvelous play of light and shade it made on our kitchen windows in the late afternoon.

But it's folly to miss trees here, where as one friend says, out of a hundred things that can happen to a tree, ninety-nine of them are bad. A lengthy drought in the 1980s killed off many of the aging shelter belts around farm houses, as well as windbreaks in cropland that were first planted, with government assistance, in the 1930s. Though it's been a good conservation practice, I doubt that there will be money available to replant them. Like so many human institutions of the western plains, these rows of trees will simply fade away.

Even the monks at a nearby monastery, who have planted and tended trees here for nearly a hundred years, tend to be fatalistic about it. They work hard—one monk I know says that in his nineteen years at the monastery he's planted nearly a hundred trees—and on hot summer days it's a common sight to see a monk on a small tractor hauling a home-rigged tank that holds 1300 gallons to water trees in the cemetery, the orchard, the western ridge. But the monks also know that to care for a tree in western Dakota is to transcend work; it becomes a form of prayer, or as St. Paul said, a "hope in things unseen." Maybe that's why they're so good at it, so persistent in their efforts.

I marvel at the fecundity of a crabapple tree that my grandmother planted at the north edge of our backyard that has drawn four generations of children to its branches and tart, rosy fruit. I worry about the two elms just south of the garden plot, weakened by drought and then disease. Will we have the energy, the hope, to replace them? Maybe with cottonwoods, the Siouxland variety developed for this harsh climate. But most of all, when I dream of trees here, when I visit them, they are the trees out in the open, trees I can take no responsibility for but consider to be my friends.

One of my favorites stands at the edge of a large pasture on the outskirts of Mandan, North Dakota. A young, small tree—what kind I don't even know, but from the highway it looks like a burr oak—nudges a fence, its branches straddling the barbed wire. There it has persisted for God knows how long with one half of it in vigorous leaf, the other rubbed bare by cattle. There are no other trees in that pasture. This tree, like a tough little juniper that emerges from the lodgepole pines of the Slim Buttes, far to the south, to stand alone on a limestone outcropping, reminds me of an elegantly carved figurehead on a sailing ship's prow, riding magnificently the dry prairie winds that will one day help to tear it down.

Many such glimpses abide: a tall, leafy locust split down the middle by a lightning strike, a lone Russian olive standing like a sentry near a pasture gate, its black branches vivid beneath the shimmery leaves. I picture the large burr oak in a ranch family's yard; it's been pruned and shaped to a striking perfection. It's the one tree I know of here that would not look out of place on a New England village common. And I mourn what I think of as the political trees, an eerie landscape of waterlogged dead and dying trees just west of Mobridge and the Missouri River, casualties of the Oahe Dam. They make me treasure all the more the profusion of trees—willow, boxelder, elm, cottonwood, wild plums—in the vast Missouri bottomland at Ft. Yates, Cannonball, and Bismarck.

The immensity of land and sky in the western Dakotas allows for few trees, and I love the way that treelessness reveals the contours of the land, the way that each tree that remains seems a message-bearer. I love what trees signify in the open country. The Audubon field book describes the burr oak as "a pioneer tree, invading the prairie grassland," and I try to listen to what these "volunteers" have to say about persistence, the strength of water, seeds, and roots, the awesome whimsy of birds scattering seed in their excrement, casting not only oak but small groves of Russian olive in their wake. Cottonwoods need more water; their presence signifies ground water, or the meanderings of a creek. Sometimes, in the distance, you glimpse what looks like a stand of scrub brush or chokecherry bushes. But if you turn off the asphalt two-lane highway onto a gravel road, you find that what you've seen is the tops of tall cottonwoods standing in glory along a creek bottom, accompanied by willows.

Nearly every morning I walk past a young tree—some sort of locust—that signifies survival against all odds. Most likely it was stripped bare in its earliest years, when, every summer, a farmer mowed the roadside ditch for hay. But it lived on, a leaf or two surviving each year, until the farmer noticed it and decided to mow around it. It's now nearly seven feet tall, the only tree for hundreds of feet around. Standing alone at the very bottom of the shallow ditch, this clever tree catches what moisture it can. It feels natural for me to converse with it, in any season, in the light just before dawn.

I share with this tree years of mornings, a moonset so enormous and red I mistook it for a fire in the distance, an ice storm with winds so sharp I couldn't keep walking westward and had to return home. Years of painterly skies at dawn. Foxes on the run, cats on the hunt. For much of my walk I am as treeless as the land around me, but on my way back into town I pass a large grove, an entrance to a drive-in movie theater, long since gone. If the wind is up, the trees roar like the ocean. Sometimes sheep are grazing there, and even though I expect to see them, they startle me with their cries, which sound remarkably like those of a human infant. This past summer the grove was the haunt of kestrels, and I often watched them maneuvering in the sky, wondering what it would feel like to ride backwards, forwards, sideways on the currents of air.

Our trees, our treelessness is, as so much in life, a matter of perspective. One summer both my father-in-law and my mother were visiting. He was raised in New York State and couldn't get over the lack of trees. I think he found it terrifying, as many easterners do. My mother kept telling him that there were many more trees here now than when she was a girl, so many that the countryside seemed luxuriant. Maybe trees are a luxury here; the question then becomes, How many do we need?

My mother has told me that she first encountered the notion of a forest from the illustrations in Grimm's fairy tales. She wanted so badly to see a forest, any forest, that she would crawl under the lilac bushes that her mother had planted by the front door and pretend she was in the Black Forest. I used to pretend—I can no longer remember what—with the honeysuckle bushes in the first backyard I remember, in Arlington, Virginia. But I spent a lot of time with them, watching from my two-seat glider swing. The one great tree in that backyard, an elm, was a powerful symbol for me, a tree of family myth, because when I was five and my brother nine, he had used it to run away from home. Climbing out his second-story bedroom window to get away from a baby-sitter he disliked, he'd spent an afternoon at a neighborhood drug store, reading comic books. I remember looking up at that tree, after the great event, trying to imagine that freedom. I also examined the branches from the upstairs window and doubted that I'd ever have the nerve to make the leap.

We left Virginia when I was seven, and moved to Illinois. I lost the honeysuckle and the other trees of my early childhood—dogwood, magnolia, sassafras, sycamore, and the enormous weeping willow and white oak of a nursery school in the countryside where my mother had enrolled me. I have only faint memories of the fabled cherry trees of Washington, D.C., and suspect that my memories of the blossoms come mainly from having been told about them and looking at family photographs.

Beach Park, Illinois, just north of Waukegan, was still rural in 1954; I walked to a four-room country school. We lived in a small, new suburb on acre lots, where the trees were saplings. But across from our house was a ploughed field with an island of tall trees in the center. Oak, elm, aspen. It was good to know that the trees were there, a brooding, comforting presence just across the road.

The trees of northern Illinois were lost to me when we moved to Honolulu in 1959, and I learned a new vocabulary. Banyan. Hala. Koa. Bamboo. I loved (and still love) the long arbor of Punahou Street. But my favorite tree on all of Oahu was (and is) the magnificent spreading monkeypod of Moanalua Gardens. Even the stench and incessant roar of traffic on an encroaching freeway doesn't diminish its beauty. The other tree I came to love in Honolulu is the eucalyptus that stands by the wooden stairway of Old School Hall on my high-school campus, a building erected in the 1860s. It made me happy to study English in a building that had stood when Emily Dickinson was alive, and the stately tree, its bark variegated like a fragile nineteenth-century endpaper, seemed a suitable companion in that happiness.

I recall testing an ancient legend on the slopes of Kilauea, on the Big Island, with some high-school girlfriends. We picked several sassy, fringed blooms of the native lehua tree and, sure enough, were sprinkled with rain on our hike back to our lodge. I also recall harvesting bananas in our backyard, a process that involved arming myself with a machete and cutting down the entire tree—it is, in fact, a form of grass, a thick and pulpy weed. I shook out the spiders and let the tiny bananas, over twenty pounds worth, ripen in a paper sack. They're much sweeter than anything you can buy in a grocery store. Years later that experience rescued me. At a cocktail party in New York City a man recently returned from Brazil declared that the trouble with America was that you couldn't buy a decent machete. While I had no idea if the family machete was a good one or not, I was the only person in the group who'd actually used one, and what had been a dreary, sodden literary gathering became more interesting.

By the time I went to college, in Vermont, I had lost the language of deciduous trees. People had to name for me the maple, oak, sumac, and beech. I recognized birches from photographs and poems. As fine and fabled as it is, now that I've been on the Plains for over twenty years, New England foliage seems profligate to me, too showy. Here, in the fall, the groves of ash and poplars planted as windbreaks glow in a golden, Italianate light, and I feel as if I am in a painting by Giotto, or Fra Angelico. A dusty, spare, but lovely place in Tuscany, or western Dakota.

When, each December, I visit my family in Honolulu, I travel from the wintry Plains to what I call the green world. It is profligate to the extreme; in a yard not much bigger than my own is an enormous mango tree, and also lime, lemon, tangerine, pomegranate, pomelo, mountain apple, lichee, hibiscus, hala, lehua, plumeria, and Norfolk Island pine. Like many Hawaii residents, we often top a pine to make a Christmas tree.

After all of that, I find it an odd joy to return to winter, to a stark white landscape. And I dream of trees, wondering if sometimes I would rather dream of trees than have so many close at hand. Even when it means adjusting to a temperature more than one hundred degrees colder than in Hawaii, it's the dryness of the Plains that most affects me. My face and hands turn to tree bark. In the heart of winter the green world is dormant, not yet hoped for. Moisture is scarce—even our snow is dry—and the vast space around the bare branches of trees is all the more a presence.

This brings me back to where I began, with Jim Burden's reflection on scarcity. If scarcity makes things more precious, what does it mean to choose the spare world over one in which we are sated with abundance? Is this the spiritual dimension that Brave Buffalo leads us to? Does living in a place with so few trees bring with it certain responsibilities? Gratitude, for example? The painful acceptance that underlies Psalm 16's "Happy indeed whatever heritage falls to me"?

Monastic men and women tell me that one question that bites pretty hard in their early years in the monastery is why anyone would choose to live this way, deprived of the autonomy and abundance of choices that middle-class Americans take for granted. We're taught all our lives to "keep our options open," but a commitment to monastic life puts an end to that. It is not a choice but a call, and often the people who last in a monastery are those who struggle through their early years reminding themselves of that fact. One sister told me that it wasn't until she had entered monastic formation that the words of Jesus in John 15 had any significance in her life: "You did not choose me, I chose you."

Stark words in a stark environment. A monk in his early thirties once told me that he'd come to the monastery not realizing what a shock it would be to suddenly not have to compete for the things that young men are conditioned to compete for in American society—in his words, "a good salary, a cool car, and a pretty girlfriend. When all of that was suddenly gone," he said, "and held of no account, I felt as if my whole life were a lie. It took me years to find out who God wanted me to be."

What does it mean to become simple? I think of the abbey of New Mellary in Iowa, the walls of its church long plastered over, until the architectural consultant the monks had hired to help them remodel discovered that underneath the plaster were walls of native stone. The monks themselves did the work of uncovering them, and now the church is a place where one can sit and wait and watch the play of sunlight and shadow, a place made holy by the simple glory of light on stone.

What would I find in my own heart if the noise of the world were silenced? Who would I be? Who will I be, when loss or crisis or the depredations of time take away the trappings of success, of self-importance, even personality itself? Could the trees of my beloved Plains, or the lack of them, help me to know? The first monks read the earth as the work and word of God, a creation that was spoken into being. "Study fish," advises St. Gregory of Nazianzus. "In the water they fly, and they find the air they need in the water. They would die in our atmosphere, just as we would die in the water. Watch their habits, their way of mating and procreating their kind, their beauty, their permanent homes and their wanderings." Look, Gregory says, "at the bees and the spiders.

Where do their love of work and their ingenuity come from? Can you explain it and arrive at an understanding of the wisdom they point to?"

The wisdom of the few, struggling trees on the Plains, and the vast spaces around them, are a continual reminder that my life is cluttered by comparison. At home, an abundance of books and papers overlays the heavy furniture I inherited from my grandparents. A perfectly simple room, with one perfect object to meditate on, remains a dream until I step outside, onto the Plains. A tree. A butte. The sunrise. It always makes me wonder: What is enough? Are there enough trees here? As always, it seems that the more I can distinguish between my true needs and my wants, the more I am shocked to realize how little *is* enough.

Late one summer night, a front moves in and I awaken. A fierce wind stirs the trees. It's been hot for so long, I go outdoors to luxuriate in the newly cooled air. A friend from far away is sleeping in my studio, and it is good to have him as a guest, good to be a host, to be settled in at home again after our time at St. John's. I want to say the prayers that will protect our friend, give him needed rest. I want my husband's sleep to help him heal from the pain of recent surgery.

The trees that fan me are the fruit of others' labor, planted by an earlier generation of Plains dwellers who longed for trees to shelter them. The land resisted, but let them have these few. I am startled by something flashing through the trees. It is the Pleiades, all seven of them plainly visible to the naked eye. This is another's work, and a mystery. And it is enough.

MONKS AND
WOMEN

It is, of course, a tangled history. It was my experience of monks in the present day that first led me to suspect that the old stereotype of the woman-hating holy man was only part of the story. I so rarely met monks who despised women, or even seemed uncomfortable around them, that I began to wonder, and to read. I soon found that even in the unlikeliest sources, such as a book about ancient Syrian monasticism, which expressed itself in the most extreme forms of asceticism, there was much evidence that relationships between monks and women were often surprisingly open and free. Theodoret of Cyrrhus's *A History of the Monks of Syria* is not a book for the faint of heart. It reflects a time, to paraphrase an old Montana joke, when monks were monks and Arians were scared. The death of the heretic Arius, as depicted in this book, "his inwards dissolved and ejected with his excrement," is one of the most disgusting things I have ever read.

But in the midst of this praise of hermits "hoary in hair and hoarier still in thought," there is also a remarkable sweetness. Theodoret himself came to know the monks through his mother. She had gone to the cave of a monk named Macedonius to seek his prayers when she was trying to conceive a child. And when she was in danger of miscarriage, she sent for him to come and lay his hands on her belly and pray over her. Theodoret later recalls the old monk exhorting him "to live a life worthy of this toil."

When Theodoret was a boy, he and his mother went to visit several of the monks on a regular basis, which was possible to do because Syrian monks lived closer to cities than their Egyptian counterparts. Theodoret recalls of the monk Peter that "he often sat me on his knee and fed me grapes and bread: my mother [had sent] me to reap his blessings once a week." His mother had met Peter when, as a young woman afflicted with a disease in one of her eyes, she had sought him out for healing. As Theodoret says, she was then "at the flower of age . . . content with the adornment of youth," and she came to the monk wearing cosmetics, much gold jewelry, and an elaborate silk dress. The monk admonished her gently; "By supposing your body to require [all this]," he said, "you condemn the Creator for deficiency." It is a remark that might be interpreted as misogyny, but in the context of the story—the monk pleads that he is only a man with the same nature as hers, and has no special access to God—it is clear that the monk believes the woman to be made in the image of God, good as she is, without unnecessary adornment.

I thought of this story not long ago when a friend who is obsessed with her appearance developed an ugly and uncomfortable rash on her face, and she decided to deal with it by switching the brand of foundation makeup that she wears daily. I longed to say—why not let your skin breathe? I thought of Theodoret's mother and wondered if it was her cosmetics that had irritated and inflamed her eye, a common occurrence, even now. If so, the monk had doubly blessed her, in steering her toward psychological as well as physical health. As Theodoret writes: "In quest of healing for the body, she obtained in addition the health of the soul."

In many instances sterile women sought out these monks in the belief that their prayers would help them to conceive. And in one case a recluse, who would not receive a woman in the monastic enclosure, nevertheless takes pity on her when she pleads outside his door that her husband will have intercourse only with his concubine and not with her. Blessing a flask of oil that the woman has brought with her, he tells her to anoint herself with it. Theodoret writes: "Following these instructions, the woman transferred to herself her husband's love and induced him to prefer the lawful bed to the unlawful one."

If monks could only market this skill, no one would ever again accuse them of escapism or irrelevancy. It certainly does not contradict my experience of contemporary monks to find their ancestors so pastorally concerned with the problems of married women. One of the reasons that people still go to monasteries for help with their most intimate relationships is that celibate men and women often make remarkably good counselors in sexual matters, and in matters of the heart.

While few people today would expect a monk to go to the heroic lengths of the unnamed ascetic who appears in a fifth-century compilation of monastic stories, Palladius's *The Lausiac History,* it would not surprise me to find a contemporary monk acting in a similar way. Identified only as "the Compassionate Monk," he is said to have preferred, like many young monks today, not to be ordained to the priesthood. Rather, he lived a disciplined life of prayer in a city, and at night made the rounds of hospitals, prisons, and streets.

The impression we receive of the monk is appealing: "To some he gave words of good cheer, being himself stout of heart. Some he encouraged, others he reconciled; to some he gave bodily necessities, to others, clothing." One winter night the monk hears a woman cry out near the entrance to the church where he is making his customary prayers. On finding that the woman is in labor, Palladius relates that he "took the midwife's place, not at all squeamish about the unpleasant aspects of childbirth, for the mercy which worked in him had rendered him insensible to such things." Considering the blood taboos that many religions establish with regard to the reproductive systems of women, the monk's behavior is a radical act of charity. But in Christian monastic history, it is not that remarkable. Monastic stories often emphasize the primacy of love over legalism.

In Benedictine monasteries, it is often the demands of hospitality as set forth by Benedict—to receive all as Christ—that free monks to express the love of God in surprising ways. One monastery I know for a number of years hosted a regional meeting of the La Leche League. At first, the monks were startled by the sight of so many mothers breast-feeding in their refectory, but as one monk put it in the community newsletter, "It reminded us from whence we came." And at St. John's one spring, when the daughter of a couple at the Ecumenical Institute was toilet training, the monks found a way to help. The family came to Mass nearly every day, and normally the toddler was quietly attentive. Now, however, one of her parents usually had to take her to the bathroom during Mass. When the monks realized what was going on, and that the parents were using the nearest public bathroom, in the basement of the church, they invited them to use the one in the sacristy instead, which was much closer. It came to seem a regular part of the Mass, little Maria and her mom or dad making a dignified procession behind the monks' choir stalls. When I complimented one of the monks on the abbey's new apostolate of toilet training, he nodded solemnly, and then made a joke of it: "And why not? We do just about everything else here!"

For all of the happy stories—the stripper left stranded when her boyfriend tosses her luggage out of a moving car, who finds that monks are men who will give her food, lodging, sympathy, and access to a phone without expecting anything in return—when dealing with the subject of monks and women it is necessary to confront the specter of fear, the fear women have that monks hate and reject them, the fear monks have that women pose a threat to their celibate way of life. It is painfully obvious that one method of coping with celibacy has been to denounce sexuality itself, and that celibate men have often projected onto women the more demonic elements of their lust. The grief this has caused is incalculable. Imagine, if you will, an eleven-year-old girl publicly humiliated by a priest, who, angrily summoning her out of a parochial school classroom, tells her that she is an "occasion of sin" for a boy she's grown up with, who for years has been one of her best friends. Unfortunately for her, the priest has his eye on the boy as a likely candidate for minor seminary, and he tells her to leave him alone, that she is an evil influence.

Now that responsible voices within the Catholic church are calling for the ability to build and maintain friendships with both men and women as a *requirement* for priesthood studies, that priest himself might be called an "occasion of sin." As for the girl, now a married woman with teenage children, she has never gotten over being called evil on the verge of her adolescence. The hatred she experienced has turned into a lasting hatred of the Catholic church. Mention Thomas Aquinas in her presence, and she begins to sputter with rage.

Early monastic literature contains many tales of monks projecting their lust onto demons who appear in female form and advice to young monks regarding women in general that, while it may have served a practical purpose, also fueled the fires of misogyny:

"do not sleep in a place where there is a woman." "It is through women that the enemy wars against [the monks]." A much more complex picture emerges, however, where real women are concerned. When women approach monks for healing prayers for themselves and their children, they are not spurned but are blessed and prayed over. When Abba Poeman sees a widow mourning at a tomb, he speaks of her as someone from whom his young disciples might learn a spiritual virtue: "If all the delights of the world were to come, they would not drive out the sorrow from the heart of this woman. Even so the monk would always have compunction within himself."

Often, when real women appear in the monastic stories, the message for the listener does not concern sexual temptation so much as the commandment to love and not to judge. When Abba Ammonas goes to a cell of a monk of low repute, after hearing that he has a woman there, and that a crowd of monks is on the way to chase them out, he sees the monk hiding the woman in a large cask. When the crowd arrives they find Ammonas seated on the cask, demanding that they search the cell. His anger is reserved for the monks who would dare to judge another: "What is this? May God have mercy on you!" To the monk he says only, "Be on guard, brother."

After a woman accepts a dare that she tempt a renowned hermit in exchange for money, she appears at his door one night claiming to be lost in the desert. The monk allows her in out of pity, but when his lust is aroused he lights a fire, saying, "The ways of the enemy are darkness, whereas the Son of God is light." The monk spends the night standing at the fire, burning his fingers as a way to overcome his desire, and the woman watches, petrified with fear. In the morning, her friends come to find her, and the monk tells them that she is inside his cell, asleep. Instead, they find her dead. The monk says, "It is written, 'Do not render evil for evil,' " and he prays over her until she is restored to life. We are told that she goes away "to live wisely the rest of her life." Who wouldn't after a night like that?

I find it encouraging that there is a genre of monastic story that Columba Stewart discovered when translating fourth-century Egyptian material for his book *The World of the Desert Fathers,* stories which, as he puts it, "show how a tempted monk may come to recognize his confusion and learn that self-knowledge can free him from his obsessions." These stories depict women who "strengthened, rather than threatened, monastic vocations," and I value them for accurately portraying the world we live in, in which, as Stewart puts it, "relations between the sexes can be creative and maturing, even for monks, rather than inevitably dangerous."

My favorite of these tales is humbling, as is much true comedy. It puts lust in its place better than any story I know. A beautiful widow suddenly realizes that her husband's best friend has fallen in love with her.

> She was wise, and knew what was going on, and said to him, "Master Simeon"—for this was his name—"I see that you are thinking about something: tell me what you feel and I will reassure you." At first he was hesitant to speak, but later he confessed to her and pleaded with her to become his wife. She said to him, "If you do what I command you, I will accept." He said to her, "Whatever you command me, I will do." She said to him, "Go into your workshop and fast until I summon you, and in truth I will not eat anything until I call for you." He agreed, but she did not tell him a specific time when she would call for him.
>
> He went off for one day, then a second, then a third, and

still she did not call for him. But he persevered, either out of love for her or because God had arranged matters and provided him with endurance. . . . On the fourth day she sent for him. He had little strength, and being unable to come on foot due to his suffering, he had to be carried. She for her part prepared a table and a bed and said to him, "Look, here is a table and there is a bed: where do you wish to begin?"

We are told that the narrator is Simeon himself, who has long been a monk and remembers with great tenderness the conversation between himself and the widow, who had told him that "with the protection of Christ, I hope to remain as I am, a widow." He had replied, "Since the Lord has seen fit to oversee my salvation by means of your wisdom, what do you advise me to do?" and she suggested that he become a monk, and become "pleasing to God."

July 11
BENEDICT'S CAVE

All tribes have their origin stories; the Benedictines tell of emerging from a cave near Subiaco, Italy, where Benedict had lived as a hermit after leaving the city of Rome. Even after he had died, the story goes, the cave retained enough of Benedict's peace of soul to have a healing effect on those who came there. One of my favorite stories about St. Benedict in Gregory the Great's *Dialogues* concerns a woman who had lost her reason. She was wandering, Gregory tells us, "day and night over mountains, valleys, forests, and plains. She rested only where exhaustion had forced her to stop. One day as she wandered aimlessly, she came to the cave of the blessed Benedict and, without knowing what she was doing, entered and stayed there. In the morning when she left, her reason was as sound as if she had never been mad. And in addition, for the rest of her life, she kept the sanity which had been restored to her."

I must confess that I like this story of a cave far better than Plato's; it's been of much more use to me. I, too, have a mind that often wanders, that doesn't know where it is. And I have found that monasteries have a way of bringing me back to myself. I am back at St. John's for a week, attending the Monastic Institute and also the Feast of St. Benedict on July 11. I've been asked to join some other women in the schola for the feast-day Mass and am overjoyed to be singing again in a choir. (Back at home, the church choir takes the summer off.)

The talk at the Institute has been strikingly honest. One sister presented a paper in which she said that when she considered her monastic life, the feelings that came were "disillusionment, discomfort, low-grade anxiety, depression, uncertainty, loss, sadness, anger, and above all," she added, "dissonance; a keenly felt gap between the desire and the reality." She said that she wondered if too much talk in recent years of setting community goals, too many high-minded sentences about maintaining a balance between prayer, work, and recreation, had effectively allowed people to deny how far out of balance things have slipped. "We're always talking about balance and integration," she said, "a sign that we probably don't have it." Workaholism, she felt, was to blame. "The truth is," she said, "my best energy goes into work, and not into prayer, and it's been that way for years." She said she'd been impressed that parents in recent years had often proved resourceful about working part-time or inventing "flex-time" jobs in order to spend more time with their children. Why, she asked, shouldn't monastic people be willing to do the same to allow more time for prayer, solitude, reflection?

She'd touched on a sensitive issue, and discussion was remarkably frank and lively. "The ideal that we so often hear," one sister said, "is that monastic people are not defined by what they do, but I don't see us living up to that. The job, the profession, the career is the thing, especially for those of us who teach." A monk said that a running joke in his community is that the Benedictines should change their motto from "ora et labora" (pray and work) to "ora et labora et labora et labora." Another monk spoke up and said that he'd often thought that work had a tendency to destroy community life. "If we find our individual fulfillment in work," he said, "does that mean that common living has become merely a common residence, a common dining hall, a matter of convenience? What I'd hope for," he added, "is that we could find a common bond, common support for our diversity of work."

Comments were made about the danger of allowing economic necessity to destroy the rhythms of community life, so that at any one prayer service or meal, a number of people are missing because of work; and about the need to put principles first and let work fit into them, rather than the other way around. One sister in a presentation on the liturgy spoke eloquently about workaholism being a symptom of the desire to control and to fabricate our lives. She said, "I find that Benedictine liturgy counters that desire very well. It speaks poetry every day, and it is not productive.

"Our way of working should be different from the world's," she said, "and we can start by nurturing a biblical imagination. If you look at Genesis," she added, "when God works, God creates." She also discussed the element of play: "Wisdom," she said, "is created at the beginning of God's work, and is described in Proverbs as a 'master worker,' but also as God's daily delight. I interpret that to mean," she said, "that play is an essential part of work."

I thought about how listening to Genesis once in a monastery choir, I'd suddenly heard Adam's naming the animals as a form of play. God does not command Adam to name the animals; God brings them to Adam "to see what he will call them." This implies that God wants to be surprised and wants Adam to play along in the continual surprise of creation. While I don't know Hebrew, I suspect from what I've read about the language of the creation story that in its original tongue this scene is full of verbal play, little jokes that are intended to convey God's delight in every aspect of the created world.

The sister compared the Liturgy of the Hours to housework, as repetitive work that is never done, but work that Benedictines keep coming back to because it forms the individual person and also maintains the fabric of the community. "But to do this," she said, "we keep interrupting our own work." Benedict termed the monastery's communal prayer "the Work of God" and said that nothing is to be preferred to it. The example he gives in his Rule is of a monk or nun hearing the bell ring for the Divine Office and immediately setting their own concerns aside. "We come back to the hours of the liturgy," the sister said, "to remind ourselves of how God is working." She added that "like Wisdom itself, we are daily with God, playing with God in the world," and said she hoped that this would keep Benedictines from being overly oriented toward productivity and efficiency.

As usual in gatherings such as this, the response to the rather exalted language of the sister's remarks was to quickly turn discussion back toward the practical. "If we want to turn from our productivity model," someone said, "then we should stop calling what we do morning and evening prayer, which are functional terms. Their right names are lauds, which means praising, and vigils, which means waiting." A monk said, "As much as we know that scripture has the power to transform us, even monastic people have a hard time just sitting and being with scripture." And on and on it went.

The heady talk has been stimulating, too much so. It is good to be sitting in silence, in the great abbey church, waiting for the feast-day Mass to begin. I seat myself in the choir with the other women as the monks gather in the baptistry. Soon they will sing an ancient chant, claiming their heritage as Benedictines. Soon they will emerge from the cave and process down the aisle, two by two, in a cloud of incense. We will celebrate, which is something Benedictines do exceedingly well. And I will be strengthened by another joyful liturgy, something to remember when my mind wanders or sinks in the slough of despond. Something to come back to.

A GLORIOUS
ROBE

Morning prayer, which can feel like sleepwalking, has an expectant air this morning. The faces around the choir seem alert, less drowsy than usual. Two black habits lie neatly folded by the abbot's throne. After the opening hymn the abbot addresses the community: "My brothers, today we welcome Joseph and John into our community to begin the year of novitiate. Let us fervently pray that during this year of testing they may come to know more fully the God for whom we are all seeking."

We recite the psalmody as usual: two psalms, a canticle, a sung psalm. The scripture text that follows, from the Book of Sirach, is read by the abbey's director of formation, a lanky man with an affable air. "My son, from your youth choose instruction, and till your hair is white you will keep finding wisdom." The image takes on a special poignancy in this context; although there are a sizable number of young monks here, men in their twenties, thirties and forties, most of the community has gone bald or gray.

This is a community of Benedictine men, one of over a hundred monastic houses in the United States—single-sex, or more rarely, coed, Protestant or Roman Catholic—who follow a way of life set down by St. Benedict more than fifteen hundred years ago. An anachronism to some, an object of romantic illusion to others, these people seem to me admirable bearers of tradition into the contemporary world, incorporating in their lives the values of stability, silence, and humility that modern society so desperately needs and yet seeks so relentlessly to avoid. Today this monastery celebrates the addition of two young men to its numbers. They have been living with the monks for three months as candidates, and as the community has recently voted to accept them for a year-long novitiate, we're now engaged in a rite for the reception of novices, or what is sometimes called a clothing ceremony.

The reading from Sirach continues, warning that wisdom requires patience, discipline, and strength in the face of testing. But there's plenty of romance as well; romance, and a promise of good things to come: "Search out and seek, and wisdom will become known to you; and when you get hold of her, do not let her go. For in the end you will find the rest she gives, and she will be changed into joy for you." The reading concludes with an exalted image of clothing, of wisdom as clothing that no longer binds but frees and transforms us. "Her yoke is a golden ornament, and her bonds are a cord of blue. You will wear her like a glorious robe, you will put her on like a crown of gladness."

After the reading, the two young men come forward with the formation director into the center of the sanctuary where they stand, backs to the altar and facing the abbot, who asks them, "What is it you seek?" That's a fruitful question for any of us, one that resists an easy answer. The ritual answer is anything but easy: "The mercy of God and fellowship in this community." The words, like the hope they express, seem to hover in the air around us, climbing the vast upper reaches of the abbey church. It is an amazing thing to hear said aloud, at 7:15 in the morning, in front of well over a hundred people. Tears well up inside me.

In his ritual response, the abbot reminds the candidates that the monastery cannot grant them an easy or quick admittance. "We must first determine whether you truly seek God, and are zealous for the work of God, for obedience and the practice of humility. We must also tell you of all the trials and hardships through which we travel to God. Are you willing so to live in our community?" The young men respond, "I am." After a brief ritual of acceptance by the monks, the abbot says, "I offer you the habit of our Holy Father Benedict. As you wear it, see in it a reminder of our monastic heritage, a sign of our life together, and a pledge of our hope to be completely clothed in Christ." The young men kneel to receive their habits, and when they stand again, the formation director assists them in putting them on.

It can be an amusing sight to observe a man working slowly, with nervous fingers, to button, snap, and smooth a floor-length habit, scapular, and cowl over street clothes, right in front of God and everyone. It is also a solemn moment in the liturgy, and in the life of any monastic community. There are men here who first put on this habit more than seventy years ago, as well as those who began to wear it just last year. They have this in common: the hope that they will wear this monastic clothing until the day they die, and even after. They hope to be buried in it, in the cemetery just up the hill.

It was this thought that disrupted my revery, as I recalled an article I'd read the night before, in the *New York Times,* about fashion's current fad for "monastic" clothing. Entitled "Piety on Parade: Fashion Seeks Inspiration," and accompanied by a photo of a runway model in dark, flowing robes, a pectoral cross slung across her hips, the article was replete with fatuous statements by designers and retailers on the subject of the new "spirituality" of fashion. It's "a calming of the clothes," designer Donna Karan said, "the antithesis of power dressing."

The president of Saks Fifth Avenue admitted that the store had received some letters from customers, asking, "What is the significance of the cross?" "It isn't the easiest image for the consumer," she said, "and I think it's gone a bit overboard." The designer John Bartlett inadvertently provided amusement in monasteries across the country with his comment, "There's nothing sexier than a monk . . . they're so inaccessible." No one has yet suggested that fashion mavens consult Hans Küng on skirt lengths, or, for that matter, the significance of the cross.

It's easy to laugh, less easy to admit that the article not only annoys me but makes me sad. The beauty of this clothing ceremony is a fragile thing, even though monks themselves are fairly sturdy and have endured with their rituals through the depredations of many centuries. Real beauty is always both tough and fragile, and the way in which these people manage to give religious significance to something as necessary, as ordinary, as clothing gladdens my soul. I resent its misappropriation by the fashion industry, though I'm not concerned primarily with blasphemy, or even with the trivialization of religious imagery. Fashion designers are always trivial—that's what makes their pronouncements on the deeper meaning of their clothes so deliciously ludicrous—and they'll always appropriate whatever strikes their fancy. Traditional religious garb is elegant, and at the very least the new fashions are a relief from biker shorts worn under lace miniskirts.

I guess I'm sad for the rest of us. Even if we're not likely to be suckered into believing, as *Vogue* magazine breathlessly exclaimed last summer, "spiritual equanimity . . . is only a credit card receipt away," the fact that such a thing can be said at all should give us pause. Told (*Vogue* again) that the somber colors and clean, even severe, lines of the new fashions constitute "a burial for the conspicuous luxury of the eighties," we have to rely on brain cells battered for years by advertisers and politicians to recognize that this burial is false: we're expected to express our newfound austerity by engaging in still more consumption of ever more expensive clothing.

Christian monks have always been conspicuous by their dress but never concerned with fashion. A tale is told of one monk in fourth-century Egypt who sold even his treasured copy of the gospels. He said, "I have sold the book that told me to sell all that I had and give to the poor." His radical conversion, like the radical way in which monks continue to shape their lives around liturgy, prayer, and simple living, can show us what is possible when we pay attention to the discrepancy between what we want and what we need.

In his rule for monks, written in the sixth century, St. Benedict is concerned that they have enough clothing but not too much, a concept that is all but lost in American culture. We think of shopping as a recreational activity. The fierce Anglican recluse Maggie Ross has described the story of Sodom as a "mordant satire on the idolatry of the great shopping mall at the end of the Red Sea, the consumer culture that can inculturate religion only as commodity." Greed is at the heart of the story, greed expressed in sexual terms, which translates into rape. Consumerism is our idolatry, the heart of our illusions of power, security, and self-sufficiency, which translate into rape of the environment.

The fashion industry traffics in illusion, selling us images of the way we'd like to be. Any life lived attentively is disillusioning, as it forces us to know ourselves as we are. Benedictines consider this attentiveness to be best developed in the rough-and-tumble of community life, where one learns to put the needs of others before one's own. The God one finds there chooses to be revealed in other people: people we love and people we can't stand; people who are hard on us, who just might love us enough to demolish our complacency.

The two young men have traveled far to this moment of asking for "the mercy of God and fellowship in this community." One was a bank vice-president, the other a librarian. They now face a year of wondering whether the vow they've made today was salvation, sheer foolishness, or both. Although they'll no doubt complain about the cumbersome skirts and endure jokes about guys in long dresses, the clothing will help to make them one among many, indistinguishable from their brothers. It symbolizes their common goal, and is black to suggest a death to worldly concerns.

I wonder why I am weeping. For myself, I'm sure, and my concerns, which are all too worldly. Perhaps it is also that these few simple words can contain so much hope and trust. These men are fortunate to have found a community in which to say them. I am crying also because I was raised to believe that rituals were meaningless in the modern world, meant to be outgrown, like superstitions. I was educated to mistrust the rich ambiguity of symbols. Yet here is ritual and symbol that has meaning.

I wonder if the pace of modern life, along with our bizarre propensity for turning everything into a commodity, erodes our ability to think symbolically, to value symbols for their transformative power. This simple clothing ceremony, just one step in the formation of two monks, has nothing to do with the ephemera of fashion, and everything to do with that which endures. It reminds me that ritual and symbol are as necessary to human beings as air and water. They mark us as human, and give us identity.

WOMEN AND THE HABIT: A NOT-SO-GLORIOUS DILEMMA

Early in the Gospel of John, Jesus turns to two men who are following him, and asks, "What is it that you seek?" The answer he receives is ambiguous: "Where is it you are staying?" Jesus replies, "Come and see," and the men go with him and become his disciples. The question, "What do you seek?" is one that is asked at all monastic professions that I have attended, including the abbreviated ceremony at which I became a Benedictine oblate. The ritual answer varies from community to community, but runs something like this: "I ask that I may follow Christ and persevere in this community until death."

Such ceremonies mark all stages of entry into a Benedictine community, and on each occasion, a sign of the monastic vocation is received. A copy of the Rule of Benedict might be presented by the formation director as a woman enters the novitiate, keeping with Benedict's suggestion that people who ask to join a monastery have the Rule read to them so they'll know what they're getting themselves into. At first vows, the prioress might present a sister with a Benedictine medal, and at final vows the ring and/or pendant that will identify the woman as a member of a particular monastery. One striking thing about this process in most Benedictine women's communities these days is that the new member will receive no specifically monastic clothing. While most men's communities kept the Benedictine habit after the reforms of Vatican II, the women were quick to give it up.

The reasons for this reflect the complex history of Benedictine women in America, and their status (or lack of it) within the Roman Catholic church. Before Vatican II, while men received the habit and other signs of monastic profession from their religious superior (an abbot or a prior), women received theirs not from their prioress but from the local bishop. Often these ceremonies literalized "bride of Christ" imagery in ways that women found overbearing. "To join my religious community," one sister said to me, "I had to borrow my sister's wedding gown. This was a common practice. But it made me feel as if I were marrying the bishop!" Women also resented the fact that before Vatican II, men were able to use the habit primarily as a church garment, as many Benedictine men do today, but they wore street clothes underneath, and could take the habit off for travel, visits to the dentist, or farm work. The women did not have that luxury. "We were expected to do everything in our habits," one sister said, "from cleaning the kitchens and bathrooms to ice skating, teaching, cooking, milking cows, and driving a tractor. The situation lacked all sense," she said, adding, "It was both dangerous and unsanitary."

The men's Benedictine habit had the virtue of simplicity, consisting of a long-sleeved cassock-like garment, belt, scapular, and cowl, but the women's clothing was complicated, difficult to wear and to maintain. A slip made of cheap material with a wide black band at the hem. A sleevelet whose sole purpose was to avoid exposing the bare flesh of the arms, with elastic at the top and a cuff at the wrist that snapped onto the inner sleeve of the habit. The habit itself, long-sleeved and floor-length, usually made of black serge and later of dacron, and over it the wide belt of the cincture, and a floor-length scapular. For the head, a cotton cap that didn't show, upon which was attached a stiff linen coif which covered the ears and came under the chin, emerging as a kind of bib with 144 tiny pleats. (Sisters more or less affectionately refer to it as "the duck bill.") Pinned to the coif was a boxy headpiece made of linen, and later of plastic (which, one sister has told me, served very well as a dam for perspiration), to hold a half-veil that covered the back of the neck and a longer, full veil that came halfway down the back. I'm told that the one advantage women had with all of this garb was that they could get by with undershirts instead of brassieres.

The elaborate headgear of the old habit is especially resented by many contemporary sisters because to them it symbolizes a subjection to the authority of the church that monastic men were never asked to make. "The veil, in many traditional societies, and in some cultures today," one sister said, "is a sign that you're the property of your husband and no one else is to see you." Another said, "In the Roman Catholic tradition, the veil represents a patriarchal interpretation of 1 Corinthians 11:10. It was used to keep us covered, invisible, in place." Some women also found the experience of receiving the veil emotionally painful. One told me, "Having our heads shaved to receive the veil was so awful that my class of thirty-seven novices couldn't talk about it for months afterward. Even if one looked upon it as a cleanliness measure, or as renouncing all for the love of Christ, I could never put it together with the gospel. What ought to have been a day of great rejoicing," she said, "instead was a traumatic experience."

With sentiments such as these simmering beneath the uniform

image of the placid nun, it is not surprising that when the lid came off after Vatican II, it flew off with a vengeance. Many Benedictine sisters have explained to me that as other, more active religious congregations of women, founded not as monastics but as teaching or nursing orders, began to look, as Vatican II directed them to, at "both the charism of their founders and the needs of the present day," they felt that they had good reason to abandon the traditional monastic dress that they'd adopted along the way. These active orders sometimes called the process "de-monasticizing."

But for Benedictine women, the new situation proved a dilemma. The American church had long ago forced them into a mixture of contemplative and active religious life—the first Benedictine women who arrived in this country had been told that they would be cloistered nuns, as they had been in Bavaria, but soon found that they were expected to serve the growing immigrant population as teachers, catechists, or nurses. The women adapted, and like many other groups of Benedictine women who followed them, they served the church well for many years. But Vatican II and its aftermath led to an identity crisis. Were they monastic, or not? Contemplative nuns, or more active sisters? As one woman told me, "In all the ferment of meetings and talk of the late sixties and early seventies, we all too often got caught up in the fervor to be 'with it,' and let a lot of our living monastic traditions—somehow distilled in the habit—fall by the way."

When Benedictine women speak of those days now, it's often with bemusement. I can scarcely imagine the situation they found themselves in; having been made to dress uniformly for all of their adult lives, they were now, as one sister put it, "free to be me, at all costs." She says of a friend in graduate school, "Her first fling was to make herself a kelly green habit, complete with veil." Other sisters have told me about the confusion of shopping for clothes for the first time. One woman was seduced by an expensive, laven-der silk slip in a store window, but having bought it, felt too guilty to wear it. Years later she finally gave it away, glad to have it off her conscience.

Unfortunately, the habit came to symbolize for many Bene-dictine women one's political stance with regard to the Vatican II reforms. "The politics and conflict between factions in the early re-newal period was something else," one nun told me, adding that because the habit had symbolized so much of the old order, it quickly became a pawn in these political struggles. "This is what makes it difficult for sisters to discuss the habit without rancor, even today," she said. In 1969, she wore the full habit as a graduate stu-dent and a part-time cab dispatcher. "In New York City," she said, "anything goes, so I never felt out of place." But when an older sis-ter who was visiting told her that the community back home had essentially split into two factions, labeling people as liberal or con-servative over whether or not they wore the habit, the younger woman said, " 'A plague on both their houses.' We were on a noisy subway," she explains, "and my sister was hard of hearing. I shouted out, *'A plague on both their houses!'* just as the car screeched to a halt and everyone could hear me."

Great diversity of opinion with regard to monastic dress still exists among Benedictine women. One former prioress dismissed the habit by saying that she felt it had become a crutch, a prop for many women in her community. "They were not mature enough to stay in monastic life without it," she said, adding, "It had be-come a form of protection." Another prioress—who believes that distinctive clothing is "an essential part of the monastic archetype, in Buddhism as well as in Christianity," and that "to take it off di-minishes the monastic impulse"—also says, "We had to take it off and dump the medieval baggage that went with it." A nun who does wear a habit—a plain long-sleeved dress with a long skirt, scapular, leather belt, and simple veil—says, "I believe that sisters who work for a secular agency, such as a school, are better off in lay dress. The sweet, stupid nun look had to be radically thrown off. But as for a monastic life, I think serious monks wear a habit."

The history is compelling. One sister wrote to me, "In the ancient world, to 'take the habit' meant to become a monk." Benedict received a habit from the hermit Romanus, and habits were worn by the earliest monks known to us, such as Anthony and Pachomius of Egypt. The scholar Peter Brown notes that in the early church monastic dress was so recognizable that small children in Egypt had a game of "monks and demons," with one child dressed as a monk in black being harassed by other children playing demons. What people today think of as the traditional Benedictine women's habit comes not from this early era, but from the medieval period. As one sister explained it to me, "It was the dress of the poorer classes, adopted precisely because it did not distinguish monastic women from laywomen."

For her, and for many other Benedictine women, the motivation behind wearing distinctive monastic dress is of prime importance. They're wary of the romance of the habit that still attracts women to more traditional communities. When I showed her what one such woman had said about her clothing—"the cord reminds me that I am bound to my Redeemer in poverty, obedience, and purity, the veil echoes my choice to be sanctified for God's purposes, and that in my life I am to be modest and obedient to God's Word"—she sensed without my telling her that the woman was new to the religious life. The younger woman's statement, "I have made a radical choice of lifestyle, and believe that I am responding to a call from God to live this way," did not surprise the older woman. "This is exactly the danger," she said. "Clothing ceremonies and the habit help to form a person in monastic life—for instance, the prayers said over each piece of clothing as you put it on—and some symbols and rituals are essential in binding us to a community. But they can also give younger members a dangerous sense of security, of being special, separate, elevated to a new level of holiness automatically without doing the long, hard, tedious work of conversion." In monasticism it's always a struggle to maintain a balance between the symbols and practices a person needs to be formed in the life and those that tend to become ends in themselves.

One Benedictine woman summed up for me the reason why the subject of the habit remains important, even for women who have never worn one (this would include women entering most Benedictine communities from the early 1970s on). "I suspect that behind the issue of the habit," she said, "are different, perhaps even warring, theologies, worldviews, and understandings of monastic life. Different assumptions about how one follows the gospel. Is holding to traditions like a medieval habit always an authentic reflection of the gospel?" Like many Benedictine women I've talked to, she feels that while some form of religious garb might be appropriate, it should not be something as "totally alien" as the old habit. "I think we can express our identification with the rest of the body of Christ," she says, "and with the poor of the world, in other ways than as an elite group receiving special treatment by virtue of our dress." She and others have said that in their experience what was meant to be a symbol of renunciation frequently was its opposite in the pre–Vatican II church, and they and other sisters were using the habit to get special favors, such as free movie tickets and ice cream cones. "That's when I decided to change," one said.

But wearing a habit was always a renunciation in that it publicly identified you as a nun, forcing you to give up any sense of privacy. As one sister told me, "The habit totally objectified you. You became all nuns. Some men would be turned on, and sexually proposition you. Or a drunken businessman on a plane would slobber all over you, and say, 'You sisters are so good, you made me what I am today.' Someone who was beaten by a nun in third grade might call you a sadist." One woman told me that when she was a novice in the 1950s, she'd been asked to escort an older nun to the doctor. As they boarded a bus in their Minnesota city, a man, his face contorted with rage, his fists clenched, came up close to the women and hissed, "Lesbians!" The older woman, who was hard of hearing, hadn't heard the remark, and, the sister told me, might not have comprehended it if she had. But she had seen the hatred in the man's gesture and it frightened her. Perhaps this incident, and the anonymous hate mail and obscene phone calls that Benedictine women sometimes receive, indicates that when a woman stands for anything in this culture she makes herself a target.

I've long been interested in the fact that most monks I know wouldn't dream of wearing their habit for travel, and many who are priests won't even wear a clerical collar. "I grew weary of hearing so-called confessions from drunks," one monk told me. Some women who wear a habit in public are resigned to the more troubling aspects of the experience. "I think I would be recognized anywhere as someone consecrated to God," one wrote to me. "I may not get a positive response," she said, "but that's what I stand for." Another woman, a member of an urban monastery, feels strongly that the public witness of the habit is important, as it offers her possibilities for ministry that otherwise would be lost. "The airline ticket agent who asks me to pray for her and her husband. The young father on a city bus, deeply troubled by burdens he cannot voice. The well-dressed woman on Madison Avenue [who] looks around as she asks for prayer, hoping no one she knows sees her doing this odd thing, and yet aching for some companionship and support in her trouble. Two teenagers dressed in the latest fashion, who want to know why some people who work in the church do unkind things, and what they can do about it." She said that while she'd been active in her church before joining the monastery, "No one ever stopped me on the street to ask me for prayers. This was not because I was not a woman of prayer, but because no one could tell that I was a woman of prayer."

To be accepted in public as "a woman of prayer," must a woman cover her entire body, head to toe? It would seem so, given the sexualization of women's bodies in our culture, the bizarre idolatry of body parts. But many Benedictine sisters feel that the asexuality of the old habit contributed to unhealthy attitudes about the body, both among themselves and in the broader culture. "We are no longer embarrassed to be recognized as women," one sister said, "with women's bodies, made in the image of God." But as always, with the issue the habit, there is a double edge. One sister told me that "some sisters feel that to express themselves as women, they need to wear bright colors, make-up, and jewelry, but I have a hard time with this. Even if we're not spending much money, the fact that our nice clothes are hand-me-downs or from the second-hand store isn't obvious to others. I wonder if we've bought too much into what society holds up to us as beautiful and acceptable in a woman." As for herself, she said that she found herself increasingly drawn to simple, inexpensive clothing, denim skirts and dresses, more black and white and fewer colors. This seems to be something of a trend among Benedictine women. One order of contemplative nuns has adopted, at least for the younger members I've met at conferences and at the St. John's graduate school, a form of dress that strikes me as extremely sensible for monastic women. For situations that demand it, such as ranch work, hiking, canoeing, or touch football games, they wear jeans and a sweatshirt. Otherwise they dress simply in black and/or white, in modest dresses, skirts, blouses, and jackets. They wear a ring and stylized cross designed for their community that marks them as religious women, but their clothing does not disguise the fact that they are women.

A Benedictine friend, a college professor who hasn't worn a habit in many years, recently spent a lengthy retreat with a cloistered community of women who wear the traditional floor-length habit and head gear. Her comments summarized the ambivalence many contemporary monastic women seem to feel. "I see lovely women . . . looking like many of the holy women of the past. There is something beautiful about that connection with the past, and something inaccessible and mysterious about them in their habits. They really do convey another world. At the same time, I also see the hiding of the body, as if they are asexual beings, and I sense denial in this. I see continuity with the way those holy women of the past were confined by their gender."

There seems to be a groundswell of feeling among many Benedictine women that they need some form of habit, if only for use in liturgical celebrations. One women's community in which most sisters gave up the full habit years ago (although many women still wear a simplified veil and black or white clothing) recently added a brief clothing ceremony to their "Rite of Perpetual Profession." Along with other traditional symbols of monastic life, the prioress hands the sister a cuculla (literally, "little tent," so called because it is a mass of pleats falling from a yoke). This long, black robe, ancient monastic dress, is the ancestor of all pulpit gowns, and the women wear it for Sunday liturgies, major feasts, profession ceremonies, jubilees, and funerals. Several women in the community have told me that they enjoy this restoration of a link to their monastic past and the visible sense of communal identity that it gives them. I wouldn't be surprised if other Benedictine women adopt a similar practice. "We need something," one sister says, "but we can't let it become something to hide behind." Another woman wrote to me, "There seems to be a deepening sense of what it means to be monastic, of the life force in a tradition that has perdured through the centuries. We've talked so much about simplicity and now we ache to see it more deeply realized in our everyday lives. And, I wonder, if as individualism wears a little thin, this movement to reclaim monastic dress may strengthen. Not a 'going back to the habit' but a going forward to reclaim it."

I've long been aware that the subject of the habit generates in Benedictine women an emotional response that, before I understood more of the history, seemed out of proportion to the subject at hand. In a way I find it reassuring that monastic women have not been able to escape the dilemma all women live with. No matter what they wear—a traditional habit or a simplified one, blue jeans or a professorial navy blazer and pleated skirt—they, much more than men, are defined by what they wear. People will take them seriously, or not, based on matters as slight as the length of a skirt or the height of a heel. I am most interested in monastic dress as a form of renunciation, a sign that one is not preoccupied with fashion and possessions. And I recognize, as one sister said to me, that monastic women "can accomplish this without resorting to an outlandish form of clothing," or as she put it, "an elaborate, expensive, cumbersome habit that is time-consuming to maintain."

I once visited a sister who, next to a shelf that held socks, underwear, and a sweater, had all the clothing she owned hung on several pegs: her spare habit and scapular, both made of denim, a simple kerchief she wore as a veil, a long winter cloak and a light-weight one for spring and fall. It took my breath away. "Thank God for the things that I do not own," said Teresa of Avila. I could suddenly grasp that not ever having to think about what to wear was freedom, that a drastic stripping down to essentials in one's dress might also be a drastic enrichment of one's ability to focus on more important things.

THE GREGORIAN
BRAIN

*It was not without reason that the ancestors and prophets wanted
nothing else to be associated as closely with the Word of God
as music . . .*—Martin Luther

Let us sing a new song not with our lips but with our lives . . .
—St. Augustine

Recent neurological research has shown that in religious
rituals from around the world, poetry is generally chanted
with a pulse of between two and four seconds, a pulse that the re-
searchers now believe to correspond to an internal system in the
human brain. This system, epitomized by the traditions of Gregorian chant and plainsong in the Christian West, seems to help
integrate the workings of the right and left hemispheres of the brain
in processing information. As a contemporary monk has written,
this may explain why "the ritual chanting of sacred texts con-
tributes in a unique way to a profound, largely subliminal, ab-
sorption and engagement having many more dimensions than
mere rational understanding." It also might help explain the current popularity of Gregorian chant albums among people who
have very little ritual life, or who have grown weary of what the
monk terms "poor talkative Christianity."

Monastic people have long known—and I've experienced it in a small way myself—that the communal reciting, chanting, and singing of the psalms brings a unique sense of wholeness and order to their day, and even establishes the rhythm of their lives. This is why they keep going back to choir, even though it may seem monotonous. This is why Benedict termed the Liturgy of the Hours the "Work of God," why Benedictines today still speak of it as the foundation stone on which they build all the other work that they do. Now it seems that their conviction has a neurological basis in the brain itself.

The scientists have also confirmed what Thomas Merton knew from experience, that "Gregorian is good, and it heals." I know from my limited experience of singing chant that it fosters faith; I believe better and more thoroughly when I'm singing it. Like so many elements of monastic life, Gregorian is a matter of focus. It teaches us what we gain when we become simple, dependent upon the beauty of the unadorned human voice. It teaches us what we lose, in music, when we add a melody and a beat. It also fosters an appreciation for community. Gregorian can't be sung alone; you need people who are willing to blend their voices in such a way as to sound like one voice. In practical terms, Gregorian makes you extremely grateful for the other people who are singing with you. When you hit a note feebly, making more a groan than music, someone else will cover for you. When the time comes, you'll do the same for them. When you need to take a breath, someone else will keep going, making a continuous flow. The flow of Gregorian music reminds me of the pulse of ocean waves, steady and incessant, but never superfluous, a satisfying sound that may swell unpredictably before ebbing back into silence. It is a music in harmony with the body, and with the universe itself. It is also, always, praise of God.

Music is serious theology. Hildegard of Bingen took it so seriously as a gift God made to humanity that in one of her plays, while the soul and all the Virtues sing, the devil alone has a speaking part. The gift of song has been denied him.

O Z

It is the eve of the Assumption. Neither virgin nor mother, I lie by the vigil light of the electric alarm clock and dream of walking to a city through a field of flowers, Dorothy on her way to the Emerald City. A crescent moon rides high in the East, and Orion lays down his sword.

A place to be: this womb of stars, this windy dawn. Fir trees begin to sift the light, their branches hung with gold. The pregnant cat sleeps in the shadow of the abbey church.

The building itself, with towers and turrets rising dramatically out of the Plains, has always reminded me of Oz. And the monks in their robes do have the air of the wizard about them; they remind me to "pay no attention to the man behind the curtain," but to focus on what lies beyond. The monastery has been a haven where I could come and stay awhile, and work things out; the monks will not surrender Dorothy.

It was here that I first learned of the baptism of desire, and the gift of tears, the purifying tears that the ancient monks said could lead us to the love of God. Once, when a little girl in a small town nearby, staring at the bright red boots I often wore to work with children in schools, asked me, "Do you live in a country?" I told her we lived in the same country. She looked dubious. But as I thought about it, the real answer came—it's our secret country, where evil spells are broken by a promise of love, and little girls can melt away the wickedness that's in them.

GENERATIONS

Once, when I spent Holy Week in a community of Benedictine women, I ended up working in the bakery with an older sister. It proved to be a happy arrangement for both of us. I'd been writing at home, so reclusive that my life there had been much like a silent retreat, and I found that the strenuous work of baking for more than two hundred women, and the sister's good company, were exactly what I needed. I had first visited the monastery bakery out of curiosity and was offered chicory coffee and a sweet roll. But it seemed that with all of the extra baking the sister had lined up for Holy Week, she needed help far more than tourists. I volunteered, and soon was working with her from 5:30 in the morning until noon or so, with time out for morning prayer at 6:30 or 7.

I was slow to learn the sister's method of forming cinnamon rolls, but I tried hard and she let me try. I soon learned that there was a right way to do everything, even flattening and storing twist ties. Had I been a much younger woman, a monastic novice only recently separated from parental authority or graduate school, this might have been hard to take. But I know so many women who have "sacred ways" around the house—I think of how I am about laundry and my own baking—that I surrendered. I felt a bit like an explorer, though, never quite knowing what wonder would next be revealed. How to pinch dough. How to fold plastic bags. Strong as she was, the sister's not a young woman, and she was happy to let me wash the heavy mixing bowl with a minimum of instruction. I learned a bit about her; a Louisiana native, she seemed shocked to find herself in Kansas—"Why, the ground here," she scoffed, "it's nothing but clay. And they don't know how to till it," she added. "They just scratch at it like chickens." Her mother died when she was small, and she was raised by a grandmother. She still misses the cat she left behind in Louisiana; her monastery there had closed, and this is where she had chosen to come.

We worked well together, although she found me a bit clumsy in removing bread from the hot loaf pans. Still, we were mostly in tune: "Kathleen, come in here and help me think!" she called once from the oven room, and I was quick to obey. On Holy Saturday, we baked forty-five pans of cinnamon rolls. The caramel sauce burned our fingers as we struggled to place the hot rolls on waxed paper. "It's enough to make you lose your religion!" the sister exclaimed, and I replied, laughing, "Oh, anything but that! Not today."

I was well aware that even though I was working, I was still a guest in the monastery, which meant that I was being treated with deference. Still, I wondered if I weren't experiencing, in a limited sense, a kind of monastic formation. The newest members of a community are usually made to work with older ones, to subject themselves to the authority of a monk or nun of an earlier generation who may or may not be sympathetic to them, who may or may not share their interests, hobbies, or political opinions. What the two of you do come to share is a fabric of stories about people, living and dead, that make a living history of the community. And you are daily adding to it.

Monastic storytelling is a form of gossip, and like the best gossip, it often serves a moral purpose. The stories that circulate often reveal the dangers inherent in the monastic way of life. Monks and nuns are not all sweetness and light—they're ordinary human beings—and I've been told by Benedictines that one of the greatest dangers in monastic life is to succumb to pettiness. Often it is the old in whom the fault lines are revealed, and others tell their stories wonderingly, both as cautionary tales and as humbling reflections on human frailty. There was the monk who became obsessed with how much toilet paper others were using; there was the sister who insisted on seeing her prioress, who had just returned from a grueling trip overseas, only to complain that some people were taking two hot dishes at dinner, both the meat dish and the vegetarian.

When younger monks and nuns tell stories about older ones, it is often with great pride and affection. I'm always finding out things I didn't know about the ministries that the "retired" members of a community have quietly practiced for years: that this sister spends some time every day recording books for the blind; that this brother makes frequent visits to the nursing home down the street. But sometimes the young take pride in the eccentricities of their elderly confreres, and the stories they relate are just plain funny. A young sister tells of being sent, with other novices, to search on foot for a car that another sister had lost. "She knew she couldn't drive any more," the sister explained. "But sometimes she'd forget, and she'd take a car and drive it out in the middle of the prairie and then walk home, forgetting where she'd left it." The sister is not making fun of the older woman, and this is understood by her audience, other Benedictines and oblates. She's making fun of herself; a former bank officer, she never imagined that a call to the religious life would lead her to wander over a prairie in search of a lost car, but why not, if this is what it takes?

A prioress tells of visiting a sister who was thought to have Alzheimer's. "We'd put her name in big letters on the door of her room, hoping that she'd remember it was her room. Sometimes she'd get stubborn, and wouldn't want to go in. The doctor had told us to ask her questions frequently, and once, when I was visiting, I asked, 'Sister, do you know who I am?' She became indignant," the sister tells us, "and shouted at me: 'Well! You look old enough to me! If you don't know who you are by now, I certainly can't help you!'"

I toss my own story into the conversation, about knitting a shawl for an elderly sister. When I presented it to her she held it close, happily exclaiming. "Oh, it's blue and green! I do love green!" She sighed and confided, "I get so tired of black." Others in our group had stories of this sister, who was known for wonderful remarks. A monk from a neighboring monastery told us that when she was well into her nineties and in declining health, she once asked him if he thought that God had simply forgotten about her.

Stories from a monastery's more remote past are less a historical record than a repository of habits, hobbies, and trivia—like the attic of an eccentric aunt or uncle who never threw anything away. Over the years I'd heard stories of the two sharpshooters at one abbey who kept up an informal competition—one would shoot from an upper floor window, putting holes in a bucket of milk that the other was carrying up the hill—but I never believed them until I saw the impressive case of shooting medals in the dusty little abbey museum. I want to believe the story about the grave-side service that one of them once provided in a parish. When a rat was spotted at the bottom of the grave, the monk reached under his vestments for a pistol, shot the rat, and completed the service.

I know that there are stories behind everything in the museum: the seeds kept in tiny vials labeled in faded ink; the animals stuffed by a local taxidermist; the ballpoint pen collection that a monk is still adding to (all the pens have business logos, most of them from area businesses that have long since closed their doors); the wooden device that makes a hideous clacking noise, which was used in the abbey years ago as a crude alarm clock; the mannequin of a boy in slacks and a school jacket from the school the abbey closed in the 1970s; the mannequin of a girl in a tropical print blouse and a hula skirt. She may simply be one of the mysteries of the universe, but chances are, someone in the monastery knows the story behind her.

Sometimes being a guest in a monastery feels to me like falling, comfortably, into a den of playful storytellers. Monastic living gives the raconteur plenty of opportunity to refine the art. "The last time someone shot at me," Fr. Francis says slowly, in his customary growl, "was in Iowa." He has our attention, of course, a group of monks and guests who had been discussing the hazards of walking outdoors during hunting season. Francis puffs contentedly on a cigar. "A cornfield," he says, finally. "I was behind a little rise. I stood up and said to him, 'I wish you wouldn't do that.'" And once, during my year at St. John's, I found myself in the waiting room of the doctor's office, a young woman doctor who serves the community of over two hundred monks, and whose medical specialty, naturally, is fertility in women. I was nervous because I was to find out if a knee injury I'd sustained in a fall had resulted in cartilage damage, but my fear was dissipated by the monks in the waiting room, two men in their eighties. The sight of a younger woman with a cane, and the story of my accident, trig-

gered all sorts of stories in them, about falls they'd had, the falls
that monks of community legend had sustained. It was an impressive collection: falls off roofs and falls from trees, falls over tree
roots in the woods, falls into quicksand, or the lake. The two were
wily, cagey, telling stories about each other that had obviously
been well-polished over the years. "He fell down once on the ice,"
one said, pointing to the other, "and he lay on the frozen lake for
over an hour before anyone found him, and in all that time he never
had one pious thought!" "No, no," the other one said, "you've got
the story all wrong . . ." A younger monk who was leaving the clinic
stopped to ask me how I was, and if there was anything he could
do for me. Gesturing to the two older monks, who were still ar-
guing amicably between themselves, I said, "Look at the company
I'm in. I'm not only fine; I'm in heaven!"

Heaven, of course, is the point of monastic life, and sometimes
the stories Benedictines tell reflect the tragicomic ways in which
we set rigid boundaries in our lives, only to have the prospect of
eternity open them wide. Some Benedictine women I know relish
the story of a monk, now deceased, who had spent considerable
energy in the pursuit of misogyny, making life miserable for the
sisters who taught with him at their small college. Much to everyone's surprise, however, in his old age he turned out to have a well-
developed shadow side. One day the abbot received a call from the
abbey nursing home; the monk was weeping inconsolably, and although he was in failing health, there didn't seem to be anything
drastically wrong. The abbot had some difficulty ascertaining what
the problem was and was startled when the older monk, still weeping copiously, blurted out, "My wife died." The monk had been
celibate all of his life, but the abbot was able to assure him that he
would meet his wife one day in heaven, and the man calmed down.
A story Jung would have loved, one that the sisters tell me con-

firms their belief in God's sense of humor, and a story that has now passed into the living memory of two monastic communities.

In any traditional society, stories are where the life is, where those in the present maintain continuity with those in the past. In the monastic tradition, from the fourth-century desert on, it is the stories that pass from monk to monk, long before they're written down, that have helped preserve the values, and the good humor, that lives on in the monastic charism.

M O N A S T I C
P A R K

Monastic humor is an acquired taste, so much so that monastic people themselves often spend a lifetime acquiring it. When I spent a week in a monastery as a reward for surviving my first book tour, the first person I encountered when I arrived was a dear friend who asked me what a book tour was like. I told him it was exhausting, and hard work, but not nearly as bad as I expected. "Maybe you were just too dumb to notice what was really going on," he said, poker-faced, and I hugged him and said, "I knew there was a reason I missed you guys."

The jokes continued. At vespers that night I discovered that the monks were reading from a desert mother, Amma Syncletica: "Just as a treasure that is exposed loses its value," we heard, "so a virtue which is known vanishes; just as wax melts when it is near a fire, so the soul is destroyed by praise." After weeks of interviews, an alarming amount of attention and praise, I'd just been kicked in the shin by a fierce fifth-century nun, and could only laugh at the delicious synchronicity that had brought us together.

The juxtaposition of the ancient and the modern in monastic life often helps monks to laugh at themselves. Not long ago a story circulated about a bear who had broken into a contemplative monastery in a remote wilderness while the monks were in church. The bear ransacked the kitchen, and probably would have left the living quarters alone, except that one monk had squirreled away a piece of chocolate in his room. "Private property, the old bugaboo," one monk said. "Maybe we need a new desert saying: 'If you try to hide a piece of chocolate, God will send a bear to find it.' " Another monk told me that in a recent excavation of a fourth-century monastery in Egypt, a small pile of gold coins had been found under one monk's bed. "There is no hiding anything in this life," he said, shaking his head, "but monks will always try."

Monks are quick to seize on the humor of their situation with regard to the rest of the world. Their habits, while they symbolize the serious matter of a religious vocation, do have a comical side. I once witnessed monks using their scapulars in an impromptu fly-swatting competition. And the long skirt can be quite a look on a man. Once, when I happened to compliment a monk on his choice of attire—he'd put a heavy sweater on over his habit—he struck a model's pose, hand on hip, and said, "Yes . . . classic, yet casual." I once witnessed several teenage girls staring moon-eyed at a handsome young monk they'd developed a crush on when they were counselors at a camp for the handicapped. The monk, being kind, had stopped by their table to visit during lunch on the last day of camp. As he walked away, one girl sighed and said, dreamily, "Oh—he looks so good in black." The monk, overhearing her, said to me, "That's fine, because I'm going to have to wear an awful lot of it."

Popular culture sometimes interacts with monastic culture in comical ways. When my sister-in-law became an Episcopal priest, and I told a monk friend that her young daughters were playing "mommy priest" with their Barbie dolls, he offered to make them vestments from scraps in his abbey's sewing room. It felt odd to deliver a Barbie doll to a monastery—he needed one for a model—but the results were spectacular: a linen alb (made of the same material that the monastery priests wear) and chasubles made from old chalice covers.

Not all monks are so willing to embrace the absurdities of American culture. When the abbot of one monastery was contacted by someone on David Letterman's staff to see if he'd allow a monk to come on the show with an item from the abbey's museum (an enormous hairball from the stomach of a pig, rumored to be the largest hairball ever retrieved from the stomach of a pig), the abbot refused. The monk who told me the story shook his head sadly, as if the abbot had failed to comprehend the momentous nature of this opportunity. Sighing in an exaggerated manner, he said, "He lacks vision," and then added, gesturing with his arm to include the monastery building and grounds, "*We* lack vision."

For younger monastics, especially, the popular culture provides ample opportunity for play. Skits and satires have a long history in monasteries; the sister I know who wrote several parodies of pop songs to celebrate her first vows—she sang them at the community party after the church ceremony—was, in a sense, being a traditional Benedictine. To the delight of her sisters, she sang, "Don't know much monastic history/Don't know much theology/But I do know all my vows by heart/Especially that celibate part/What a wonderful world it will be." Her version of "Pistol-Packin' Mama" ("I was drinkin' beer in a cabaret/havin' lots of fun/and then one night He got to me,/and now I am a nun") brought the house down. Benedictines in Alabama recently welcomed monastics from the rest of the country to a conference by singing "Dixie" as a Gregorian chant. They also had what I'm told was a hilarious collection of redneck jokes—"You know you're a redneck liturgist, monk, nun . . . when . . ." Unfortunately, no one I spoke with could recall a single one of the punch lines. Monastic humor tends to be of the moment, and in-house, which seems appropriate for people who build communities set apart from the world.

I once heard young Benedictine sisters threatening to put their monk friends into a "Hunk Monk" calendar. And several monks and I once made up an elaborate series of names for Punk Monk bands. Some were of the "you-had-to-be-there" variety— "Theodore and the Studites and their Monster Hit, 'Circumscribed'"—was funny only if you'd sat through the reading at morning prayer during which Theodore used the words "Circumscribed," "Uncircumscribed," and "Circumscribability" for what seemed like a hundred times. It would have made even Emily Dickinson's head spin. "Abbot Pons and the Gyrovagues" was another we liked, gyrovagues being a restless kind of monk of whom Benedict did not approve; of Abbot Pons, the less said, the better. "Monks with Attitude" was our favorite, because we all know some. When the movie *Jurassic Park* came out, I happily participated in the invention, during lunch in a monastic refectory, of "Monastic Park," a fantasy monastery in which the fourth-century desert abbas and ammas had been brought back to life. (Some monks said it gave them a whole new outlook on the monastic life to think of their abbey as a kind of theme park. Others said they felt that they were already living in "Monastic Park," dinosaurs and all.) Sometimes monks speak of casting their own monasteries, trying to figure out who would play them. The choices range from Clint Eastwood to E.T. One middle-aged monk insists that he would best be portrayed by Angela Lansbury, and he may be right.

What I treasure most about monastic humor, however, is not the elaborate constructions that monks frequently engage in, but the little remarks, the simple pleasures that add spice to the day. When, after I'd had a bad fall and was limping along with a cane, feeling a bit sorry for myself, I was cheered up by a monk who greeted me with an enormous grin, and asked, "Did God *finally* strike you down?" When, after the first time I'd been asked to participate in a liturgical procession and reading at St. John's, I told the abbot after Mass, "You guys sure know how to show a woman a good time," he shrugged and said, "Practice, years of practice." What he meant, of course, is centuries. He was also making a play on the Greek word "praktike," long significant in monastic history as a term for asceticism.

But I believe that my favorite instance of monastic humor came as I arrived for a schola practice during Holy Week at St. John's. As I took my seat among the other women, I noticed that the monk behind me, a friend, was gazing at the ceiling. I said, "Ooooh, a monk in rapt contemplation, something I have longed to see." He replied, "It was just an erotic fantasy, Kathleen." "Oh, is *that* all," I said. Another monk said, "What he means by 'erotic,' Kathleen, is what most people mean by 'eremitic.' " The schola director, more amused than impatient, waited for the laughter to subside. And then we began to sing.

August 28

A U G U S T I N E

Who can be good, if not made so by loving?—St. Augustine

Not long ago, I was asked by a college student how I could stand to go to church, how I could stand the hypocrisy of Christians. I had one of my rare inspirations, when I know the right thing to say, and I replied, "The only hypocrite I have to worry about on Sunday morning is myself."

The church has had a hardening of the arteries in the sixteen hundred years or so since Ambrose, then the bishop of Milan, welcomed the convert Augustine into the body of Christ. Theological fine-tuning, some of it unfortunately inspired by Augustine himself, has led us to forget that Christian worship is not, in the words of Margaret Miles, "primarily a gathering of the like-minded" but a gathering of people "to be with one another in the acknowledgment that human existence originates in and is drawn towards love."

Even when I find church boring, I try to hold this in mind as a possibility: like all the other fools who have dragged themselves to church on Sunday morning, including the pastor, I am there because I need to be reminded that love can be at the center of all things, if we will only keep it there. The worship service will most likely not offer an aesthetically pleasing experience, great theological insight, or emotional release, although any and all of those things are possible, and precious on the rare occasions when they occur. When I look at the way my life has unfolded, my presence in the Christian assembly is miracle enough. The congregation in Lemmon, South Dakota, has seen me come and go; mercifully, they've allowed my conversion to unfold in their midst without pestering me to see if I've been "saved" in just the right way, or if I know the Confessions in the *Presbyterian Book of Order* by heart.

And this is why St. Augustine is so precious to me. He helps me see, in the lengthy story of his own conversion—with its fits and starts, its meanderings and deep desires for faith—that mine has been a traditional Christian journey. When I'm at church at home, or worshiping as a guest in a monastery choir, I often think of the Augustines in our midst, who are still wandering in and out of the faith. I think of my own inconstancy in prayer, my own hypocrisies that I know by now are among the reasons I go to church: to burn them off in singing hymns, and in listening and responding to scripture.

And I am always grateful to the hypocrites around me, imperfect strivers like myself, because they're the reason I now have this freedom. I am grateful also for Aidan Kavanagh's comments on Augustine in his book *On Liturgical Theology*, which first led me to claim Augustine's story as an inspiration and model for my own. "Augustine was a wandering catechumen for thirty years," he writes, "attending worship, backing off from it and the community of the church. But he kept returning, and the result was that Augustine found himself being baptized and communicated at Ambrose's hands in the midst of those whose singing and Amens had helped bring him home."

I suspect that his gratitude to the worshiping assembly would allow St. Augustine to grasp more fully than many modern people the profound hospitality of Cecil Williams, the pastor of Glide Memorial Church in San Francisco, who insists that "the church is not just for believers." In his book about the church, *No Hiding Place,* he says, simply, "When people come to Glide, we don't ask them if they are atheists, Methodists, or Buddhists. We ask them what their names are and how they're doing."

On Easter Sunday at Glide the pastor invites people to tell their own stories during the service. One year he said, "There's an empty tomb somewhere in this room this morning. I invite you to come forward now." And people got up to speak of living two years with AIDS, nine months free from drugs. Then a man came forward who, Williams says, had a skittish look in his eyes "that told me he was still in the tomb . . . still tied up in the grave clothes of crack cocaine." The man told the congregation that the drug counseling at the church had been enough to keep him off drugs for days at a time. He admitted that he had a little crack still in his system that morning, but he said, looking around the church, "I wasn't gonna miss this!"

A healing straight out of the gospels, in which repentance and healing happen simultaneously, as in a lightning strike, in which the desire to worship is a step from death into life. And a cause for celebration in the body of Christ, who welcomes all who seek him. Blessed be those who throw the church doors open wide.

THE LANDS OF
SUNRISE AND
SUNSET

I must live here because of the quiet. On my dawn walk last Saturday the world was so still that I began to wonder if the nearly full moon, still high in the western sky, was about to speak. Eventually I heard several vehicles in the distance—no more than three in the forty-five minutes I was out—and I caught a little movement to the south of the highway that turned out to be five mule deer. Stopped, watching me, wary. One stood behind a round hay bale so that just its ears showed—the Charlie Chaplin of deerdom. Back in town, the only moving thing was a girl delivering newspapers.

This morning we had our first snowfall, and the world was even more still, more drawn into itself as the sky fell. Tomorrow, sun is forecast, and temperatures that will bare the ground, bringing us back to fall. But the first snow of the season always feels momentous here. A seasoned television cameraman once told me that the light in our snowy plains and sky is uncommonly blue, and I sometimes think I endure Dakota winters because of this blue light. Ever since I was six months old and seriously ill, and had what people now describe as a "near-death experience" of wandering down a tunnel of light, I've been drawn toward blue.

I live here because no one in Lemmon, South Dakota, thinks that being a writer is a big deal. They regard me with a healthy mix of pride and wariness. If my neighbor the cop is up early, ready to start the day shift, and he happens to notice that the light's on in my studio, I'm just another person doing my chores. If a rancher delivering calves to the local livestock auction sees me walking by at 6 A.M., he knows that in some obscure way, I'm working too, up at that hour because that's when the job gets done.

I live here because, after being out in what is purported to be "the real world," after too much time in the literary hothouse, this is a good place to cool off. At its very best it becomes my monastery, which progresses like a river, by running in place, its currents strong and life-sustaining. This is my real world, where life proceeds at its own healthy pace, where I can revel in the luxury of paying more attention to sunrise and sunset than to clock time.

Yet I'm still a city person, at least by South Dakota standards, because I live in a town of 1600 that is by far the largest "city" in the enormous northwestern quarter of South Dakota. Country people are those who live on ranches forty miles from town, along gravel section line roads. In winter they stock up, because it may be a week or more before they can get to a grocery or hardware store. But in over twenty years of living here I've become enough of a prairie person to feel hemmed in by the houses and tree-lined streets surrounding me. Most of the trees in town were planted when my mother was a child, but I've become a throwback to an earlier generation. At least once a day I need to walk the three blocks to the edge of town and see the land, see how the sky is playing with the horizon.

I often think I live here because I'm a frustrated painter, drawn to painting this landscape with words. And even when I'm not writing about this place—when I'm writing a memoir of my twenties in New York City or trying to recapture the religious sense of the world I had as a child—it is the sunrises and sunsets here that ground me in the present. Not long ago, I spent three days immersed in grueling work, writing a personal narrative that seemed too personal, too painful to ever see the light of day. Sitting with my notes around me, gazing at a blank computer screen, I tried to forget that a deadline loomed, and I was still spending hours just sitting and brooding, letting the thing work itself out inside me.

When I finally finished shaping the first draft and knew that I was well on my way toward having a piece of writing, I glanced outside for the first time in hours. I noticed that the sky was doing glorious things. Quickly, I pulled on my boots and a jacket and began walking west, toward one of those sunsets in which both the eastern and western sky are vivid with color—dawn in reverse, gold gone to peach gone to scarlet. And as I walked I began to have a biblical sense of God's presence in the sky, of God speaking through the colors. It seemed a blessing not only on the day, and the coming night, but on the closure of this particular piece of writing, which I'd been trying to draw out of my heart and onto paper for nearly ten years.

As I've spent so much time immersed in Benedictine liturgy, which is centered on the psalms, I know many of their phrases by heart. One of the goals of monastic life is to let the psalms become so much a part of one's consciousness that they surface unexpectedly, in response to the circumstances of daily life. As I walked on that afternoon I suddenly recalled a blessing from Psalm 121: "The Lord will bless your going and your coming, your resting and rising forevermore . . ." It is the aim of contemplative living, at least in the Christian mode, that you learn to recognize a blessing when you see one, and are able to respond to it with words that God has given you. *Yes,* in response to that wildly colorful yet peaceful sky; *yes,* I could say back to God, with a line from Psalm 65: "The lands of sunrise and sunset you fill with joy."

THE NURSING
HOME ON SUNDAY
AFTERNOON

Every Sunday afternoon at 2 P.M. there is a worship service at the nursing home. The pastors in town share the duty, the Lutherans one week, Presbyterians the next, then the Catholics, then the Church of God. The pastors prepare a Bible reading and brief sermon, and church women bring cookies and coffee. It's a popular event with the residents of the home, those who are mentally alert and those who are less so. I always find it absurdly joyful, a restorative to the soul, but I don't attend as often as I'd like.

What I love most about the services is the Lord's Prayer and the singing. It reinforces my belief in the power of poetry, and also in the aptness of Auden's definition of it as "memorable speech." People who may remember little else can still say all the words of the Lord's Prayer (the King James version they grew up with), and they also have a remarkable ability to recall the words of hymns. The last time I conducted the service there—our minister was out of town, and had asked me to fill in—we sang "Stand Up, Stand Up for Jesus," "Blessed Assurance," and "Amazing Grace." One woman would not stop singing "Amazing Grace," so we just let her go happily on, eyes closed, smiling and swaying in her wheelchair, while I said a prayer and a benediction. A pastor later told me that "Holy, Holy, Holy" has the same effect on her.

I know there are several people in the home who appreciate hearing the Bible read, and they also like what they call a "good message" based on the scriptures. With the others, you can't tell how much gets through; in this regard, preaching at the home is a kind of reality check. While you have no idea how much, or even what, is getting through to people any time you preach, here that fact is simply more obvious, and more humbling. For my Sunday service, I had picked out some Bible readings in advance—a psalm, a gospel text—but didn't bring a written sermon to read, just a few notes scrawled on a bookmark. The lectionary reading for that Sunday was Luke 21:5–19, but I decided that there was too much apocalyptic gloom to read the whole thing. I did read the opening lines about the beauty of the temple in Jerusalem, and Jesus' dire prediction that "the days will come when not one stone will be left upon another," and also the reassuring words that end the text, "By your endurance you will gain your souls." I said I thought that they, of all the people in town, knew best about endurance, and about what it means to watch things come and go. I mentioned the lovely old department store on Main Street, built in 1906, that had recently been demolished. I knew that some of them had gone in a van to observe its coming down. And—I felt on risky ground here, but I thought it a risk worth taking—they also knew, more than most, what it means to have the temple of the body taken down, to live in bodies that no longer work as well as they would like. A few people nodded; a few smiled wistfully. "But you endure," I said, "because you know God loves you." And here, I surprised myself, and some of the residents, by adding, rather forcefully, "You know that you are still beautiful in the eyes of God."

I hadn't thought about it beforehand, but the elderly don't often get told that they're beautiful. Not much that comes on the large television set in the corner of the recreation room tells them that; not much in the magazines on the reading rack. Even if I hadn't believed what I was saying, it would have been worth saying, just to see the expressions on their faces. It was an inspiring moment, for me and for them. Later, after coffee and visiting and lots of old-time stories, when I joined the Presbyterian women in cleaning up, and we were talking, one marveled at how her great-grandmother was able to live totally in the past. "I remember her as she was," she said, "and it's hard on me, but she seems content to be this way."

"It's a kind of mercy," another woman said, and the poem of our conversation began to flow. Another added, "They make no distinction between the living and the dead," and another said, "It must be like eternal life." My flippant demons wanted to add, "And they'll never have to fill out another income tax form," but I resisted.

I thought of a passage in Esther deWaal's *Seeking God,* a book that changed my life. She had helped me to understand what I loved so about Benedictine liturgy, and allowed me to see that it was also what I love about coming to the nursing home. "The geriatric ward in which so many older people now end their days is inescapably full of pain and distress. It would be absurd to pretend otherwise. Yet, bound as most of us are by the relentless demands of the clock and the calendar, we find here a world which accepts another kind of time, where requests and reminiscences repeated endlessly remind of us of something which the Orthodox liturgy knows with its continual repetitions again and again and again. These people [who] many would prefer to banish and forget, might be speaking to us . . . of that time outside time of which we need a constant reminder."

Isaiah's seraphim sing "Holy, Holy, Holy," and in the landscape of worship around God's throne, John, too, sees them, four living creatures, "full of eyes all around," who are full of song. "Day and night without ceasing they sing, 'Holy, holy, holy, the Lord God the Almighty, who was and is and is to come" (Rev. 4:8).

ONE
MAN'S LIFE

I first heard that Kevin was missing on the "Prayer Chain," when I called home to get my phone messages. The "Prayer Chain" is a telephone tree of church members, and when there are deaths in the congregation, or when people have requested prayers before surgery, or for any other reason, the prayer chain goes into action. My husband and I were at a Benedictine monastery in North Dakota, not far from home, and we puzzled over the message: Kevin, a young, affable, devoted family man and hard worker, a truck driver, was missing. This was serious business, as it was early winter, and very cold, with snow on the ground and temperatures well below zero. I asked the monks to pray for Kevin and his family. Monastery bulletin boards are the ultimate "prayer chain."

David and I assumed that Kevin's pickup had gotten stuck somewhere on a country road. We couldn't imagine why he'd be out on a country road, but that seemed the best bet. You learn quickly here—sometimes by having to spend a night in your car— that in winter it's not wise to drive down the roads that aren't on a school bus route, as they're the last to be plowed. When we got back to town, my husband went to the tavern where Kevin's wife worked, hoping to hear that he was all right. Instead, he learned that Kevin's body had been found, and that the police considered it a murder.

It's hard to convey the disbelief that I felt when David phoned me. Murder had been the last thing on our minds. In the twenty-one years that we've lived in Lemmon, South Dakota, there had been just three murders in the area. Two elderly men were killed for their money; in both cases the murderers were incompetent and foolish enough to be caught and punished. Another sad case involved several young men high on drugs—angel dust is what I've heard—who beat another to death in a dispute over drugs and money.

Piecing the story together from all the talk downtown—wherever you went, people were talking of little else—we learned that Kevin had last been seen offering a ride home to a man who'd been in the area for a few weeks, working on a crew taking railroad ties from abandoned lines. A large, bullying man from Montana, he'd made his presence felt in the bars and cafes. A troublemaker, quick to pick fights, he stood out. People here can be plenty tough, but except for a few cowboys during their growing-up phase, they don't usually feel called upon to prove it. In the more than ten years that my husband worked in a popular working-class bar downtown, he very seldom had to break up a fist fight, and never saw a weapon drawn, a fact that is all the more remarkable because so many people here own and use knives and guns as a matter of necessity (if you're forty-five miles from town on a gravel road and a deer bolts from the ditch, breaking a leg on the front of your pickup, a gun is good to have).

David and I listened as people who had searched for Kevin told their stories; they knew his pickup truck had been found abandoned, and that they might have to abandon the search and wait for spring snowmelt to uncover him, but well over a hundred volunteers searched a 900-square-mile area in the subzero cold, on foot and horseback, in planes, and on snowmobiles. Two of Lemmon's largest employers, the livestock auction and a jewelry manufacturing plant, let their employees join the search at full pay. Food and fuel for the searchers were donated by the local grocery stores and gas stations. Gruff ranchers interviewed at the cafe on Main Street spoke of "a sense of being violated," and lamented that their sense of trust was diminished. It occurred to me that in this region, which most of the world considers "Godforsaken," we still have the grace of being able to feel the loss of one man. There are no "crime statistics" here, only people, and a crime such as murder is taken as a personal affront. Still, you know that the next time you see a car broken down at the side of the road, you'll stop and offer help. We don't know any other way to survive in these open spaces.

No one knows exactly what happened that night. Kevin was a peacemaker; out for a few drinks with friends on a Saturday night, he'd helped to break up a fight earlier in the evening. Maybe to show that there were no hard feelings, he'd offered a ride to the man who'd started the fight. Kevin was half-Lakota, and proud of it. I wonder if his murderer—who, we later learned, had a long record of violent assaults—thought that since he was killing an Indian, no one would care. He was wrong. He's in prison for life.

Here, we still know that murder is a momentous thing. We have no way to escape it; the man who finds the body, the policeman investigating the crime, the priest who prepares the eulogy are not faceless strangers but neighbors, people you know. And there is no way to avoid having your own heart broken; at the visit to the widow's house—you bring food, tears, hugs—the three-year-old looks up at you and says, "My daddy died."

Here, you can still feel what the death of one person does to the world. It's a bitter luxury, but it's all ours.

"IT'S A
SWEET LIFE"

*Old monks are wild as well as simple. They perch more lightly on
the globe than the rest of us.*—Peter Levi, THE FRONTIERS
OF PARADISE

While monasteries are renowned for their sacred spaces,
the imposing churches and cloister walks that speak eloquently of silence, their holiest places are often not silent at all, but
resound with conversation. In the "retirement center," "care center," or "hospital wing"—pick your euphemism—where many of
the oldest members of a community reside, the oral history of the
monastery is most alive. Such places in the outside world are commonly called "nursing homes," and are much dreaded. Monasteries cannot help but reflect their culture, and Benedictines are not
immune from the fear of old age and lack of respect for the elderly
that mar American society. Community life, as Benedictines practice it, is so intense that over the years a perceived slight or the abuse
of power can become heavy baggage; thus you sometimes find
middle-aged monks who feel they have a score to settle with an
older monk, who years ago may have been their teacher, boss, formation director, or abbot. But when community works as it should,
its elderly have the self-respect of people who have spent a lifetime
listening and being listened to.

Monasteries also demonstrate, often in surprising ways, that when several generations of people are living together, the place of the very old is to teach about possibility. The monk or sister who can speak of planting the venerable trees in the cloistered garden or of building the stone fence that marks off the monastery enclosure may prove inspiring to a newcomer who feels stuck in the tedious, unglamorous tasks of the novitiate: cleaning and waxing floors, washing windows, working in the compost pile and flower beds, wondering what all of this has to do with a life dedicated to God.

The monastic retirement center is a place where one often encounters old people in whom pretense has been so stripped away that their holiness is palpable. Turn the lights off and you suspect that they might begin to glow in the dark, radiating the "openness to all" and transparency of heart that scholar Peter Brown tells us made Anthony of the Desert recognizable to fourth-century pilgrims even in a crowd of black-robed monks. The novices assigned to care for the aged and infirm members of a community frequently discover that this sort of holiness is most evident in people who have endured with patience and grace many years of debilitating illness and prolonged physical pain. This is not at all a romanticizing of illness but a recognition that people can sometimes transform physical sickness into health of soul. The example of a sister who is a calm, centered, quietly joyful and generous person, and who has suffered for years from a degenerative neurological disease, means more to a young nun than any book of theology or class on monastic history. In her own community she's found a woman who helps her to put many great souls of the Christian tradition into perspective: Hildegard, Julian of Norwich, Thérèse of Lisieux, all of whom converted their physical suffering into a love so profound that we are still reaping the benefits.

The stereotypical monk has a faith that is serene and certain. The reality is otherwise, especially for younger monastics, who often struggle mightily with issues of faith and belief. Near the end of a recent Monastic Institute, a week full of illuminating talks by a contemplative French Benedictine, Ghislain Lafont, an anguished young Trappist spoke up: "We've spoken of the loss of faith in American society. But what of loss of faith within the monastery itself?" He indicated that he was living, as a monk, with profound doubts, and that while the monastery was where he felt he belonged, at times his life there was nearly unbearable. Fr. Lafont nodded; none of this, evidently, was a surprise to him. What he said in response struck me as both practical and thoroughly monastic: "Of course we are weak, unable to cope. But if we can maintain faith, hope, and charity, it will radiate somehow. And people who come to us may find in us what we can no longer see in ourselves."

If Benedictine life is about loving others, about seeking God within the human community, then the means of salvation is at hand, right there in the other monks. Both those who offer love and support, and those who are incompatible or unsympathetic, can teach the young monastic what it means to incarnate Christ, to become the sort of person who radiates love. In this context, friendships within the monastery can become an inspiration to all. Over lunch one day with several Benedictine sisters, I was treated to stories of two nuns, long-deceased, who had become inseparable as they aged. One of the women had lost most of her hair and had taken to wearing a bright red wig. One morning the wig was even more askew than usual, but as the two walked arm in arm into chapel for lauds, her friend was overhead to say to her, "My, you look lovely this morning." When one of the women had to enter the convent nursing home and leave her friend behind, she said to her, "Don't forget about me." And her friend replied, "How could I forget you? You're my better self."

Younger monastic people revel in such stories, such lives. They may never have known their own grandparents well, but they come to feel, in the monastery, that they've found many grandparents, guides to life within community, exemplars for the arduous journey. The living-out of vows is not respected in America. Our commitments are disposable, and if a marriage, or life in a monastic community, isn't working out, we tend to move on. And young monks and nuns can't help but suffer from the tension; committed as they are, they retain an edge, a tension that only time in the monastery can wear away. But when younger monastics, still attuned to the competitive values of the world, are delegated to care for older ones, the dimensions of commitment become clearer. As they steer a recalcitrant older sister toward the bathroom, or the chapel, an inner voice reminds them. *This is what you can hope to become.*

It's a message that can transform them. Young monks pray with sick old men whose piety seems terribly out-of-date, only to discover that as monks they have more in common than not. Listening well, they can hear the things that will help to make them monks. "On Candlemas one year," a young monk told me, "I was overwhelmed to hear a brother say that as he grew older, he'd become more content to be like Simeon, an old man who spends his time sitting in the temple and waiting for the promised savior."

I once said to a good friend, a monk in his thirties, that while I loved him very much, it was the guys who'd been in the monastery for fifty years or more who really appealed to me. He sighed, and said, "This life is like being in a rock tumbler, which is really great, if you want to come out good and polished." It's not a bad comparison. Older monks and nuns often do attain an enduring and radical beauty, the many years of discipline having uncovered a freedom that others find inviting. While they usually have no certification as "spiritual directors," something of a craze these days among younger monastics, these elderly are often the ones people turn to. Although they are genuinely humble and would refuse the designation, they have a wisdom and holiness that others recognize and draw from. Encountering them can be a dazzlement, a revelation of holy simplicity.

At the end of the Monastic Institute one year I paid a visit to one of my favorite people in the world, an elderly monk who is going blind. He is going blind as he has lived, with feistiness and grace, and without losing gratitude for the many blessings of a long life. As always, he apologized for his messy room, and then he proudly showed off his latest accoutrement: a tape recorder on which he listens to the current issue of *America,* and also the latest books on the liturgical theology that has been his life's work.

He asked if I would come with him to call on another monk who had taken a bad fall the day before. This was a monk I'd not met, a priest who had only recently retired, in his mid-eighties, from many years of serving as a chaplain in a prison not far from the monastery. Other monks had spoken of this man with admiration, as someone who was humbly realistic about his ministry. "He knew that a lot of the prisoners came to Mass for something to do, just to get out of their cell," one young monk had told me, adding, "and that was enough for him. He just kept at it, hoping to do some good."

The nurse was leaving his room. She told us he'd been napping off and on all morning, awaiting transport to a nearby hospital for a CAT scan. He'd hit his head in the fall and the doctors needed to know the extent of his injuries. I was nervous about disturbing a man who might be sleeping or in great pain, not wanting company. Nothing could have prepared me for what happened. Another nurse entered the room and called out, "You have a visitor. Two visitors." We heard a weak voice respond, "Ah . . . it's a sweet life." As we entered the room, and he got a look at us, he said again, "It's a sweet life."

Gregory the Great tells a story in his *Dialogues* about a man who visited St. Benedict in his hermitage, explaining that as it is Easter, he has brought a gift of food. Benedict says to him, "I know that it is Easter, for I have been granted the blessing of seeing you." Standing in that monastery nursing home, I felt that I'd just been blessed in the same earth-shaking way. The monk's greeting was the epitome of Benedictine hospitality—in his Rule Benedict says simply, "All guests who present themselves are to be welcomed as Christ"—and it also brought home to me the incarnational nature of monasticism. It is not a theory or even a theology, but a way of life.

All week at the Institute we had pondered and discussed the fundamentals of "the monastic way," such essentials as sacred reading, liturgy, work, silence, vigilance, and stability. Now, in the presence of two elderly monks with well over a century of lived monastic experience between them, the point of all this was made clear: to so form people in community, stability, and hospitality that they can welcome each other, and life itself, as sweet, despite the savage ups and downs, despite the indignities of old age and physical infirmity.

The elderly monk in that hospital bed would probably be startled to hear how beautiful he was to me as he lay there with a hideously bruised face; how he radiated the love of Christ; how I felt as if a desert *abba* had given me words I didn't even know I needed—*"It's a sweet life."* I don't know what he was like as a young man, but I'm sure he struggled, like every other Benedictine I've known, to become a monastic person. He'd probably hasten to assure me that he struggles still, that he is still in need of spiritual guidance and correction in pursuing "conversion of heart," a vow unique to the Benedictines. Yet with one simple gesture, he had powerfully demonstrated to me the incarnational nature of Christian faith, how, to paraphrase Teresa of Avila, we are the only eyes, mouth, hands, feet, and heart that Christ has on earth.

He was an ill, old man, and not one but two people had come to see him. What could it be but sweetness, and God's blessing? His welcome refreshed me and made me see something that's easy to lose sight of in our infernally busy lives. That we exist for each other, and when we're at a low ebb, sometimes just to see the goodness radiating from another can be all we need in order to rediscover it in ourselves.

COMING AND GOING: MONASTIC RITUALS

The Lord will guard your coming and going, both now
and forever—Psalm 121

Any small town has rituals that mark the season: in Lemmon, South Dakota, they include the Christmas Fair and Snow Queen Contest, the Boss Cowman Rodeo in July, the Junior Livestock Show in the fall. A monastery follows the liturgical year, the great cycles of Advent, Christmas, Lent, and Easter, as well as the calm flow of Ordinary Time. From the repetition of saints' days, feasts, and solemnities over the course of a lifetime, a Christian monastic seeks to experience what Paul Philibert has described in *Seeing and Believing* as "the mystery of our living between two worlds, one of space and time, the other of promise and expectation."

The daily round of a monastic life—coming to the day, to church, to meals, to evening, to sleep—is marked by the Liturgy of the Hours. But other momentous comings and goings—to the novitiate, to first vows and then life vows, to a new job in a dependent monastery halfway round the world, to a silver or golden jubilee, to a deathwatch, to a funeral—are marked by rituals of great solemnity and beauty. Even what would be mundane events in the world are often sanctified in a monastic setting. I once attended the installation of a new president of the American Benedictine Academy. The ceremony was incorporated into a worship service and involved a laying on of hands, as over three hundred people stood in a monastery choir, hands upraised, and a blessing was said over the new president. After our final hymn, I happened to be with a friend, a retired business executive. "Is this how they did it at Honeywell?" I asked. She rolled her eyes and said, "Not quite."

Rituals bind a community together, and also bind individuals to a community, and while this is something that monastic people have long been aware of, I find that these days they're talking about it more, and setting about to reclaim some of the ritual aspects of their life that were cast aside in what I've heard more than one Benedictine call the "mindless modernizing" after Vatican II. *The American Monastic Newsletter* recently established an open forum on rituals, inviting Benedictine men and women to describe the rituals that their communities have found most valuable. People have sent in reports on everything from a "commissioning ceremony" held in August, when jobs are assigned for the year, and a prioress presents each sister "with a symbol of her Benedictine life and a paper with her ministry written on it," to a ritual held in a monastery cemetery on All Souls' Day, in which a vigil light is placed on each tombstone, and the abbot blesses each grave with holy water. A monk describes a communal anointing of the sick held quarterly in his monastery, in which those confined to infirmary rooms are assigned to pray for specific purposes. "This gives them," the monk says, "a greater sense of participation in the monastery's life and work."

I have witnessed monastic communities bestowing a ritual

blessing at vespers the night before an abbot or prioress departs for a lengthy trip, or when a monk or sister is about to embark for a sabbatical or a new job in Jerusalem, Ireland, or Brazil. At one monastery I know, the community recently devised a new ritual for monks who decide to leave before making final vows. At vespers one night, shortly before the man would have made his lifelong commitment, the monks had a brief ceremony to bless him as he went on his way. It was clear to me that the ceremony was also intended to leave the door open, in case the man ever decided that he wanted to return.

The great return in a monastic life, of course, is the return to God. While I have not participated in any of the informal deathbed rituals that often mark a death in a monastery—these tend to be in-house affairs, for family and members of the community—when I've heard of them, I've been struck by how loving they seem, and also how of a piece they are with the rest of monastic life. In some communities, each member comes individually to be with the dying person for a while, to talk over old times, to pray, to read the scriptures out loud. Sometimes groups of monks or sisters will gather, to sing a confrere's favorite hymns or psalms. Often, people hold a deathbed vigil, taking turns reciting psalms out loud for someone they may have been reciting the psalms with for fifty years or more. A sister who participated in such a vigil for a dying monk, a mutual friend, told me that his death lasted a long time. He was struggling, resisting, but while he seemed unconscious, he did respond to some of the psalms. In fact, she said, they were the only thing that seemed to calm him as he finally slipped away.

At the Medieval Congress at Kalamazoo one year I witnessed a remarkable exchange between scholars of the medieval era and contemporary Benedictines. I've always noticed, at Kalamazoo, a bit of tension between the scholars who study monasticism and the people who live it—I find it similar to the unease literary scholars sometimes feel with living poets; it's so much easier to study dead ones. In this case, a medievalist, a Benedictine monk, presented a paper on aging and dying in medieval monasteries. His point was that much of what modern psychology tells us is vital for families in the grieving process—the need for forgiving, for touching, for listening to stories—was provided for, in the medieval monastery, by a series of rituals that moved from the infirmary to the church to the cemetery. Most important, he said, these rituals helped people comprehend death not as a sharp breaking off from life—which is how modern people tend to see it—but rather as a new stage in a process of dying that we've been undergoing for some time. In a recent best-seller, *How We Die,* a medical doctor makes the same point; the death of the body is something we live with all our lives.

At Kalamazoo, Benedictine men and women responded to this presentation on medieval funeral practices by commenting on the rituals surrounding deaths in their own communities, and it was fascinating to watch the response of scholars both shocked and intrigued to learn that so many medieval rituals were still alive and well. A monk commented on the medieval practice of not leaving a dying person alone, but staying with them, and reciting scripture in order to keep the devil at bay, by saying that while modern Benedictines didn't talk a great deal about the devil, the medieval bedside vigil sounded much like the ones in his own community. A nun said that in her monastery, when a sister dies, it is the job of the prioress to wash and dress the body. As a former prioress herself, she said that having to do this had been a forceful reminder of how deeply she'd loved these older women, and also compelled her to confront her own fear of death. Another monk, a Cistercian, commented that while the habit was no longer used as a burial shroud, as in medieval times, in his monastery another ritual—the monk's cowl being closed over his face—served much the same purpose.

In the *Lives of the Desert Fathers,* it is said of the monks of Abba Isidore's monastery that they were so attentive to God's will that "when the time came for each to depart, he announced it beforehand to all the others and then lay down and fell asleep." The going of monks from this world is not usually accomplished with such tidiness. What one does often find is that a lifetime of listening to the Bible, of celebrating on a daily basis the rituals of the Christian church, leads monks to call on the Bible in their last moments, and to identify more completely with the Jesus Christ they've been seeking all their lives. A retired abbot told me of the last words of a dear friend, words that he said were spoken suddenly, and with clarity, by a man who'd been suffering for days, in and out of consciousness, apparently unable to speak. "I didn't know," the dying monk said, "that the agony in the garden of Gethsemane would last so long."

"THE REST OF
THE COMMUNITY"

I first began to understand how different monasteries were from any places I'd known when the monk who was training me as an oblate said one day, "It's time for you to meet the rest of the community." We walked to the cemetery, and through it, and as we passed each grave, the monk told me stories about the deceased. Having been at the monastery for over sixty years, he'd known nearly everyone buried there. A hundred years ago in America, in many small towns, such a cemetery tour might have been possible, led by an old-timer, or the town's amateur historian. Such practices as tolling bells to announce a death and holding an all-night vigil in the church were still common. Now, I suspect that monasteries are about the only places in which these traditions are kept alive.

Hospital chaplains in large cities have told me that the number of people who die without family or friends is increasing. Often, it's the hospital staff who arranges for the disposal of the body, and the chaplain who conducts the funeral for a person he or she may never have met. Monasteries couldn't be more different. The vow of stability, which places people in a particular community, in a particular place, means that Benedictines live their monastic lives knowing exactly where and how they will be buried. I once asked a young monk how this felt as we walked back to the monastery after a graveside committal service. He said that he seldom talked about it, because most people found it morbid. But to him, it was one of the strengths of monastic life. "My friends are there, my mentors and guides in the religious life," he said, gesturing back at the cemetery, "and one day I'll join them."

The funeral we'd just attended had been for a monk I'd never met, but after the eulogies felt I knew, a man from a tiny Montana town who'd become a scholar of medieval literature and had been baptized at the age of thirty-six, entering the monastery six years later. After retiring from a career as an English professor at a Benedictine college, he'd founded an AIDS hospice. In preparing his eulogy, the abbot had raided the abbey archives, and in quoting from letters the monk had sent home he made his voice come alive for us. "Having lost all my family in the last few years," the monk had written to his abbot, "I've had to sort a few things out, and it is comforting to know that I have another family which has been very good to me." A self-assessment made at the time of his retirement from teaching brought many smiles around the choir: "I am a sixteen-stone monk-medievalist enthusiastically arrived at the mid of my seventh decade. I am tolerant, compassionate, and bossy—probably the result of having been lucky all my life. I have, since childhood, always felt the strong support of family and friends—so strong that it has prevented my dwelling on my numerous shortcomings because it's shown me that my shortcomings are acceptable to those I care about."

After one Holy Week, the monk had written to the abbot, "My sense of renewal this Easter was highly emotional. . . . As I prepare to enter my seventh decade I am unreasonably happy. . . . Please convey to Fathers Alexander and Hilary my experience of gloriously humiliating joy! They will both know I have done absolutely nothing to deserve it." And of his AIDS hospice he'd said, "The first person who lived with me weighed seventy-five pounds. . . . But I was in awe of how he functioned, how he never lost his sense of humor, his capacity to enjoy things. I couldn't imagine myself functioning that way with what he had to bear. You can't pity someone you're in awe of."

Many people said that the monk, a humble man, would have been highly amused at the drama of his funeral. Right at the prayer of consecration, during Mass, an enormous thunderclap sounded— it had been a sunny day—and several monks saw lightning arc through the upper reaches of the church. A gentle rain came just as we began to sing the Agnus Dei, but it had stopped by the time we were following the casket through the church and out the back door of the monastery. The storm was marching away from us, through the eastern sky, which looked like a scroll from the Book of Revelation; I half expected to see angels tugging at its edges.

The psalm we sang as we walked—"I rejoiced when I heard them say, let us go to God's house, and now my feet are standing within your gates, O Jerusalem"—gained new resonance, as did the other psalms we'd sung all day, doing the Office for the Dead instead of our regular prayer services. I realized that the familiar words—"My soul takes refuge in the shadow of your wings, I take refuge until the storms of destruction pass by," or, "Awake my soul, awake lyre and harp; I shall awake the dawn"—carried a new poignancy in the presence of death. And I suspected that the next time I encountered them in the ordinary, four-week cycle of psalms,

I'd find them to be more deeply textured, changed by this day of mourning, which opened onto eternity.

One never has so strong a sense of what monastic community means as at a funeral; it is the apotheosis of monastic storytelling. And it also reminds us that monks seek to live this life with hearts focused on eternity. As my friend Patrick Henry, director of the Ecumenical Institute at St. John's, once said to me, "Monastic funerals always blur the line between this world and the next; one feels that the present is just a moment in the continuum, between this community, and the community of the saints." The "rest of the community" turns out to be very large indeed, and in the funeral liturgies, it makes itself known. Monks do not flinch from the reality of death—during the night-long vigil and Office for the Dead, the coffin lies open near the altar—but there is also a powerful sense of Benedict's vision of monks here and now being brought by Christ "together into everlasting life."

Anyone with a sacramental understanding of the world knows that it's the small things that count. And in a monastery, the gestures, songs, antiphons, prayers, and scripture readings that unify a monastic profession service, the Holy Week and Easter liturgies, and the funeral become small things writ large. In one community I know, the lines from Psalm 119—"If you uphold me by your promise, I shall live; do not disappoint me in my hope"—that a sister repeats three times when she makes her profession of monastic vows, are also sung three times by the community at her death: at the reception of her body, at the beginning of the funeral service, and at the grave. In another community, the hymn called the "Ultima" that is sung at the end of all feast-day meals is also sung at the end of a monk's funeral. The goal of a monastic life is to let oneself be changed by community ritual, ceremony, and the repetition of the psalms, until, in the words of one hymn, our lives *become* a psalm in praise of the glory of God's name. The connections that Benedictines painstakingly thread through their everyday lives reinforce my sense of monastic life itself as a great poem, one that honors and celebrates Jesus Christ, who, Oscar Wilde tells us in *De Profundis,* "is the poem God made."

"THE ONLY
CITY IN
AMERICA"

You have come to Mt. Zion and the city of the living God . . .
—Hebrews 12:22

When Thomas Merton first encountered the Abbey of Gethsemani, where he was later to live as a monk, he wrote: "I had wondered what was holding the country together, what has been keeping the universe from cracking in pieces and falling apart. . . . This is the only city in America—and it is by itself, in the wilderness . . ." A monastery is a city in the ancient meaning of the word, as "civitas," a place which stands for human culture in the largest sense, and exists to serve the common good.

I have often had the odd feeling that the monastery is the real world, while the dog-eat-dog world that most people call "real" is in fact an artifice, an illusion that we cling to because it seems to be in our best interest to do so. The true city, the holy one, allows us, in the words of Paul Philibert, an alternative "vision of human relationships where beauty is more desirable than financial profit, friendship more precious than advantage, and solidarity in a common vision of human dignity more compelling than self-fulfillment." A simple paraphrase of Dorotheus of Gaza—I'd much rather do things with others and have them come out wrong than do them by myself to make sure they come out right—demonstrates the distance between a monastic perspective and the modern American individualism that allows us to ignore a basic reality: human beings are remarkably dependent on one another.

A city is a place where the worst and best about humanity come to the fore, where we're forced to be realistic enough to lock our doors even as we rejoice in being able to celebrate the greatest achievements of our culture. The Christian vision of heaven is of a city, the New Jerusalem, and Christian theology suggests that the Godhead itself is a kind of city, a community of three persons, or in the Benedictine Aidan Kavanagh's words, "a collective being, with unity." Kavanagh laments that in contemporary society the city's sacred potential as a symbol of community has been "invested in sovereign individualism," which allows us to retreat into a myopic unworldliness. "[Our] icon is not a city," he writes in *On Liturgical Theology*, "whether of man or God, but the lone jogger running through suburbia, in order, we are told, to feel good about himself."

Cities remind us that the desire to escape from the problems of other people by fleeing to a suburb, small town, or a monastery, for that matter, is an unholy thing, and ultimately self-defeating. We can no more escape from other people than we can escape from ourselves. As Basil the Great wrote to a friend after leaving the city of Caesarea in the fourth century, "I have abandoned my life in the town as the occasion of endless troubles, but I have not managed to get rid of myself." Images of the city are impossible to avoid in the monastic choir, as scripture is full of them. You're reminded, over and over, that in fact you have come here to be a part of the city of the living God, and you're challenged to make something of it. Do you reflect Benedict's belief that "the divine presence is everywhere"? Do you work, as Jeremiah reminds us to do, for the welfare of the city to which God has sent you? Can you say, with Isaiah, "About Zion I will not be silent, about Jerusalem I will not rest, until her integrity shines out like the dawn, and her salvation flames like a torch"?

NIGHT

Compline, which means "complete," is the traditional name for the night office. The compline Psalms, 4 and 91, remind us that we all need protection from forces beyond our control, even as they reassure us that protection is ours. The night will come with its great equalizers, sleep and death. It will pass over us, and bring us forth again into light.

"Ponder on your bed and be still," Psalm 4 reminds us, "make justice your sacrifice and trust in the Lord." One night I sat with a friend who had just learned of her sister's death in a suspicious accident. Beyond the grief over losing a sister much younger than herself, whom she had always looked out for, was an unbearable question: Had the husband, who had been abusive in the past, now committed murder? In the morning she'd be traveling to the city where her sister had lived, and would be interviewed by the detectives investigating the death. But for now, sleep was necessary and, of course, impossible.

I said, feeling helpless, that maybe I could read her the best bedtime story I knew. She smiled faintly and said that she would like that. So I read Psalm 4 aloud, catching my breath at the last lines: "I will lie down and sleep comes at once, for you, alone, Lord, make me dwell in safety." We both wept, and were able to sleep a little, before the empty dawn.

The great desert monk Anthony once said that "the prayer of the monk is not perfect until he no longer realizes himself or the fact that he is praying." Frank O'Hara speaks in a poem, "In Favor of One's Time," of an angel engaged in an immortal contest, "which is love assuming the consciousness of itself . . ." Between these two poles, it seems to me, we seek to become complete: between shedding our self-consciousness and taking on a new awareness, between the awesome fears that shrink us and the capacity for love that enlarges us beyond measure, between the need for vigilance in the face of danger and the trust that allows us to sleep. Night comes, or as Miss Dickinson put it, it *becomes,* and we turn our lives over to God. We are able to rest, in the words of an old hymn, "on the promises," we are willing to lean "on the everlasting arms."

ACKNOWLEDGMENTS

I would like to thank the Bush Foundation and the John Simon Guggenheim Memorial Foundation for supporting my work. I am grateful also for the friendship and support of Patrick Henry and Dolores Schuh, C.H.M., of the Institute for Ecumenical and Cultural Research, and for the many colleagues there who have become friends. The Institute has consistently inspired and challenged me in rewarding ways. My debt to the congregations of Hope and Spencer Presbyterian Churches, and the monastic friends who have contributed so much to this book is incalculable; I hope they'll accept the book as an expression of my gratitude. Among the Benedictines I owe special thanks to Josue Behnen, Jeremy Hall, Katherine Kraft, Dunstan Moorse, Julian Nix, and Robert West.

As always, it has been a joy to work with my editor, Cindy Spiegel, and my agent, Lynn Nesbit. I also want to thank Bart Schneider, editor of the *Hungry Mind Review,* who commissioned the title piece of this book, and first took a chance on me back in 1987, when I needed it most. To my husband and parents, my sisters Becky and Charlotte, to Marilyn and my brother John, who gave up two of his Thursdays at Mai'ili, my deepest thanks.

Thanks are due to the editors of the following periodicals and anthologies, in which versions of several chapters of this book were originally published, including:

"The Rule and Me," *North Dakota Quarterly,* Fall 1990.

"Jeremiah as Writer" and "A Story with Dragons," *Communion: Contemporary Writers Reveal the Bible in Their Lives,* David Rosenberg, ed., Anchor Books, 1996.

"Borderline," in *Sister to Sister,* Patricia Foster, ed., Anchor Books, 1995.

"Paradox of the Psalms," in *Out of the Garden: Women Writers on the Bible,* Christina Büchmann and Celina Spiegel, eds., Fawcett, 1994.

"Degenerates," *Ploughshares,* Fall 1994.

"Between 'Point Vierge' and 'The Usual Spring.' " *A Tremble of Bliss: Contemporary Writers on the Saints,* Paul Elie, ed., Harcourt, 1994.

"Road Trip," *Northern Lights,* Summer 1992.

"Places and Displacement," *Imagining Home,* Thom Tammaro, Mark Vinz, eds., University of Minnesota Press, 1995.

"The Cloister Walk," *Hungry Mind Review,* Winter 1992/93.

"Celibate Passion," *Hungry Mind Review,* Fall 1995.

"At Last, Her Laundry's Done," first appeared as "It All Comes Out in the Wash," *The New York Times Magazine,* August 22, 1993.

"A Glorious Robe," *Parabola,* Summer 1994.

"The Lands of Sunrise and Sunset," *The Earth at Our Doorstep,* Annie Stine, ed., Sierra Club, 1996.

Portions of the chapters on Hildegard of Bingen and Mechtild of Magdeburg were presented at the Medieval Congress in Kalamazoo, Michigan, under the auspices of The American Benedictine Academy.